MY GARDEN IN AUTUMN
AND WINTER

My Garden in Autumn and Winter

by
E. A. Bowles

with a New Preface
by Charles Elliott
and Nomenclatural Update
by Peter Barnes

Timber Press
Portland, Oregon

First published in 1915 by T. C. & E. C. Jack

Reprinted in 1998 by
Timber Press, Inc.
The Haseltine Building
133 S.W. Second Avenue, Suite 450
Portland, Oregon 97204, U.S.A.

Printed in Hong Kong

Library of Congress Cataloging-in-Publication Data

Bowles, E. A. (Edward Augustus)
    My garden in autumn and winter / by E. A. Bowles ; with a
preface by Charles Elliott and nomenclatural update by Peter
Barnes.
      p.   cm.
    "First published in 1915 by T. C. & E. C. Jack"—T.p. verso.
    Includes index.
    ISBN 0-88192-459-8
    1. Myddelton House Garden (Enfield, London, England)
2. Bowles, E. A. (Edward Augustus)—Homes and haunts—
England—London. 3. Plants, Ornamental—England—London.
4. Autumn—England—London. 5. Winter—England—London.
I. Title.
SB466.G8B683   1998
635.9'09421—dc21
                                              98-17491
                                                   CIP

CONTENTS
of the 1998 edition

KEY

A. Old Conservatory
B. Poison Bed
C. New Conservatory
D. Terrace
E. Hosta Bed
F. Iris Beds
G. Pergola Garden
H. Market Cross
I. Rose Garden
J. Tom Tiddler's Ground
K. Standard Roses
L. Foxtail Lily Border
M. Petrified Tree
N. Terrace
O. Lunatic Asylum
P. Wild Garden
Q. Wisteria Bridge
R. Lodge
S. Reception

To Alpine Meadow and
Rock Garden

Pond

New River (now lawn)

MYDDELTON HOUSE GARDENS

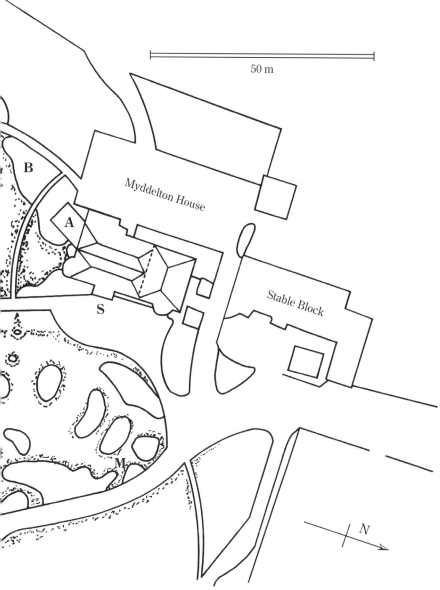

50 m

Myddelton House

Stable Block

B

A

S

M

N

Map courtesy of E. A. Bowles of Myddelton House Society and Lee Valley Park Authority. Special thanks to Charles Kingdom and Christine Barker.

PREFACE
by Charles Elliott

It would be difficult to find anyone to match Edward Augustus Bowles (1865–1954) as an all-around garden expert. Creator of a great garden at Myddelton House on the northern edge of London, authority on crocuses, colchicums, daffodils, and anemones (to name only his particular favorites), painter of flowers, much loved friend of nearly all the leading gardeners of his time in England, he was in addition a still rarer thing—a man who could write about his garden and his botanical charges with passion, wit, and unrivaled charm. His three classic volumes—*My Garden in Spring, My Garden in Summer,* and *My Garden in Autumn and Winter*—have delighted thousands of readers since their first publication in 1914 and 1915 on the very brink of World War I.

This third volume is slightly different in organization from the first two. Less a simple tour of the Myddelton garden, it is more a graceful, knowledgeable, and often amusing account of the way a garden makes its way toward the "calamity" of a killing frost, and then endures the "unwelcome presence of winter." Bowles readily admits that he dislikes cold weather and is depressed by "the certainty of a final catastrophe ahead." But in his hands the story is never a gloomy one; there are always points of horticulture to discuss and plants to admire. (Or to rail against: *Autumn and Winter* contains some of his most splendid diatribes on, for example, collarette dahlias, which he regards as

My Garden in Autumn and Winter

"only fit to be grown in the garden of an asylum for the blind.")

A plantsman at heart, Bowles is in a position to offer insightful firsthand information about many demanding species. His technical studies—*Handbook of Crocus and Colchicum* and *Handbook of Narcissus*—present such information in abundance and are still regarded as invaluable. But in his "My Garden" series, Gussie (as he was familiarly known) does far more than simply give us information, and that is what makes these books so memorable. Discussing particular varieties of plants, considering problems he has had in growing or propagating them, assessing their virtues in the garden or as cut flowers, digressing into history or personal anecdote whenever the mood strikes him, it sometimes seems that he is writing for himself as well as for us. What other authoritative garden writer would go on to confess, after noting that *Sedum pulchellum* needs moist conditions to show itself at its best, that he learned this only after "one of those horrid, interfering blackbirds" broke off a piece of root and dropped it in the bog garden.

Like most keen plantsmen, as opposed to designers, Bowles favored the living, thriving plant over the dead, winterkilled version, however dramatic and architectural it might appear when covered with a coating of ice or frost. Thus *Autumn and Winter* is mostly about the former season and the flowers and shrubs that come into their own when high summer is past: asters, lilies and their relatives, Japanese anemones, such precious survivors as *Salvia patens* and the last roses, the coloring trees, the plants that have made it through the first sharp frost—*Erigeron mucronatus* (*E. karvinskianus*) and *Borago laxiflora* (*B. pygmaea*)—caryopteris, a few special veronicas. Of cyclamens, those tiny

Preface

jewels of autumn, he admits to an "insatiable desire . . . and could never have too many," a sentiment that is easy to agree with, especially after reading Bowles on the subject. Predictably, this volume deals extensively with autumn crocuses, including *Crocus sativa*, the source of saffron, which calls forth a fascinating digression on its history as a medicine and a spice. Curiously, Bowles remarks that saffron "is no longer much used for flavoring food except in Cornwall and some parts of Switzerland, Germany, and Austria," which will come as news to plenty of cooks today. But it is not only attitudes about food that change over time. Conservationists at the close of the twentieth century are likely to be shocked by the way Bowles and his friends like Reginald Farrer blithely collected plants from the wild in wholesale lots on the assumption that they would never run out. ("If all the collectors in all the world with all their sacks," Farrer once wrote, "combined to toil at the task for months and years, I do not believe they could strip even one range of the Alps of their *Eritrichium*.") Bowles specialized in collecting rare crocuses.

Gus Bowles was forty-five when his three "My Garden" books were published, and though he lived for nearly forty years more he wrote nothing else of the kind again. Instead, he concentrated on gardening, on painting (mostly flowers), on committee work and judging for the Royal Horticultural Society, on charitable good works in the neighborhood of Myddelton, and on writing regularly for a children's magazine, signing his pieces "Uncle G." He also pursued, with all the enthusiasm and assiduity of the self-taught, the botanical studies that led to his handbooks on crocuses (1924) and narcissi (1934). Had fortune

My Garden in Autumn and Winter

not frowned on him, he would have had two more such hand-books to his credit, on snowdrops and anemones, but both were undertaken when he was an old man. The first project was more or less hijacked by a collaborator, and the second proved to be unmanageably large and was never completed.

Almost half a century after Bowles's death, his garden at Myddelton has been restored to something approaching its former glory, and is open to the public. It is certainly worth a visit. Yet in another sense it has never been closed, thanks to the descriptive powers of Edward Augustus Bowles and the "My Garden" trilogy. If ever a garden achieved immortality, it is in these books.

MY GARDEN IN AUTUMN
AND WINTER

Facsimile of the Original Edition of 1915

Scots Pines and Venetian Sumach. (*Frontispiece.*)

My Garden in Autumn and Winter

By E. A. Bowles, M.A.

London: T. C. & E. C. Jack
67 Long Acre, W.C.
And Edinburgh
1915

CONTENTS

ILLUSTRATIONS

BLACK AND WHITE PLATES

My Garden in Autumn and Winter

COLOUR PLATES

Publisher's note:
Unfortunately, original color illustrations could not be obtained for
reproduction in this facsimile edition. Timber Press regrets any incon-
venience and includes this list for the sake of historical accuracy.

viii

MY GARDEN IN AUTUMN
AND WINTER

CHAPTER I

The Passing of Summer

IN the garden Summer melts into Autumn as gradually
as the fading from one to another of the dissolving views
that delighted the children and enlivened parish enter-
tainments some half a century ago. A touch of gold or
crimson on the heavy dark green foliage of late Summer
gives promise of the new picture that will grow clearer as
the old one fades. Maturing fruits weigh down the boughs
instead of flowers, leading us to believe, in spite of authoritative denials, that Autumn is closely connected with the
Latin word *auctus* although the spelling of *auctumnus* was
never legitimate.

Seed time and harvest is perhaps the best definition of
the third season of the year; but for the good gardener it
only expresses one side of its character. The cooling rains
of Autumn produce a similar result to that wrought by the
warming sunlight of Spring, and awaken so many bulbous
plants to their annual round of growth, flowering, and seeding, that in gardens where good collections of them are

grown a second Spring seems to fill the beds. Many autumnal species of Crocus, Cyclamen, and Oxalis closely resemble their relatives of the Spring, and though Tulips and Daffodils are not represented they have their counterparts or understudies, in *Colchicum speciosum*, especially in its white form, for the Tulip, and Sternbergia for the Daffodil.

The average, country-bred Englishman dates the commencement of Autumn from the day upon which it again becomes lawful for him to shoot partridges. Heads of families, and their young people too, are inclined to synchronise it with the reassembling of schools and the termination of the Summer Holidays. The most correct of all possible reckonings of the seasons is that observed by astronomers; and from them we learn Autumn lasts from the twenty-first of September to the twenty-first of December; but popular custom is against them, as seen in the generally used term Midsummer Day for the twenty-first of June, which according to their reckoning is but the first day of astronomical Summer. I often consult an old Latin-English Dictionary when I wish to obtain an idea of the views current in the close of the seventeenth century, when it was new from the press, and from it I learn that Autumn is the period from the sixth of August to the sixth of November. That fits in with the idea that Midsummer falls on the twenty-first of June, and Midwinter on the twenty-first of December. Many a time I have wished it did so when Winter's cruel rigours were still afflicting us in the middle of March!

But what is most material to this chronicle of **my**

The Passing of Summer

garden is the approximate period in which I feel there is more of Autumn than of Summer in the flower beds. In the average season, in this peculiarly rainless section of England, this seldom occurs before the latter part of September, but premonitory symptoms may be observed quite early in August. If I am a little behindhand in the replanting of my Crocus corms that have been lifted and cleaned, I am sure to find a few autumnal kinds shooting out long, white growths, like spills made of twisted paper, as they lie in the pots. If a corm lies sideways or upside down in the pot an unkind fate induces that one to shoot the first and the most strongly, and at planting time it is a puzzle to get it so placed in the earth that the tip of the shoot may point upwards and the base of the corm lie so that the roots may descend.

It always strikes me as remarkable that autumnal flowering plants such as Colchicums and Crocuses should start to grow, and sometimes should succeed in flowering, when stored away and kept comparatively dry. Of course there is a certain amount of moisture in the corm that is available to pass into the developing cells of the blossoms, and they may be able to derive a little more from the atmosphere ; but even these combined sources of moisture must fall far short of the amount provided by active roots, which is indispensable for most other plants. Of Crocuses, *C. zonatus, speciosus,* and *cancellatus* will flower quite respectably without making any roots, when standing in pots, empty but for the Crocuses, in an ordinary shed or greenhouse.

I have often seen *Colchicum autumnale* flowering well

3

My Garden in Autumn and Winter

in a cottage window in Cornwall, simply lying on the inner sill, without any soil to root into. The only plant I can think of that can be treated in the same way in Spring is *Sauromatum guttatum*, that weird, spotted aroid that of late has been sold for flowering without the help of soil or potting, and somewhat incongruously named the Monarch of the East.

Even in dry seasons, before the autumn rains have soaked the parched earth, the more sensitive of the Crocus and Colchicum genera recognise that it is time to push up a flower or two, relying on the dews that begin to refresh the fainting garden by the middle of August. " St. Bartholomew and his cold dew" is a popular saying, and I always feel, even in years of drought, when his day, the twenty-fourth of August, has arrived, my Primulas and more delicate Saxifrages that have survived thus far, will be able to regain strength and plumpness within the next few weeks. The end of the struggle against combined heat and drought, and a rest from hard labour with watercans each evening are welcome first-fruits of Autumn's presence, even if one has to pay for them with the realisation that Summer is passing away, that the evenings are drawing in and it is now too dark to do much in the after-dinner stroll in the garden unless the moon is at the full. Then a Herald-moth flutters in to the lamp through the open window, the Lime and Horse-chestnut leaves on the lawns entail daily sweepings, most of the Vines in the pergola begin to show bronze tintings on the older and more exposed leaves, the Claret Vine turns purple from head to foot, and the Early Chrysanthemums yield a basketful

4

The Passing of Summer

of flowers for the vases. At such a time it is better to be grateful that the wealth of colour, store of fruit, and long-lived flowers one receives from Autumn's bountiful hand are now added to the rich store left us by vanishing Summer, than to dwell upon the obtrusive signs of decay to be seen in falling leaves.

One of the greatest virtues of gardening is this perpetual renewal of youth and Spring, of promise of flower and fruit that can always be read in the open book of the Garden, by those with an eye to see, and a mind to understand. It is pleasant to note the formation of next year's catkins on the Hazels while the leaves are still green, the rounded buds that mean flowers on *Chimonanthus fragrans*, or even the plentiful seeds that the Balsams shoot about every time you shake the old plants. What hopes of future beauty one can read in the fat, nut-shaped bud of a *Pinguicula grandiflora*, the mealy winter rosette of *Primula cashmiriana*, or the hard central crown of tightly rolled fronds of some good fern.

Some people prefer to read a sad note in Autumn and to dwell on the fading and passing of Summer's joys, and as it takes all sorts to make a world, and there must ever be those who *enjoy* bad health, who would miss their death's head as much as their salt-cellar on their dinner tables, we must allow them their minor harmonies and depressing remarks about departing swallows. But the good gardener should have no time to look back on departing joys; he should be all alive to take advantage of the yet warm soil, that, combined with a cool and moist atmosphere, makes the days of September and early October the most propitious

5

My Garden in Autumn and Winter

of all the year for planting out recently collected alpines, nursed into vigour in shaded frames, or seedlings pricked out in boxes or beds, as well as for dividing and moving many of the plants of the garden; and yet again for that most fascinating part of gardening, the ordering and planting of the Season's bulbs.

The autumn manœuvres of the garden, if properly planned and carried out with vigour at the right time, do more to ensure a successful flower pageant next season than any amount of after care. Then is the best moment to pull down and rebuild portions of the rock garden, if only you have planned the alterations early enough to label the plants that die down entirely, before their disappearance. Many large clumps can be lifted out and stood on the path until their bed has been remade for them, and can, even after many days, be snugly tucked up in it again without suffering from the delay. If so treated in Spring, a flowering season would have been ruined. I find many things, such as Cistuses, the large yellow Helianthemums, such as *H. halimifolium* and *H. formosum*, Lithospermums, Veronicas, and many other sub-shrubs can be put in as cuttings in Autumn in the open ground, and even though they may not actually root before Winter comes, they retain sufficient life to produce roots with the return of Spring much more surely than cuttings not detached from the old plants until the Spring. So there is always plenty to be done in Autumn, more in fact than the days allow for, and no time to waste on sad regrets.

Another joy of Autumn that I do not fail to take advantage of is the knowledge that one can cut sprays of

6

The Passing of Summer

Roses without regard for the immature buds. Tea-roses with long sprays of purple-red foliage and many young buds, that do so much to complete the beauty of form and balance when placed in a vase, are luxuries I never dare allow myself early in the season, but in late autumn days it is often kinder to flowers to cut them and bring them into the house than to leave them outside to run the risk of nipping frosts. There is, too, a wonderful satisfaction in having filled every available bowl and vase with Cherry-pie, Nasturtiums, *Saxifraga Fortunei*, Dahlias, Mignonette, Crinums, Marguerites, and Salvias the day before the blackening frost came, and having a fine show indoors for perhaps a week or more after Jack Frost robbed you of all these typically summer flowers outside. The little gamble with the Clerk of the weather, in covering a few beds with matting during the cold spell, and so keeping their bright contents unharmed for the warm days of St. Luke's Summer, gives a zest to gardening for me, and I can enjoy the salvage of Summer for the further ten days without stopping to realise that I have only postponed the calamity for a spell.

There are joys, too, for the sensitive and appreciative nose in the scents peculiar to Autumn. I especially enjoy the fragrance of newly-fallen Walnut leaves; it is more delicate, and of course more easily got at in its pervasiveness than the scent of a young leaf or two plucked and bruised.

This last season, St. Cecilia's Day, the twenty-second of November, was made notable by the sudden fall of the Mulberry leaves after a white frost, and when the sunlight was on them the air was full of a sweet scent quite new to

7

My Garden in Autumn and Winter

me, something like the flavour of ripe Mulberries, but peculiarly clean and refreshing in tone, reminiscent of the silkworms we tended as children as they ate holes in Mulberry leaves.

I have never been able to get any pleasure from the scent of dying leaves of Strawberries, that was so highly praised of old by Bacon and others. It is reasonable to suppose that the careful selection of the Strawberry from the point of view of its fruit only may have led to the loss of the characters that produced the fragrance in its dying leaves. If the fragrance was as delightful as the testimony of many writers affirms, it would be worth while seeking out any still existing old-fashioned varieties, as well as the wild parents that gave us our garden Strawberries, and planting them separately in order to discover which, if any, possess the charm of fragrant foliage. Bacon writes that, next to the white double Violet and the Musk Rose, the sweetest fragrance of the garden is that of "Strawberry leaves dying, which yield a most excellent cordiale smell."

Then Sir John Suckling, who lived in the middle of the seventeenth century, wrote in one of his plays :

"Wholesome
As dying leaves of Strawberries."

Mrs. Gaskell endows one of her heroines, Lady Ludlow, with the power of enjoying this scent. But it seems to have died out amongst us now, and the latest reference I can find to it is the statement made by the late Mr. Burbidge. Burbidge wrote in his charming book, *The Scented Garden*, that the scent of dying Strawberry leaves in the early sun-

8

The Passing of Summer

shine of a frosty morning is one of the rarest and most delicious of all scents of the garden. Is it then the same with the Strawberry as with the Mulberry, that the atmospheric conditions are seldom right for a feast of perfume just when there is an appreciative nose at hand? Or should we conclude that the modern Strawberry has lost its fragrant leaves, or that we no longer possess the power of enjoying them?

It is chiefly in late Autumn that *Impatiens Roylei*, the great, pink, annual Balsam, scents the air with an odour of ripe plums, even stronger than that one can sniff out of the flowers of *Iris graminea*. But beyond these special and localised perfumes, the whole air bears a scent of newly fallen leaves, a rich woodland brand of scent, most noticeable on damp mornings and towards evening, while calm sunny hours at midday, before the advent of sharp frost, are full of balm and spices from Asters, *Alyssum maritimum*, Tea-Roses, and Heliotrope, and there always seems to me a richer bouquet in their incense on these days than earlier in the season.

CHAPTER II

Autumn Crocuses

I SEE that I noted September the twenty-sixth as the day when the garden was really full of autumnal Crocuses. But many had put in an appearance much earlier in the month, and one, the rich orange *C. Scharojanii*, flowered in the middle of August.

It needs a sharp eye to detect the first reappearance above ground of some of these autumnal species, for so many of them flower before producing any leaves, and in their case it is no more than the very tip of the white, or green-veined sheathing leaves, that appears. Once this is through, it is marvellous how quickly the flower itself lengthens and pushes up between the strong, leathery sheathing leaves that have by sheer force pierced a way for it through the hard ground. The white nose of the sheathing leaves may have been noticed one day no more conspicuous than a baby's newly cut tooth, the next a blue bud has emerged and is perhaps an inch long, and by the following day a large blue flower is opened to the sunshine. Thus a day of rain followed by two of warmth and sunshine will often transform a yard or two of bare brown soil into a brilliant patch of rich blue *Crocus speciosus*. I have watched the vernal Crocus of the Alps developing under a

Autumn Crocuses

daily thinning coverlet of snow, sometimes pushing its flowers along horizontally between the snow and the ground until at last their lifting force is sufficient to break through the thin layer, and they can straighten up in the sunshine while the last snow crystals are melting round them.

Now, I long to watch the reappearance of an autumnal species in its own home, for that I have never done, and I can well believe that the coming of the autumn rains may work as wonderful a miracle as the departing of the snow, and the Crocus-clad ground be as beautiful in either case.

Rather more than a third of the autumnal species flower before their leaves make any appearance above ground, but I can only think of one, namely, *C. gargaricus*, of the vernal species that does so. This looks as though the habit was of some use to the autumnal section, but as it is not correlated with any geographical range, peculiar type of colouring, or any other character that I can detect, and as with most of them the leaves follow so soon after the flowers fade that they do not thus escape injury from winter frosts, I cannot offer any solution of the problem, but simply state the fact, that eleven out of the twenty-nine autumnal species I have cultivated, flower before their leaves appear.

This habit tempts one to plant them among other plants that form carpets, and certainly the effect of the flowers rising through some Acæna or Saxifrage is good, but unless the Crocuses are scattered rather thinly there is a risk of the carpet being bothered and worried into a nervous breakdown or anæmic debility from having to struggle with a mass of long Crocus leaves lying on it. I have not yet hit upon what I consider a thoroughly satisfactory pair of stable companions or messmates, one of which shall be a Crocus. *C. speciosus* with *Geranium atlanticum* is not bad; *C. zonatus* in *Acæna inermis* has proved a fair success. I have tried such kinds as *C. longiflorus* and *C. asturicus* in *Cerastium tomentosum*, but although the effect was charming in October, when the Crocuses were in flower, their long, green leaves spoiled the effect of the silver carpet in Spring. Now I am trying *C. speciosus* in a carpet of Ivy, and hope it may be able to make itself at home there, and agreeable to its fellow-lodger.

There is a widespread idea that Autumn Crocuses are hard to grow, and so there is many a well-furnished garden that still lacks their special charms. I cannot believe, however, that there is a garden in England that can produce a healthy cabbage and a Marigold in which *C. speciosus* and *C. zonatus* would not become so thoroughly at home after a few years that it would be as hard to entirely eradicate them as it is to banish Ground-Elder. Yet people will spend money annually on Early Tulips and Hyacinths and such fleeting joys, and grudge a few shillings that would provide carpets of blue and mauve for every recurring October. I think some people have had disappointments with Autumn Crocuses through ordering and planting them too late in the season, and that has procured them an evil reputation that they do not deserve. It is, I know, easier to preach the early ordering and planting of bulbs than to practise these virtuous acts. The July and August

Autumn Crocuses

flower beds are so full and gay one can only with difficulty bring oneself to think about next season's gaps, and it seems cruel to pull up some annual not yet on the retired list. Yet I am convinced no one would repent prompt action in ordering Autumn Crocuses the very day they receive lists containing them, and then hunting out suitable homes for them as soon as possible after their arrival. Everyone should commence with the four most reliable species, namely, *C. speciosus, C. zonatus, C. pulchellus,* and *C. longiflorus,* and I will boldly prophesy that these will give as much pleasure as any plant of the whole year, and that it will not be long before plans are made for further plantings. Like their brethren of the Spring they all rejoice in free, gritty soil, even pure sand, for the corm to lie in, but they do not object to rich, even stiff, soil below for the roots to enter and feed on, so long as there is enough drainage to prevent stagnant moisture wetting their toes and producing the Crocus equivalents of catarrh and consumption. It follows, then, that sunny slopes of the rock garden and well-prepared beds with an established reputation for good drainage suit them best, but *C. zonatus* and *C. speciosus* may be planted almost anywhere with reasonable hopes of success.

Let us now turn from generalities to the plants themselves, and in order to demolish the miffiness myth, we will go and see for ourselves what *C. speciosus* has done with itself during the twenty years that have passed since it first found a foothold in this garden.

I first saw it in Ware's Hale Farm Nursery at Tottenham, in full bloom on a sunny September morning, and

My Garden in Autumn and Winter

ordered a dozen corms, to try whether I could grow it. These forerunners were planted in the warm southern bed in front of the peach-house, where unknown treasures are still planted, that they may be, not only warm and sheltered, but also easily kept under observation. I will not trace the intermediate steps but simply chronicle the fact that last August we determined to thoroughly replant this bed, removing the old soil for new. We sifted that old soil through sieves, and thereby caught many bulbs missed in the lifting, and among them were hundreds of *Crocus speciosus* corms ; but even after that process of elimination, the old soil, spread out in the kitchen garden, produced a crop of blue flowers of this Crocus last Autumn, and such a mass of leaves this Spring that I expect our Celery trenches and beds of Brussels Sprouts will be decorated with *C. speciosus* in September and October as long as the garden lasts.

You must know that this species is not only a great seeder, but nature has ordained that each healthy corm should produce satellites in the form of a ring of minute cormlets, after the manner of the " spawn " of a Gladiolus. These tiny babes are about the size of a Carter's Little Liver Pill, and as round in shape, and are as difficult to find and remove when considered undesirable, as the offsets of Alliums like *A. roseum* and *A. triquetrum.*

The mature corms of *C. speciosus* are easy to recognise as they belong to the annulate section of the genus, which means they have a shining smooth skin, that splits on the under side into a series of rings which can be easily seen, and also rubbed off with the finger. They may be con-

Autumn Crocuses

fused with its near ally *C. pulchellus* if grown together, but are usually larger and flatter, and if carefully examined the tunic of *C. speciosus* is found to be thinner in texture, and the rings are continued one after another to form the basal tunic, while in *C. pulchellus* there is a rather large flat disc that serves this purpose. From all spring-flowering annulate species they can be separated by their habit of shooting out long, white growths shaped like tusks in the middle of August, when spring-flowering species are still dormant. The small fry, the pilules, are uncommonly hard to separate out if they get mixed among those of *C. chrysanthus*. After I had sifted and sorted the products of this lifting of the peach-house border, and obtained many potfuls of *C. speciosus* corms, I was able to plant a thick carpet of them under the Wistaria standards on the lawn, and another where the *Geranium pratense* forms can be cut down under the old Bay by the pond, and on this September morning we can walk about the garden and find many a blue patch, all the result of that original dozen from Ware's. But I soon bought more, for I found Barr had a specially large and pale form of it mixed among the ordinary type, and I found varietal names existed in catalogues. So in the big herbaceous bed there are some broad stretches, and the Eremurus clumps, now entirely devoid of leaves, are marked out by carpets of blue Crocus flowers, for I find they can be planted deeper than the great wheels without tyres of the Eremuri, and left below to look after themselves when their gigantic neighbours are replanted. Again under the old Snowy Mespilus is a round bed, green and yellow with Winter Aconite in early Spring, but throughout

My Garden in Autumn and Winter

September and October blue or lilac with this and other Crocuses.

Let us pick a bloom of the type and note its charms. First I reckon its tall and stout perianth tube which does duty as a stem. Stronger than that of most Crocuses, it stands against wind and weather really well for so frail a type of flower. After two days of opening, and the consequent fertilisation of its ovules, the flower is easily knocked over, but even so it remains attractive for another day or two in dry weather, lying on the ground, and room is made above for another to take its place. This type is generally freely speckled with fine purple dots on the outside, which lend a richness to the general effect of colour when the blossoms are closed. But when they open out in the sunlight no Crocus of either season produces such a near approach to an effect of true blue colouring. This is chiefly due to the inner segments, which are generally freely veined with a true ultramarine shade of blue on a pale lilac ground colour; but individual plants vary considerably in this character of the veining.

Dean Herbert endeavoured to distinguish three distinct varietal forms, but seedling plants have refused to be tied and bound by his narrowing distinctions, and they freely combine all his points of difference with a bewildering freedom of conscience. There are, however, some really good varieties of modern introduction. The finest of all was given to me by Mr. Elwes, and I believe was collected by himself in the far East. It is known as var. *Aitchisonii,* and is the largest flowered Crocus known to me. I have a specimen that I dried on purpose to con-

Crocus speciosus from Artabir. (See p. 17.)

.

Autumn Crocuses

vince people that the drawing I made of it was not exaggerated, and I find the segments measure over two and a half inches in length. It is much paler in colour than the typical form, and less veined with blue ; in fact, almost a uniform lavender of a very pale shade outside, but a bright rosy-lilac within. It is a magnificent thing when in full flower, and seldom appears before the middle of October, when true *speciosus* is waning, so it is a pity such a fine and useful plant is still rather scarce.

Messrs. Van Tubergen received a form from one of their collectors that approaches this var. *Aitchisonii* both in size and colour, but is not so large, nor so late in flowering. They call it var. *Artabir* from the locality it was found in, and the photograph facing p. 16 shows a little group of it at the foot of the rock garden. This fine form is both plentiful and comparatively cheap. The same firm got a good strain from Schemacha, among which were several pure white specimens which have provided us with a good hardy white Crocus for early Autumn. The rich scarlet stigma of this species is very lovely in these white forms.

About six years ago I was delighted to find two very acceptable gifts from the gods in a row of seedlings from the old blue *speciosus*. They are not quite white, but have only just enough blue to give them a look of healthy solidity, and they have preserved the blue veining on this light ground. Of course a seedling in one's own beds is always more nearly a swan than a goose, but even allowing for this weakness I believe my two grey seedlings are fit for any honourable post open to an autumnal Crocus.

17   B

My Garden in Autumn and Winter

A useful late form of *C. speciosus* came here from Smith of Worcester, under the name of *C. speciosus v. globosus.* Its value is provided by two characters, lateness of flowering and an extra amount of blue in its colouring, rather than by the roundness of outline that provided it with its varietal name. Here it flowers from mid-October till late in November, and so is always the last of the *speciosus* forms of each season. This one species of Crocus, then, can be looked to for beautifying otherwise bare patches of ground from mid-September onwards for at least two months, so take my advice, and write at once to the firm who lists any varieties of it, asking them to reserve you the six or six hundred that the tightness or laxity of your purse-strings permit, for next year's planting season ; for if you wait till you see it in flower, or until you are ordering your other bulbs, you will be too late to make it and yourself happy.

C. pulchellus is a near relation of *speciosus,* and like it is annulate as to corm tunic, leafless when flowering, and has a much divided bunch of stigmata. It is distinguished at a glance, though, by its rich orange-coloured throat, cool lavender shade of ground colour, fewer and more parallel purple veins, and pure white anthers, characters that combined make it a very lovely and refined flower.

It is at its best rather later than the typical form of *speciosus,* but wherever the two are grown in considerable numbers their flowering seasons overlap, and in a peaceful garden, where beds are not too often turned out, a very interesting set of hybrids between the two species is sure to appear sooner or later.

18

Autumn Crocuses

These vary much, and so far as I have yet observed they mostly resemble *speciosus* in general appearance, but are easily detected by pale cream-coloured, or rarely pure-white anthers, and the addition of a patch of yellow of varying size and depth of colouring to the normally white throat of *speciosus*. The depth and number of the veins on the segments also vary, and to a quick eye proclaim their hybrid origin, but they also give them sufficient distinction from a decorative point of view to make some of the more distinct forms well worth lifting and careful attention, in order to obtain a sufficient number to plant a good-sized patch. It is the best instance I know of an undoubted hybrid between two distinct species of Crocus, and therefore, even if it were not the daintily beautiful thing it is, it would be welcome in the gardens of the curious, as the old books call such plots as mine. *C. pulchellus* now and then gives its admirers a white seedling of exquisite beauty, so seeds are well worth garnering and sowing. The orange-coloured throat is even more conspicuous in this albino than in the type, and as it is a sturdy form it is a great addition to the none too numerous or robust white forms of autumnal Crocuses.

C. zonatus suggests at a first glance a pink form of *pulchellus*, for it has similar white anthers, orange in the throat, and a scheme of parallel veining on the segments. It belongs to a totally different branch of the family, though, and has a corm that is unmistakable, differing from that of all other Crocuses known to me. It is wide and flat, and never quite symmetrical in outline, for it always possesses one or more protuberances somewhere on its outer edge, which I believe are the points from which it produces the curious clusters of cormlets that aid its rapid increase. These differ from the pilules of *C. speciosus* in being both in shape and colouring very much like a grain of wheat, and are so small, so slightly attached to the parent at lifting time, and, moreover, so much like dry earth in colour, that if one wishes to get rid of this vigorous species from any border it has claimed for a possession, these minute cormlets will render the task difficult, if not impossible.

Few would wish to eject this Crocus, though, for it is one of the first to greet the autumn rains with flowers, and though their segments are of thin substance, and so do not stand rough weather well, it is very generous in the supply provided. Their light pink shade of mauve is suggestive of the colouring of a Colchicum, and distinct from that of any other Crocus. Sometimes a seedling, flowering for the first time, will open nearly white, and flatter my hopes of obtaining that long-felt want, a pure white *C. zonatus*, but hitherto they have always responded to my raptures by blushing as soon as they found themselves famous, and losing their proud position and clean new label, to be mixed with the potful of the typical form at the next lifting. I have been beguiled into spending many shillings on *C. zonatus albus* so described in catalogues, but they also, just as much as the home-grown ones, have coloured up like a bashful schoolgirl, and I still lack the white *C. zonatus*. It will come some day, however, for I believe every plant, except perhaps those with yellow flowers, of too primitive or conservative a plan to break out in new lines, is likely

Autumn Crocuses

to produce an albino form wherever it is grown from seed in large quantities. This has led me to hunt diligently in alpine regions for white forms, and I have frequently found them myself, and boldly directed others to do so. Once I was almost ready to apologise for my belief in this capacity for producing white forms, for upon hearing that a friend with an eye for a good plant was going to Cintra in October, I begged him to visit the central home of *C. Clusii* and to find for me the white form thereof, but omitted to tell him it would be the first one on record. He sent me a goodly supply of the typical purple one later on, saying that it was plentiful enough, but so far he could see no trace of the white one, and if anyone else had bidden him look for it he would have long ago given up hunting, feeling sure it did not exist. I was on the point of writing to confess my lack of certain knowledge of its existence when a blessed postcard informed me that no fewer than three of the pure white treasures had fallen to his trowel, and had been potted up that they might reach me without risk of damage. They are some of my most precious possessions, and have led me to demand similar careful searches of other gardening gadabouts.

C. longiflorus has so far as I know yet to be found in its white form. I have pale seedlings in plenty, but nothing that leads me to expect a white one from them, and I long to get among its flowers on some Italian hillside. It is a very beautiful thing, however, in any form, whether it be the soft rosy lilac, with rich orange-yellow throat and scarlet stigma of the type, the pearly grey forms known as var. *Wilhelmii* or those from Malta, and therefore known as var. *melitensis*, with featherings or stripes of rich purple on their outer segments. It is a sturdy, happy plant, making itself at home in any warm, well-drained border, and certain to greet you every year at the end of October and throughout November with a mass of its fragrant flowers, which are all the better for the support of its stiff young leaves. It has been known as *C. odorus*, and I wish it might be legitimately always so called, for it is as fragrant in Autumn as *C. Imperati* is in Spring, and a few blooms brought into the house will soon give you a reminder of Primroses and Irises, and the coming of Spring. I hope that all who read this will plant a patch or two of this cheap, reliable, and lovely plant, if only for the purpose of giving their noses a treat when autumn frosts have cut off most of the outdoor flowers that can provide so good a perfume.

In Sicily saffron is collected from *C. longiflorus*, but only from wild plants, and I have never heard of this species being cultivated for the purpose. This seems rather extraordinary when one considers how hardy and free-flowering *C. longiflorus* is, even under the comparatively sunless skies of England, and how very shy of its blooms the real saffron-producing Crocus, *C. sativus*, is under similar conditions. The true Saffron is one of the most remarkable of our cultivated plants. It has been renowned for its value as a drug, a perfume, and a dye from the earliest times, and is mentioned in the Song of Solomon, and praised by many Greek writers. Yet it is now retained in the pharmacopoeia solely for its use as a colouring agent, though quite superseded elsewhere as a dye by less costly productions, and is no longer much used for flavouring

Autumn Crocuses

food except in Cornwall and some parts of Switzerland, Germany, and Austria. This one cannot wonder at, for it is not a flavouring that appeals to everyone, and is, in fact, an acquired taste. I myself like it in cakes, as one meets with it in Cornwall, but it may be I was predisposed to like it, from its associations and interest, and I must own that though I like to meet with it in Cornwall I have never had a saffron cake made at home. In the year 1671 a book of two hundred and eighty-three pages, wholly devoted to the history and uses of saffron, was published at Jena. It was written by John Ferdinand Hertodt, and if only one might believe him, saffron aided by other substances should cure pretty nearly all the ills that flesh is heir to, including Hypochondria, Arthritis, the Plague, toothache, and madness. Hertodt generally advises the mixing of a variety of other things with the precious saffron, it is true, such as Dragon's blood, flowers of Chamomile dried and pounded, swallows' nests, the worm-eaten wood of oaks or the fat of the mountain mouse ; but even though such powerful ingredients as opium, myrrh, and aloes, or the oil of Henbane enter into his prescriptions for draughts or ointments, yet saffron is the all-important drug that is the leading feature of each, and without which the rest are accounted worthless. It is even recommended as a hair dye if it is a yellow colour that is desired as the result. But I fear no one consults or follows the advice of the Crocologia nowadays, and the cultivation of the Saffron Crocus and the use of the drug are steadily declining. Spain produces the largest quantity of saffron now, but it is still grown in parts of France and as far away as Afghanistan, Kashmir, and China, and by the

My Garden in Autumn and Winter

German inhabitants of a district of Pennsylvania. Therefore, even now it is cultivated over a far wider extent of the earth than that in which the many species of the genus Crocus have been found to grow naturally. Yet it is by no means an easy plant to cultivate successfully, for it is liable to attacks from parasitic fungi, insomuch that several investigations of these diseases have been carried out and suggestions for preventing them published. Then, again, not only are the plants easily injured by bad seasons, but the flowers are sometimes destroyed by bad weather at their flowering period. So saffron has always commanded a high price, and has tempted those who sold it to adulterate it in many ingenious ways. In these days of increasing numbers of officials, when at last it happens that all other things have their inspectors, we may once more hear of the appointment of Inspectors of Saffron as in the Middle Ages. Let us hope they will prove more lenient than those of Nuremberg who in 1444 burnt Jobst Findeker in the same fire as his adulterated saffron. Even in the days of Dioscorides and of Pliny it was a common thing to moisten and otherwise adulterate saffron, and Pliny tells us "Nothing is so subject to sophistication as Saffron, and therefore the only triall of true Saffron is this, if a man lay his hands upon it, he shall heare it to cracke as if it were brittle and readie to burst: for that which is moist (a qualitie coming by some indirect means and cunning cast) yieldeth to the hand and makes no words." From Pliny we also learn that "Our Wine-Knights when they purpose to sit square at the taverne and carouse lustily, if they drink Saffron, never feare surfeit nor the overturning of their braine; and

24

Autumn Crocuses

they are verily persuaded that this keepeth them from drunkenness, and maketh them carie their drink well," which may partly account for its popularity in ancient days. The marvel to us, however, is how sufficient can be produced to meet even the comparatively small demand of modern times, for it has been reckoned that eight thousand of the flowers will only produce about three and a half ounces of dried saffron. I do not know how freely it flowers in sunny Spain, but here it is a very shy flowerer, and I fear I could never make a fortune by picking all the saffron produced here. It appears to have been a lucrative crop as grown at Saffron Walden and near Cambridge in the early half of the eighteenth century, as Miller, in that monument of industry and learning, *The Gardener's Dictionary*, gives a table of charges and profits, and reckons at the price of thirty shillings a pound for saffron the net profits of an acre should be about five pounds four shillings yearly, without counting any return from the sale of the increase of the roots. The industry is now dead in those neighbourhoods, and I cannot find any evidence that the plant lingers in the district as a naturalised alien, or even as an ornament to cottage gardens.

Another point of interest of *Crocus sativus* is the fact that like many other cultivated plants its exact origin is unknown, and the wild forms of both Greece and Italy differ so much from the cultivated plant that all of them have been regarded by botanists at one time or another as distinct species.

To my mind the form known as *C. sativus*, var. *Cartwrightianus*, which is, or was some fifteen years ago,

My Garden in Autumn and Winter

abundant round Athens, is the most likely form I have seen from which the cultivated plant might have sprung. For centuries it has been increased only by vegetative reproduction, as it is perfectly sterile and never sets seeds unless fertilised by pollen of some wild form. Thus it must be one of the oldest of cultivated plants that has been derived from one individual and yet still retains unimpaired vitality. Some of our double-flowered old garden plants such as the Rockets, Roses, and Clove Carnations, and possibly such easily divided herbs as Mint and Horseradish, may have gone on for a great length of time without the raising of a fresh stock from seed, and are wonderful enough, but I can recall no other plant that can boast of such antiquity of sterility and such extended cultivation as the Saffron Crocus. It is rather curious that the nearest approach to these two characteristics is found in another member of the genus, to wit, the old Dutch Crocus, which likewise never seeds, and is one of the commonest of garden plants and as vigorous as ever.

So in spite of the Saffron Crocus needing a good deal of attention, good light soil, frequent lifting and dividing, and a very choice sunny spot for its residence, I like to have some generously planned plantings of it ; and I value its handsome lilac flowers, so richly veined with purple, all the more, perhaps, because in some seasons the plant is so niggardly in presenting them. The long stigmata, which are the portion dried for saffron, are of a wonderfully rich scarlet hue, and hang out of the flower. Their thickened upper ends and slender lower portion greatly resemble nails in shape, and look so much as though they had been

Autumn Crocuses

soaked in blood that being three in number I wonder there is no monkish legend extant connecting them with the nails of the Crucifixion.

Once the flowers open they never entirely close again, and, therefore, unless protected overhead, are easily destroyed by rain or even a plentiful dew, a fact which greatly detracts from their garden value. The Italian form var. *Thomassii*, which I owe to the generosity of Kew, behaves more sensibly, and closes as tightly as you please on dull days and at night, and, moreover, is a handsome plant. It had died out in England, but the arrival at Kew of a fresh stock from its classic home near Taranto should help to spread it again among Crocus lovers. Here it seeds freely, and varies sufficiently to make the raising of seedlings exciting.

Next in garden value comes the var. *Cartwrightianus*, for though the flowers are small they are freely produced, but rather too late in the season to live long in the open. The stigmata are almost as long as those of the officinal plant, and especially gory in colour. Among corms I collected on the Lycabettos when I was in Athens, I found a good deal of variation, some being nearly white, but none lacked the veinings characteristic of the typical form. There is a good pure-white form in cultivation, however, and also a larger plant sometimes sold as *Cartwrightianus albus*, but more like an albino of the true Saffron. This last is one of the most lovely, for it is richly marked with a fine shade of blue-purple at the throat. Although it does very well in a neighbour's garden, it dies here after a few seasons of apparent prosperity, in spite of my constant

My Garden in Autumn and Winter

experiments to find a corner that really suits it. In some seasons I have had a clump with over a score of blossoms open at one time, and that was a sight worth looking at in the dull days of late November.

All of these varieties I have mentioned have the long nail-shaped stigmata that add so greatly to their beauty, but there are several in which the stigmata are no longer than in *C. longiflorus.* Such are those known as var. *Pallassii,* a variable plant ranging from a rich rosy-lilac to white, and perhaps most beautiful when the lilac of the outer segments shades at the edges into a nearly white, marginal band. Though it seeds freely it is not a very robust plant, and the old corms are inclined to die after seeding. The var. *Elwesii* is generally a large and pale lilac form, but I have some that are pure white. The best white form has been grown for some years at Kew as var. *Cashmirianus,* but it has no right to that name for Royle's figure is as purple as paint can make it, and he afterwards came to the conclusion that it was but an escape from cultivation of the true Saffron.

The poorest of all the varieties as regards substance and colour of flower is known as var. *Haussknechtii ;* but it is a very good tempered plant, marvellously floriferous, seeds almost as freely as a Groundsel, and varies a little from starchy lilac to nearly white. As its betters in its own family lack its kindly nature so conspicuously, one is inclined to make rather a fuss over this reliable and amiable mediocrity, and its flimsy flowers brighten up several ledges of the rock garden here. Even its stigmata are wanting in the distinction shown by its congeners, and they

Autumn Crocuses

are paler and shorter than in other varieties of *sativus ;* not worth likening to nails, scarcely more than brads, in fact, but the plant will " grow for you," so Haussknecht's Crocus is sure of a welcome here, where my love of the genus inclines me to grow all I can get. This catholicity leads to the inclusion of a misshapen, humpbacked, bandy-legged form of *C. zonatus,* that seldom produces a flower, and when it does the poor thing looks sparrow-bitten and slug-sliced. But then you must know it is so exceedingly interesting from a teratological point of view, spathes being transformed to segments, segments to antheroid bodies, stigmata perhaps to segments, and scarcely ever twice running on the same plan, so that not only do I allow it an honoured padded cell in the lunatic asylum border near the other demented plants, but carefully nurse a stock in the cold frame and in a cosy nook of the rock garden. I owe it to my good friend Mr. Walter Ledger, whose garden at Wimbledon is ever producing some new plant to be figured in the *Botanical Magazine,* a gall new to Britain or, as in this case, a Crocus that is beyond explanation or reduction to rule. But let us turn from the curious to the beautiful, and admire the whiteness of the flowers of the varieties of *C. hadriaticus,* which in the most marked forms are easily recognised by the yellow of their throat as being distinct from white forms of *C. sativus.* It seems very doubtful, though, whether they should be allowed to rank as anything but mere colour forms of that protean species, for I have found it impossible to distinguish some seedlings raised from *C. hadriaticus* which were lined or tinted with lilac, from similar ones with yellow throats raised from *C. sativus*

My Garden in Autumn and Winter

Pallasii. It is, however, a useful custom for garden purposes to reckon the white forms with long flowers as
hadriaticus, whether they are the variety *Saundersianus* with
purple throat, or var. *chrysobelonicus* in which it is golden,
and more or less marked externally with reddish brown.

There is a remarkable variety known as *peloponnesiacus*,
which, unlike all its near relations, produces its flowers
before its leaves in some seasons, but now and then
confuses its owner and observer by sending up as fine a
crop of them as any true Saffron Crocus is wont to do.

A group of closely allied species inhabits Western
Europe, and may be conveniently termed the Spanish
group, although one, *nudiflorus*, is plentiful north of the
Pyrenees in France, *C. Clusii*, already mentioned, is
commonest in Portugal, and *Salzmannii* is the one
autumnal Crocus found in Northern Africa. All of them,
however, are plentifully distributed in Spain itself, and are
hardy and useful species for English gardens. *C. nudiflorus* is the best, and yet, except when the owner of the
garden has visited the Pryenees, one seldom sees it over
here, and I do not know of any nursery that lists it. Yet
in the Basses-Pyrenées, even round Biarritz and St. Jean
de Luz, it is almost impossible to dig up any plant in
any spot at any time of the year without also obtaining a
plentiful supply of small corms of *C. nudiflorus*. It is the
only species in cultivation (the yellow flowered *C. lazicus*
still living in hiding somewhere near Trebizond) that
produces running stolons that separate from the corm and
grow into fat round corms after passing through several
intermediate stages between the shape of a worm or a

30

Autumn Crocuses

wood-louse, and the orthodox figure of a virtuous, blossom-promising Crocus corm. Anyone unfamiliar with their strange appearance might be forgiven for throwing away such ungainly looking objects, mistaking them for Couch Grass when decidedly vermiform, or the pupa of some evil fly when half-way through their programme of quick changes, and contracted to a short cylindrical figure. As its name implies, *C. nudiflorus* flowers without leaves. It is a tall, handsome species, larger and deeper in colour than the closely allied *C. asturicus*, and easily distinguished from it when in bloom by the absence of green leaves, which are generally to be seen protruding a little above ground in *asturicus* when the flower is fully out, or at any rate may be easily found by turning back the tips of the white sheathing leaves. Even should this test fail there remains another, for *C. nudiflorus* has a beautiful edging of deep purple to the lower half of the outer segments that is easily noticed, and does not exist, so far as I know, in any other autumnal Crocus. With its fringed scarlet stigmata and large, purple flowers and kindly habits of increase this species ought to be in every garden. I hope all who go to the land of its birth, whether to the Basses-Pyrenées or the higher slopes, will dig diligently for it; perhaps some enterprising nurseryman will combine a week's holiday with a commercial enterprise and be the means of distributing it widely. All success to both amateur and professional in so desirable a venture. About one in every fifty thousand is pure white and very beautiful. I have heard a tale of the late Mr. George Maw in connection with this white form, which relates that he was breakfasting with

My Garden in Autumn and Winter

Mr. G. F. Wilson, who had just received a box of flowers by post from the Pyrenees, and among them a white bloom of *C. nudiflorus*. Mr. Maw spent most of his time during breakfast looking out trains, and as soon as possible he set out for the locality from which the treasure had been sent, but I have never heard whether he was successful in finding it. From the mention in the monograph of none but those found near Biarritz by Mr. Osborne I fear he was too late. A good supply of white ones has been brought to one of the best of Norfolk gardens just lately, and I have hopes one may come here before next flowering season. If you cannot get *C. nudiflorus* you should grow *C. asturicus*, but it makes rather a poor substitute, not much better than that so ingeniously discovered by the heroes of this delightful story.

A tactless doctor prescribed a diet of champagne and oysters for a patient whose means would not provide it. On his next visit the patient was much worse, so he asked if his instructions had been carried out, and was told, "Well, you see, we couldn't afford it; so we gave him the nearest we could, ginger beer and whelks."

But as ginger beer is not altogether to be despised, so some of the best forms of *C. asturicus* are worth having. The best is var. *atropurpureus*, which is darker than the type, and a really good purple. I have had pale lilac varieties collected for me in Spain, but have never yet seen the white form, though kind friends in that country have been looking for it for several seasons. *C. Salzmannii* is the species that occurs both in Spain and Northern Africa, and has a fine bold flower as far as shape goes, but it lacks good colour

Autumn Crocuses

and substance. It is a good doer in spite of its southern habitat, but mice are especially fond of its very large corms, and unless a breakback trap is put down as soon as one notices on the surface of the ground the tell-tale shreds of corm tunic, they will invite their friends to the feast and finish off the whole colony. The plant produces long leaves at flowering time, which improve its appearance, but I cannot forgive it the flimsy transparent texture of its flowers, which remind one of the cheap ribbons worn by dolls at a country bazaar. As I have already mentioned *C. Clusii* there only remains of the Spanish group *C. serotinus.* It is a beautiful flower of cool lavender as to ground colour, prettily feathered with purple, and the latest of this group to flower, yet it is a very scarce plant. Its native home is unknown, the specimens from wild sources under its name in herbaria being generally either *nudiflorus* or *asturicus.* Dean Herbert wrote of it as a hardy species, and Salisbury gives a good figure of it in *Paradisus Londinensis,* and describes it as the latest of the autumnal Crocuses "flowering close under a south wall till the beginning of December." I cannot make it happy here, though it has been planted in the choicest places I can choose for it, and I know of no other garden than Glasnevin where it does well. I wish someone would discover its wild home and start us again with a fresh, healthy stock.

C. medius, fortunately, is easily enough catered for, and it is one of the loveliest. In colour it is warm, rosy-lilac with a number of radiating purple lines at the throat, which make a distinct, star-shaped patch the like of which no other Crocus possesses, for though *sativus* has lines in the throat they are connected with the veinings that extend to the tips of the segments, while in *medius* they run no further than the throat. It gained its name of *medius* as it was considered to be intermediate between *sativus* and *nudiflorus*, but has no close affinity with either, and nothing more than the superficial feature of the star ornament in the throat to connect it with *sativus*. The finely-cut scarlet stigmata, which are even brighter and larger than those of *nudiflorus*, together with its leaflessness at flowering time make it look a little like *nudiflorus*, perhaps, but the coarsely reticulated corm tunic of *medius* is a sufficiently reliable character to distinguish it from either.

Mr. Bartholomew found a lovely white form of *C. medius* in his interesting and well-filled garden at Reading. It is a singularly beautiful thing, as it has managed to retain the blue-purple star in the throat, and the pure white ground finished off with the scarlet feathery stigmata almost incites one to sing "Hurrah for the red, white, and blue." *C. medius* has a limited range as a wild plant, being found on the spurs of hills along the Riviera between Mentone and Genoa, but it is a very hardy and easily grown species, quite happy in light soil in a sunny, well-drained spot.

C. byzantinus is also often called *iridiflorus* from its peculiar shape, the outer segments being very large, and the three inner very small, so that when fully expanded it looks more like an Iris than a Crocus, especially in forms in which the outer segments are deep purple and the inner nearly white. The earlier name of *byzantinus* must stand ; but it is a pity, because it is misleading, seeing that the

34

Autumn Crocuses

plant grows in Hungary and Transylvania, and does not occur in Asia Minor.

It is one of the few Crocuses that does best in a rather shady position, such as a northern or north-western slope of the rock garden, or under light deciduous shrubs.

Mr. Allen, of Snowdrop fame, raised some robust and handsome seedling forms, and those named President and Rosamond are among my special treasures in the Crocus frame. Next to them, and in the front of the frame, that its low wall may shade it from the southern sun, I grow a beautiful, pure-white form given to me by Mr. Hoog of Haarlem. It is interesting, too, because of its stigmata. In the typical lilac forms the much-branched stigmata are of much the same shade of lilac as the perianth segments, but in this albino form every trace of lilac colouring has vanished, and the stigmata are pale yellow.

There are three other robust, easily-grown Autumn Crocuses that must have honourable mention in this chapter, and each in its commonest form is white. *C. cancellatus* is white in its western homes, but becomes more and more tinged with lilac and striped with purple as it ranges eastward, till it becomes altogether lilac richly suffused with purple. It is small wonder then that it has had many names applied to it. It seems right and best to regard them all as forms of *cancellatus*, and to expect a handsome early-flowering plant, leafless at flowering time, and of every shade from white to purple in endless gradations ; and you may buy them as *damascenus, pylarum, Schimperi, Spruneri, Dianthi, idealis, Mazziaricus, palaestinus, Kotschyanus,* or *cilicicus.* If you like you can group all the

35

lilac-grounded forms as var. *cilicicus*, but I advise you not to attempt to sort them out further, nor to try to fit them to the other names, for its powers of variability seem endless. I collected a few bulbs near Athens once, when they were out of flower, only finding them by the white stripes on the leaves that made them show out among the grasses, and when they flowered here no two were alike.

Crocus caspius had never been in cultivation before the firm of Messrs. C. G. van Tubergen of Haarlem sent a collector to its far-away home on the shores of the Caspian in 1902. I had a small share in the undertaking, and was delighted when I heard that the collector had been successful, and still more so when I received a goodly store of living corms. Most of them had flowered, but I noticed two had belated flower buds in them, and I carefully nursed them and was rewarded with a sight of this newcomer's beauty when they both flowered in late November, and one of them had a tinge of rosy-lilac that promised a new variety. At lifting time the corms had grown plump and sturdy, and showed the red tunic with a satiny sheen to it that is peculiar to the species ; and in 1903 I was able to show both the white and the lilac one, variety *lilacinus*, before the Scientific Committee of the Royal Horticultural Society, who awarded it a Botanical Certificate. We had grave fears that coming from such a southern home it might not prove hardy, but it has settled down very well here, and now blooms early in October instead of as at home from November onwards to March, a few at a time. I have kept the best of all white autumnal Crocuses to the end, and this is *C. marathonisius*, from Mount Taȳgetus in

Crocus marathonisius and C. caspius. (See p. 36.)

Autumn Crocuses

Greece, and named after its birthplace, Marathonisi, and not the better known Marathon. It has been confused with the smaller and more delicate *C. Boryi* at times, but has really little affinity but that of geographical range with that species, and is much nearer to *C. longiflorus* in its characters and would be very hard to distinguish from a white form of it should one exist, were it not for the superior size of *marathonisius*, and the still more important point that its flowers are wrapped in a pair of spathes whereas *longiflorus* has but one.

This great white Greek species is a fine sight on a sunny morning in late Autumn, with its orange throat and scarlet style branches, but writing of it makes me feel I am getting into late Autumn and the happenings thereof before I have dealt with the splendour of the flowers of September, so we will leave the Crocuses for a while and return to the late-flowering species, and those that need the shelter of a frame, in another chapter.

CHAPTER III

Early September

FOR many years I have spent the greater part of September in other people's gardens, but in the last two years circumstances have been too strong for me and I have had to forego my usual visits and stay at home. So I have watched the pageant of the unfolding of Autumn and the procession of its flowers with all the more zest as the consecutive stages were new to me. First came the Cyclamens, that are peculiar to Autumn, and produce flowers before leaves, like so many bulbous plants that flower in that season. I generally get the first bud or two in the latter part of August, either on some plants of *C. neapolitanum*, that grow beside the steps of the front door, or else from a grouping of a hundred or more old roots that live in a dusty, dry stretch of ground under the great Cedar. It is marvellous how they, and *Antirrhinum Asarina*, can exist there, for during the greater part of the year the soil is so dry that the sparrows use it for the mixed bathing in dust, so popular with those evil birds and the farmyard fowl. *Nettoyage à sec* would be a good name for it, if one did not feel it was too euphemistic, and there was more dryness than cleanliness about the pastime.

These two plants somehow manage to get a little moisture, and turn what would, but for them, be a very dismal, dusty spot, into an interesting one all the year round, and at times they make it a regular beauty spot.

38

Early September

Cyclamen europaeum sends up its cheerful, dark-green leaves with their zonal markings of grey-green on the upper surface and ruby-red lining below, before the Neapolitan species has quite lost its even handsomer ivy-like foliage. From July onward, *C. europaeum* gives a succession of its sweetly-scented, rosy-red flowers, and they with the Antirrhinum furnish the element of beauty till the leafless flowers of *C. neapolitanum* appear. But even while *C. neapolitanum* is without flowers or leaves the leathery seed capules on their coiled stems, like wire springs, should provide interest and employment. They are well worth examining for the sake of their curious construction, and should be carefully collected that the seeds may be sown either directly where wanted or in seed pans. I have an insatiable desire for Cyclamens, and could never have too many, for I know of no other plant that will turn patches of dust under thick trees into stretches of beauty so permanently and thoroughly. So when the autumn rains come, hundreds of flowers, both pink and white, of *C. neapolitanum* appear under the Cedar, to be followed by glossy leaves of wonderfully various shapes, some being as roundly cordate as those of a Violet, others as hastate as those of the Field Convolvulus, but the handsomest are those which imitate the leaves of Ivy, and have projecting fingers all round their palms. I have kept an open eye for vagaries of colour, as well as of form, and have acquired a few in which the silver zone has almost overspread the leaf ; others in which it is almost absent, and the finest of all, a form that, like so many other good things, came to me through the generosity of Canon Ellacombe. This one has very ample, ivy-shaped leaves of rich green with a brilliant silver

My Garden in Autumn and Winter

zone an inch wide on them. I was much struck by the
beauty and vigour of the Cyclamen in Mr. Wilks' delightful
woodland garden at Shirley, where it grows better than
anywhere else out of Cornwall, smothered up in a carpet
of Ivy. So three years ago I commenced to imitate his
success by planting it among a carpet of Ivy that has covered the ground under a rather widely spreading Deodar
on one of the lawns. This last Autumn has proved the
wisdom of imitating one's betters, for I had quite a show of
pink and white blossoms which looked all the more attractive for their setting of green Ivy leaves ; and when the
flowers fade it is delightful to watch for the appearance of
the zoned leaves among the plain green ones of the Ivy, as
interesting as looking for those outline faces and figures to
be discovered in puzzle pictures. It requires as sharp an
eye to detect all the patches of Cyclamen among the Ivy as
one needs in the Natural History Museum at South Ken-
sington to count how many young birds or eggs of Ring
Plovers may be found on the stones and shingle ; or how
many moths or beetles of cryptic coloration are sitting on
the bark in their respective cases.

You get as good value year in and year out from
Cyclamen neapolitanum as from any one plant I can recall,
and I think it must be one of the most long-lived of all
that are not trees. There is one immense old root here,
that would not go into the crown of my hat, and my dear
old mother used to tell me she brought it from Atkins'
garden at Painswick (the same who originated *C. Atkinsii*)
soon after her marriage, and it is now many years since
my parents celebrated their golden wedding. Sixty years
is a long life for any one plant, for *C. neapolitanum* does

40

Ailanthus glandulosa pendulifolia by the New River. (See p. 40.)

Early September

not renew itself annually as most bulbous plants do, but just grows a little wider from season to season, and the older and larger it grows the more vigorous it gets, and the greater number of flowers it produces. I have grandchildren of this old plant which are of quite a decent size, and some of them are white-flowered, but for the most part they take after their grandmother and are pink. I believe that the type of leaf, both as to form and banding, is inherited fairly truly by the offspring in specially well-marked forms, and seeds saved from my most silvery forms have produced some plants quite as good as their parents.

I used to regard *C. cilicicum* as a much later bloomer than *neapolitanum*, but a little colony of it under the old Snowy Mespilus, bought, as often happens, for *C. Coum*, now that the plants have become settled, is not many days behind the larger species in producing flowers. They are rather small, and pale, but have a graceful effect as their segments are long and narrow, rather like those of the spring-flowering *C. repandum* in shape. *C. cilicicum* can be distinguished from *neapolitanum* at a glance by noticing that the little auricles, tiny wing-like projections, so conspicuous at the mouth of *neapolitanum*, are absent in *cilicicum*. Later on, the peculiar way in which the round leaves are spotted with silvery grey rather than banded will distinguish it from other Cyclamens.

In other years, I had always thought I had missed a great deal in not seeing *Artemisia lactiflora* at its best. In friends' gardens, I had deemed myself unfortunate in always finding it either in a condition of greenish white bud, or past its prime and turned to a dull creamy-yellow. But now that I have at last watched its daily progress,

My Garden in Autumn and Winter

I find that it has no period of brilliant whiteness, no full bloom, but is one of those plants you watch hoping that to-morrow it will burst into full beauty, instead of which it wanes and turns dingier than ever without achieving anything great, a dog that has no day, but only the promise of one. *Aster Shortii* I have seldom seen at its best before, and it is a plant with a really lovely best, but unfortunately rather a short one. It blooms quite early in September, too early in fact to be really useful as a Michaelmas Daisy, either to decorate a roast goose, as I am told was once the custom in this house, or to stand out in the garden when frosty nights have toned down other rivals. Its graceful habit, feathery sheaves of blossoms, and peculiarly pleasing shade of clear lavender are rather wasted owing to this early timed and short visit. *Aster umbellatus* is an early, and a stately, white-flowered species of striking appearance, but very seldom seen in gardens, probably owing to its early flowering. It has a pleasing way of turning white again in old age, and when covered with silvery seeds is almost as beautiful as when in flower ; and yet another virtue does it possess, in spite of all the show of silver pappus I have never yet seen a self-sown seedling, so there is no need to cut away the seed-heads before the last pinch of down has been blown out of them. Close beside my group of *Aster umbellatus* there is a fine old plant of one of the best of the Mallows, *Althaea cannabina*. It grows twelve feet or more high, and is wonderfully elegant and light in the plan of its branching, and when set with dozens of light crimson blossoms, the size of half crowns, on thin wiry stalks, is indeed a goodly possession. It is such a

Malva Alcea, var. fastigiata. (See p. 43.)

Early September

well-behaved perennial plant too; quite content to be left alone, but all the better for a thinning of the stems each spring to allow the remaining ones to strengthen; and then in July, when it has reached to its full height, and before it gets heavy with flower buds, it is a wise course to tie a girdle of strong tarred twine round the dozen tall stems that they may support one another in stormy weather. *Malva Alcea var. fastigiata* (see plate) is generally overblown here by the end of August, but a specimen that got cut down has shot up again this season and is a mass of soft rosy-pink bloom, and I have made a mental note to try whether this second-flowering can be induced in other seasons by a similar decapitation. *Crinum Powellii* is now at its best, and there are few outdoor plants that surpass it for beauty when growing and flowering well. Here it needs rather more food and drink than it receives, but a group of some eight or more old clumps, of the white, the rose-coloured, and the pale intermediate forms, makes a brave show with the great tall stems and pendant flowers that look too tropical and magnificent to be so thoroughly hardy. Another plant that suggests southern lands is a specimen of *Ailanthus glandulosa var. pendulifolia.* We cut it back severely each Spring, and allow only two, or at the most three, eyes to shoot. The result is that on a seven-foot high stem we have a crown of leaves like those of some tropical Palm, for treated thus they will, in a good season, reach a length of six feet, with large leaflets of a brilliant green arranged in pairs on either side of the immense mid-rib.

I also treat a specimen of the ordinary form of the Tree

43

of Heaven, as the Ailanthus is called, to a similar annual snubbing, and very few people recognise it, with its palm-like effect, as the same plant as an old unpruned tree that grows a few hundred feet further on. The old tree looks somewhat like an Ash or Walnut, with extra large leaves, and is not very interesting except when in flower. Then the scent is delicious enough to warrant its celestial name, which I always imagined was given it in China on account of the delightful perfume of its flowers. It seems, however, as stated in Elwes and Henry's great book on trees, that both Ailanthus and the English name come from a word Aylanta, which in the Amboyna language signifies a tree so tall as to touch the sky, and was really applied to *A. moluccana*, a species found in the tropics. I have never heard of anyone having found out what use is served by the two curious glands at the base of each leaflet. Doubtless, they are useful somewhere, and at some time of growth, and are not placed there simply to help botanists to distinguish it from the Black Walnut and somewhat similar trees. Anyway, a blind man should never fail to recognise *Ailanthus glandulosa* if he knows of the existence of these hard round glands. There is a parallel instance in another tree, *Idesia polycarpa*, which has a pair of large glands shaped like the heads of big pins, or the horns of a miniature giraffe, and situated on each leaf stalk. They do not seem to secrete any fluid, but you can recognise the tree in the dark by feeling for them.

It is said that the pollen-bearing flowers of *Ailanthus glandulosa* give out an evil scent, but I have never smelt it, though I have often enjoyed the delightful fragrance of

44

Early September

our tree here when in flower in July; and also, when driving under trees in flower in southern France, I have only noticed the sweetly-scented ones. The leaves, on the contrary, have an exceedingly unpleasant scent when bruised. It reminds me of one of the scents I most dislike, that of burnt milk.

There are several plants worth looking at in early September growing in the pergola garden. First of all the Claret Vine, which is then at its best for the depth of purple its leaves assume, as later on they grow lighter until they become a bright crimson. It covers two neighbouring uprights of the Vine pergola and makes a fine deep-toned bit of colour, and is so hardy and reliable that where there is room for but one Vine I should certainly advise that this kind be chosen. Close behind, a Thistle towers up quite ten feet, and was beautiful in late Summer on account of its graceful, branching habit, and the number of its white flower heads. Now it is still more beautiful for the flowers have turned into silvery tufts of thistle-down. It was brought by Mr. Hiatt Baker from the Caucasus, and though for many years I admired it immensely in his garden, I was afraid to bring home seeds in case it should seed about too freely, and perhaps fill the cornfields with ten-foot high Thistles. But after seeing it still a favourite at Oaklands after the lapse of several seasons, I plucked up courage to give it a trial, and so far I have never had more than I wanted after weeding out a few that were too near good little plants for the health and safety of the latter; and giving away a few more, leaving only three or four to grow into giants. *Cnicus candelabrus* is its name, and the specific

My Garden in Autumn and Winter

portion well describes its stately branched appearance. Next to it is a clump of *Coriaria terminalis*, one of the most striking of all berry-bearing plants. It has arching stems some three to four feet high, set with pairs of handsome, light-green leaves throughout their length, and ending in a terminal spike of curious little reddish-green flowers that are nothing remarkable. But as the seeds begin to ripen, the petals, instead of falling, swell out and first become fleshy and dull orange, but end by being transparent and juicy and of a lovely shade of yellow like clear amber. The long spikes of these berries, each made up of five separate lobes, like a star of yellow glass, and enclosing the black carpels, have a most remarkable appearance. These terminal spikes are generally ripe in the end of July and August, but soon disappear, being eaten by birds. The lateral spikes of flowers are then developed, and in September these, to the extent of three or four on each shoot, have an even richer effect than the single terminal ones. *Cestrum Parqui* has grown into a large clump by the pavement round the sundial, and is now about five feet high and as much through, bearing thousands of its greenish-yellow, tubular flowers. They would need to be just a trifle brighter in colour to make it a first-class plant, but when fully out they are so unlike anything else that the plant always attracts attention. It has a strong odour, very similar to that of the Gladwin or Stinking Iris, or of *Clerodendron foetidum*, which has been said to resemble the scent of roast beef. Not that of an underdone juicy undercut, of course, but of a burnt bit, a protuberance on the joint that has had too much of the fire. If the shoots of this Clerodendron have

46

Early September

come through the past Winter without getting cut down to the ground, it too should be in flower in September, and its great flat heads of crimson buds, opening into pink flowers, are very handsome among the ample, dark-green leaves. The flowers are as sweetly-scented as the leaves are—well, stinking is the best word for it, so I shall use it, unrefined though it may be. On the wall *Escallonia floribunda* is full of flower, and so brilliantly white that few shrubs can equal it for beauty and purity at this time of year. Its older name of *montevidensis* always sounded very suggestive of a hot climate and the need for shelter, but it seems very doubtful whether it is right to regard *montevidensis* as even a variety of *floribunda* and not merely as a synonym, and as *E. floribunda* was found in the Andes at a height of 8400 feet, we have the explanation of the plant's happiness here in the open air. I cannot think of a more lovely autumn-flowering shrub for a warm corner. The pure-white of its flowers is beautifully enhanced by a rich green tip to the stigma, like a tiny emerald set in its centre. In front of it, and some distance away from the wall, is a fine, large shrub, for the eastern counties, of *Eupatorium Weinmannianum*, now just beginning its season of attractiveness to the butterflies, and thereby rivalling *Sedum spectabile*. The Eupatorium is white with a flesh tint on the young flower heads, and is very generous in producing bunches of bloom from early September until Jack Frost gets really vicious, and destroys even the buds of the Monthly Roses, which generally occurs a week or two after he has slain the Dahlias. Now if there is a Red Admiral Butterfly or two in the garden they are sure to be

My Garden in Autumn and Winter

found either on the Eupatorium or on the flat pink heads of *Sedum spectabile.* I do not know which I like the better, the old pale pink form of this Sedum, or the newer, deeper crimson one, and the butterflies are equally uncertain, and go from one to another. When unfurnished with butterflies, the dark-coloured variety is perhaps the showier plant, but its crimson tint is not quite so happy a background for the scarlet of a Red Admiral and the glittering fire-tint of the Small Copper, as the lighter pink of the older form.

One of the best patches of soft, creamy-yellow in the whole garden is provided by a variegated form of *Sedum Telephium,* and will last in beauty for quite another month, but it is a tricky plant, and unless you keep your eye and thumbnail busied with it, you will find nothing but a lanky plant with sea-green leaves and very dowdy, reddish-purple flowers. Two possibilities have to be guarded against ; the first needs vigilance in Spring, when the shoots reappear, that all the shoots which have reverted to the normal green form may be removed root and branch, lest they overpower the weaker-growing, variegated ones. Then as soon as flower buds are developed they should be nipped out, to induce the development of side growths, which in turn will try to flower, and must be just as severely suppressed in this very natural desire. Then the leaves, unshaded by bunches of flowers, will assume a wonderfully brilliant, but soft, buttery-yellow colouring that looks almost good enough to eat. I grow two clumps, one on either side of one of the flagged paths, and the effect of its round-headedness, due to my active thumbnail, is a good match for some old stone cannon shot that occupy the other two

Early September

corners of these beds, and the four corners of the opposite pair, as I had only six stones for the eight spaces. These stones were found on the beach at Sandgate one Autumn after a great storm had washed away the shingle, and it has been supposed that either a ship-load of them was lost there through the sinking of the vessel, or else they were used in a bombardment. They vary a good deal in size, but are wonderfully picturesque, not being too exact in spherical outline, and a good deal chipped and weathered. Some friends who live at Sandgate rolled them up into their garden, and generously gave me several of them. Two large ones stand on either side of the porch, two more on the steps by the pond, and these six form the corners of the beds in the paved garden. As a contrast to the golden *S. Telephium*, I recommend one of the good purple-leaved forms of the closely allied *S. maximum*, which are generally found in gardens labelled *S. atropurpureum;* but according to Baker's monograph, the last word on the subject, the name should be *S. maximum var. haematodes*. I hope before long Mr. Lloyd Praeger, who is now at work on this intricate genus, will set us all straight on Sedums, and what joy it will be if labels need not have more than three words written on them ! This purple Sedum, however, is one of the few plants that scarcely needs a label, for it is so distinct when active, being as purple as a Copper Beech in its prime, and the old stems will stand all through the Winter to mark its site until the young buds begin to push up. I have always been fond of Sedums, and acquisitive both in gardens and on hillsides for many years, so that the garden is perhaps

My Garden in Autumn and Winter

rather too full of them as I always try to bring home a bit of any form that seems to differ from those already here, and Sedums very seldom die out in our dry soil and climate. The most difficult to keep is the beautiful *S. trifidum*, from the Himalaya. It is a gem for the choicest part of the rock garden, with neat annual growths of about four inches here, but said to reach eleven in its native haunts. The leaves are deeply toothed and arranged in a loose rosette at the tips of the growths, and in late September, come the rich red flowers in a close central bunch. It is a very rare plant in gardens, and if it had not been for the kindness of Mr. Richard Beamish, I should not possess it. It grows better in his wonderful quarry rock garden than anywhere else I have seen it, but even there it is not easy to increase, and it was a season or two before even his most generous of dispositions was justified by circumstances in cutting off a portion of this plant to fulfil his kind promise that the first cut from the joint should come to me. *S. Ewersii*, also known as *S. turkestanicum*, is one of the brightest rose-coloured species, and would be a treasure for the rock garden even if it flowered in May, when there is such an *embarras de richesse* in any well-furnished one, but coming to its best in September it is worthy of a very choice position. Prostrate, slender branches, neat, light-green leaves, plenty of pink flowers, perfect hardiness here, in spite of a book reputation for tenderness, and as easily propagated by division as a common Daisy, are five good points it possesses, yet it is not often planted. Later in the season *S. Sieboldii* takes its place, and is larger and even more beautiful, but is seldom grown in the open; I imagine because it is so useful and beautiful as a pot plant that it has become stereotyped in gardening minds as suitable for that purpose only. On a sunny ledge, where its branches can sprawl over a hot stone, it is as happy as Hampstead and as hardy as Canute or Philip of Burgundy. *S. pulchellum* is another beautiful species that has a reputation for tenderness. It was one of the rare treasures of Bitton Garden for many years, and was figured in the *Botanical Magazine* from specimens sent by Canon Ellacombe, as long ago as 1875. I write a *rare* treasure because it never increased over freely there, but nevertheless had to sustain a continual drain on its detachable portions, due to the covetousness of all who saw it, and the liberality of its owner. I owe my plants to his generosity, and he owes his present abundance of the plant to a happy accident that occurred here to his gift. I grew it for some seasons on the warmest ledge of rock available, and sadly starved and slow of increase it proved there. One day a portion was scratched off by one of those horrid, interfering blackbirds, and the scrap fell into the bog garden below, and before I noticed its descent, had rooted and begun to spread, and looked so fat and healthy, I left it there and watched the result. It soon began to choke out the other denizens of that bog garden, and I had learnt the lesson that *S. pulchellum* needs moist conditions to show itself at its best. It is perhaps less hardy in cold climates in such a position, but it is so easy to keep a piece in the drier uplands for renewal in case of accident, that it is best to treat it to plenty of gravy with its dinner. When grown in a sunny and dry place it turns a better colour in

My Garden in Autumn and Winter

Autumn than when in moister ground, and often produces such a glorious range of red and crimson shades as to justify the ill-treatment of starvation. So I still grow a patch or two in high and dry quarters for the sake of its red leaves. Since I found out its taste for moisture, I have seen it growing magnificently in Ireland in wetter conditions than I can provide for it here, and I strongly advise all who can, to give it an honoured position on the edge of the bog garden in full sunshine. The branching inflorescence is most graceful, possessing, as a rule, five or six branches. It always reminds me of a star fish, and I half expect to see the arms curl inward a little more, or stretch out flat before it walks away. Sometimes a poorer flower head gives only four arms and forms a cross, and in America it is called the Widow's Cross, I suppose from this effect; but it must be a gay widow who wears a cross of such charmingly soft rose colour.

It would be easy to fill a fair-sized rock garden with nothing but Sedums and yet make it attractive throughout the year, as so many of them are quite independent of their flowers for beauty. Several of them colour finely as Autumn draws near, and especially if grown in exposed and dry positions. *S. Middendorffianum* is already bronze, and some of the lower leaves are becoming touched with crimson, and it will increase in beauty daily until some extra sharp frost causes it to fall asunder. *S. obtusatum* can be made to look like two quite distinct plants by different treatment. One piece should be planted in a cool, half-shaded position, in which it will wax fat and produce dark green leaves that look juicy and succulent,

and shine as though varnished. The other should be
planted in light soil on a stone in a hot, exposed position,
and this will grow into a compact mass of fleshy-looking
substance and turn as red as a ripe cherry in Autumn.
S. spathulifolium, if given rather a slim diet of poor soil in
a dry place, will generally acquire a red tint on the edges
of its oldest leaves, that greatly adds to the beauty of its
rosettes. *S. Stahlii* turns a rich red each Autumn, and its
fleshy, round leaves look so much like berries that if it is
left out-of-doors here for the Winter, the birds eat the leaves
so greedily that it is reduced to nothing but bare stems, so
I am obliged to grow it in a pan and take it into a house
where its charms can mature safely.

A little biennial species is trying its best to take possession of my newest and most successful moraine beds, those
which I call the fish hatchery moraine, from the underground plan of its waterworks, and which I have described
fully in the Spring volume. This Sedum was a come-by-
chance, which appeared in a pot of seedlings of *Campanula
excisa,* and was so pretty and glaucous, I planted it in the
sandiest portion of these moraine beds. It flowered and,
after ripening seed, died in its aggravating monocarpic
fashion, but, as it succeeded in ripening some thousands
of seeds there is no scarcity of young plants, so that on
most days of the year I can pull up a few that never will
be missed. It makes really charming little tufts of glaucous foliage in the Autumn, and if it would but remain
small and neat and be contented with a few dozens
of its pale pink flowers all would be well, and it should
possess the land as it desires. When the flowering fit takes

it, however, it spreads out rapidly and becomes a rather coarse mass of stems, flowers, and seed pods, with incredible rapidity, and it is best to pull it up before it gets as far as scattering its dust-like seeds. I find it is *S. hispanicum*, not a very common species, and that the name *glaucum* belongs to it too, but merely as a synonym, and it appears that the little plant so often used for bedding has no right to the name of *glaucum* it generally bears, and yet has no other at present.

The autumnal resurrection of *S. amplexicaule* is as remarkable as that of any plant. When the drought and heat come in mid-June, as come they are sure to do here, it dries up into curious brown fleshy joints, and looks more like a dead and dried wood-louse than a living Sedum. But as soon as the autumn rains have soaked it and its surroundings, glaucous green leaves sprout out at the tips of the dried-up joints, roots appear on the undersides, and it grows again into a soft, spreading carpet of glaucous stems with short leaves. I have been told that it covers parts of the roof of the Escurial in Spain, and that it is curious to notice the quick change in colour in Autumn.

It would take too much space to review the many Sedums that have found homes here, so we will conclude this chapter by admiring the downy rosettes of *S. pilosum*, which look so much more like a Sempervivum than a Sedum, and we will wish them luck through the coming Winter, that they may survive to flower and bear seed next year, before they die off, as die they then must, because they are, alas, as strictly monocarpic as *Sedum sempervivoides* itself.

CHAPTER IV

Mid-September

As September approaches middle age two great events take place in the Rose world of this garden. They are only great by comparison and because of the absence of the masses of Tea Roses and Hybrid Perpetuals that other more fortunately endowed gardens can show. Rayon d'or will be giving me a flower or two to fill a vase with living gold. Frau Karl Druschki and La France and Lady Waterlow are still generous at that time, and Souvenir de la Malmaison begins to provide solid, stout-stemmed blooms far superior to the earlier ones of the summer months. But the two Roses I look to for my own delight and lead friends to see are *R. Moyesii* and *R. bracteata*. The former had its days of glowing beauty throughout June, when its deep red flowers, lit up by sunshine, glowed out like the lamp over a chemist's door or the red bottle in his window. Now the hips are ripening, and are quite equal to the flowers for colour effect and interest. They even beat those of *R. macrophylla*, at least in the forms I possess of it, in size and wonderful beauty of outline. Captain Pinwill gave me hips of *R. macrophylla* some years ago that live in my memory as the finest thing in Rose hips I have ever seen. Alas, they contained no seeds, so I have not

55

yet found out whether their glory was due to its being a superior variety, or to the favouring environment of a Cornish garden. So *R. Moyesii* provides my leading lady among the Roses when fruiting time comes round. Its hips are pendant like those of *R. pendula,* our old friend *R. alpina,* but under its latest authorised name ; well developed ones are nearly three inches in length, as the sepals are persistent, and close into a pointed inverted cone at the end of the flask–shaped neck that gives such grace of outline to the whole vase-shaped hip. The colour is as worthy of praise as the shape, for it is that of scarlet coral in pretty talk ; red sealing wax in household words. Admiring friends have also discovered another beauty in them, that of fat, healthy seeds which carried to distant gardens germinate readily and help to spread the plant.

The other great event is the flowering of *R. bracteata,* the Macartney Rose, a plant so distinct from the rest of its family that it seems to have borrowed the characters of several genera. Its glossy evergreen leaves have such small and leathery leaflets one would not be greatly surprised if one saw pea-shaped flowers among them, and the buds, wrapped in the many silvery grey bracts that give the plant its specific name, look at an early stage more suggestive of the flower of one of the Compositæ than of a Rose. Then, again, the substance of the great white flowers is stouter and firmer than in most Roses, and the number of anthers is so large that the golden centre falls but little short of that of a Romneya for beauty. Even after the petals have fallen the anthers retain a

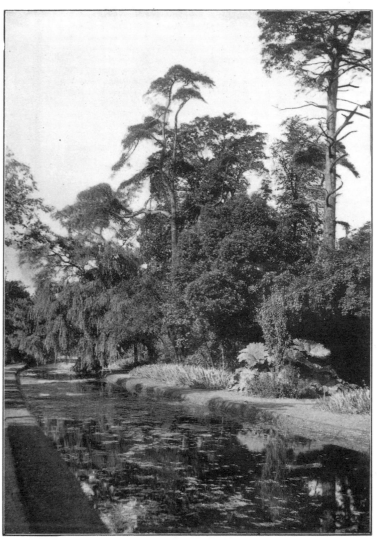

The New River.   (See p. 57.)

Mid-September

good deal of beauty as they gradually deepen in colour
to orange and then to tawny-brown, and the disc turns
scarlet, making a wonderful contrast of colour with them.
Unfortunately, it is slightly tender and needs a south wall
or some other effective shelter to be really happy. Perhaps
it would be fairer to the Rose to put this fact in another
form of words, and say that considering it is found in
India and China, it is fortunate that it is hardy enough
to grow and flower as well as it does in the open air.
The largest plant here grows on a buttress of the old
Enfield Market Cross now in the centre of the rose garden.
I chose for it the one that faces most nearly to the South,
and though in severe winters the Rose has been cut almost
to the ground, it has managed of late to ripen some fine
long growths, and each Autumn for the last three years
has produced many dozens of its glorious flowers, so pure
in their white and so rich in their gold. To add to their
other charms they have a delicate scent rather like that
of *Romneya Coulteri,* or the slightest whiff, the very ghost
of the real thing, of the scent of *Magnolia grandiflora,* all
three flowers having a dash of lemon scent about them,
but each in varying degrees.

The Iris beds alongside the walk by the New River
would be for most of their lengths only a thick mass of
leaves of various shades of grey or glaucous green, were
it not for the quantity of brilliant, scarlet fruits produced
by *Arum italicum.* Small scraps of its tubers have been
dug in deeply when there has been a general turn out
and replanting, and though at first we struggled against
the claims of these poor submerged wretches to their

57

My Garden in Autumn and Winter

share of light and air, our efforts at digging them up, or our cruelty in pulling off their heads seemed to make but little difference to their vigour. So we let them be, and now that they flower and fruit we are glad of the lucky accident that provides such a bright colour in the silly season for beds of Bearded Irises. The berries are larger than in our common wild Cuckoo-pint, and are produced in longer bunches, which stand up on higher stems, so that a clump of some dozen or so makes a brave show. The leaves of some are beautifully veined with white, and very handsome in Spring among the young Iris leaves. Others, with plain green leaves, I make use of by picking those that are likely to choke their more precious neighbours, and arranging them in vases with Anthuriums or any other aroids, even with the white Arum, *Richardia africana*, which would overfill a small vase if accompanied by its own immense leaves. Another plant makes itself at home among the Irises, and does so little harm that it is welcome to most of the places it selects. This is *Linaria purpurea*, a plant naturalised on old walls in some parts of England, but not often enough seen in gardens. It has such a neat, upright habit that it is very effective, rising here and there above more lowly plants. It is a sort of Lombardy Poplar among Toadflaxes as regards figure, and its tall spires of blossoms are a very good bright purple. When the central spike is going to seed it is better to cut it out, then the lateral spikes will soon tower up to carry on the show of bloom, and will hold on bravely till the frosts come. Nearer the edge are spreading clumps of *Ceratostigma plumbaginoides*, the

Mid-September

plant we used to call Plumbago Larpentae, and were quite
happy in doing so while we knew no better, being perfectly
contented in thus honouring the Lady of Sir George
Larpent, in whose garden, Paxton tells us, it flowered for
the first time in England, in 1847, the seeds having been
sent thither by Mr. Smith, who collected them on the
ruined ramparts of Shanghai. This extract from *Paxton's
Magazine of Botany* destroys my belief in a story I heard or
read somewhere, but cannot now put my finger on, that a
soldier plucked the seeds and put them into his pocket
when our troops entered Pekin, a far more romantic
origin for the plant. Anyway, the name Ceratostigma
tells a true tale, for a pocket lens will show the curious,
minute, glandular processes that grow like horns out
of the arms of the stigmas, and which distinguish the
members of this genus from a true Plumbago. It is a
beautiful plant when it does well, providing a fine display
of true prussian-blue flowers for several weeks in the
Autumn, and then, when the frosts have destroyed the
flowers, the leaves turn to brilliant shades of crimson and
scarlet. It certainly loves a light, warm soil, and is the
better for a sunny place and any protection that can be
spared for it. It grew well in the peach-house border,
until its space was wanted for newer and rarer plants;
while there it found its way under the wall into the peach-
house itself; and under glass the flowers were earlier,
larger, and brighter, and were produced for a longer
period than outside, and I feel sure it would be worth
growing in pots for the autumn decoration of conservatories. *Ceratostigma Polhillii* is a newer introduction, more

59

My Garden in Autumn and Winter

tender, and of half-climbing habit. It has grown well for the last three years on the south wall of the pergola garden, and has climbed the wall for a height of three or four feet. It flowers freely in September and on into November; the flowers are of a particularly lovely shade of blue, that of *Commelina coelestis* or a Gentian. I fully expect that the next hard Winter that visits us will play sad tricks with this plant, and I must make the most of its beauty before it comes. Another climbing plant that is now in full beauty is *Loasa lateritia*, very beautiful, but very vicious, for it can sting as sharply as a nettle. All the members of the genus, and those of the closely allied one, *Blumenbachia*, are covered with hairs of such beautiful design and mechanism that they are well worth observing under a microscope. Some are only simple, but as transparent and glittering as the finest glass, and are placed on a pulvinus or cushion, which is a skin distended with liquid, just like that of a stinging-nettle, only larger. A slight touch breaks the little glass-like tube of the spine, leaving a sharp, ragged edge, which easily pierces soft skin, and being pressed down on the cushion of liquid, its contents are forced through the broken tube into the wound, and a wonderfully sharp sting is the result. I find it hurts me more at the moment than the sting of a nettle, but does not pain for long, seldom lasting for more than five minutes, whereas a nettle's sting will become irritable and inflamed even on the following day. I first saw this pretty plant in a garden in Devonshire, where it and its near relations were largely grown, twining about standard Rose-trees along the drive. My host told me he lost so many of

Mid-September

his choice flowers through the love of the errand-boys of the district for buttonholes, that he bethought him of planting members of this stinging family freely at the entrance to the garden, and he declared the shock they gave to those who helped themselves to flowers had made a marked difference in their habits, and they had a general mistrust of unknown flowers lest they too might sting as viciously. I fear I often invite those who greatly admire them to pick some to look at, and enjoy the jump and squeak that follow their discovery of the stinging hairs. Besides the plain hairs, whose function is to sting, there are others of a marvellous variety of shapes. Some are hooked, others barbed, and some have heads fashioned like javelins, grapnels, or harpoons; all of them are made of transparent silica, and, being filled with clear liquid, are very beautiful objects when highly magnified.

The flowers, too, are wonderfully interesting to examine. They have five boat-shaped petals, white in *L. vulcanica*, orange in *L. lateritia*, and yellow in *L. bryoniaefolia*. Into the hollow of each boat-shaped petal there is neatly fitted a bunch of stamens, and as the flowers are pendant the petal forms a perfect tent to keep the pollen dry until it is ready to go out into the world, and take its chance of getting carried off by insect visitors. We will return to the method of its dispersion in a minute, and stay now to admire the most beautiful part of the blossoms, a ring of fleshy protuberances, staminodes, as a botany book would call them, but which brings so little idea to the ordinary mind unhampered with technical terms, that we will try if homely words can describe them. Staminodes they may be because they are certainly organs formed by the fusion and alteration in form of several stamens, but their form and colouring is the wonderful thing rather than their morphology. So in plain words they are five fleshy bodies, in shape rather like a small section of moulding, such as one looks over in shops when choosing a frame for a picture. They are brilliantly yellow for the most part, and are variously striped with white or scarlet bands, and are so placed in the centre of the flower that they form a cone-shaped boss, out of the centre of which the stigma appears. The whole centre is thus a gorgeous series of rings of colour, and forms the most attractive portion of the flower both to a human eye and a nectar-seeking insect. A few of these anthers dehisce at a time, and when their pollen is ready for dispersal their filaments curve inward, bringing their pollen-dusted heads out of the protection of the hollow petals to stand out freely in the centre, so that a visiting insect must knock against them in trying to reach the honey, secreted by the gorgeous staminodes. The style does not lengthen until the stamens have finished their work, and then the stigma receives pollen from visiting bees that is of necessity brought from the anthers of another flower. In Knuth's great book on pollination, Delpino is quoted as declaring the stamens bent back to the petals *after* the pollen has been shed. This is not true of any species I have observed, nor do I think it likely a plant would possess a habit so obviously useless, nor hollowed petals that were so perfectly adapted for pollen protection unless they were used for that

Mid-September

purpose. It seems that the habit of ripening the anthers before the stigma is much more common among plants than the other way about—that is, protandrous flowers are more numerous than those that are protogynous. Therefore it greatly added to my affection for the plant of *Hyoscyamus aureus* that grows in a crevice of the rock garden when an eminent Irish botanist pointed out to me this Summer, after looking at my plant, that the stigma ripens before the anthers. But let us return to the family of Loasaceae and their stinging propensities, for we must notice another plant, *Blumenbachia insignis.* It closely resembles one of the white Loasas in appearance, but the flowers are not quite so handsome, and I should not want it if it did not possess two endearing properties besides the power of stinging as viciously as any of them. I have an affection for it because it sows itself very amiably, and reappears without giving us the trouble of seed saving and sowing, pricking out in pots, and then putting out into the ground that all the Loasas I have grown demand of us. And, again, it has a very beautiful seed-pod, far in advance of the hairy, rather shapeless ones of the Loasas. For in Blumenbachia it is composed of several parallel divisions all spirally twisted to form a most elegant pendant, vase-shaped pod that would make a good model for an electric-light globe. As the pod grows large it becomes distended with fluid which makes it semi-transparent, and it looks as though it were some beautiful piece of old Venetian glass of a dull sea-green colour. But one requires gloves, or a good deal of pluck to pick the pretty object, for the hairs on it

63

My Garden in Autumn and Winter

are as ready to sting as those on any other part of the plant.

Two members of the Corydalis family are often at their best here in September, and both of them are annual or, at most, biennial plants. Perhaps it is wisest to call them monocarpic, a splendidly useful word lately come to the fore, which in expressing the fact that the plant bears seed but once, evades the question of how many seasons it takes getting ready for that great finale. *C. racemosa* is a rather coarse-growing species, with handsome light green leaves rather yellowish in colour, and has large orange-coloured flowers of the usual Corydalis bunny-rabbit make, with the characteristic spur behind. This spur, by the way, provided the family with its name, for it reminded a Greek of a lark's hind toe-nail, so the name of the bird was transferred to the flower, only changing the final *o* to an *i*. The most distinct points about the flowers of *C. racemosa*, though, are the curious brownish-grey tips to each flower, which contrast so pleasantly with the orange colouring of the rest, and the extremely unpleasant rank scent given out by the whole plant if broken or bruised, a scent that reminds one of castor-oil, not the best fine-drawn, but the sort you give to dogs. Ugh ! *C. glauca* is inoffensive to the most fastidious of noses, and has very elegant, blue-green leaves, a true sea-green justly termed glaucous, and the flowers are a charming mixture of bright yellow and red. I generally hope for the best and leave it to sow itself ; but if the autumn-germinated seeds are not in the most favourable of cosy corners they perish in the Winter, and I have to rely on a pinch of saved seed, which if sown in Spring produces

Mid-September

flowering plants early in September. The plant likes good living, and a share of a newly-made bed well enriched with leaf mould will produce plants four times as large and as handsome as those in a worn-out old corner.

For foliage effects at this season it is difficult to find prettier plants than two other newly introduced species of Corydalis. *C. ophiocarpa* is one, and it gets its specific name from the extraordinary shape of its seed pods, which are waved in a serpentine manner that makes them resemble miniature snakes, or green eels hanging from the stem, and the Serpent-pod Fumitory should be its English name if it needs one. Its leaves are very finely cut, and enlarged into lobes at the extremities of the division, and are of a rather unusual grey or brownish tint of green. The flowers are dull and small, and it is only for the sake of its pretty leaves and curious pods one would want it. It generally chooses to sow itself round some octagonal pieces of stone on which Italian oil-jars stand in the vine pergola, and does best on their shady sides, where it makes a charming tuft of cool colouring. The other, *C. cheilanthifolia*, is also happily named, its fern-like leaves closely resembling the fronds of some of the species of Cheilanthes, a genus of ferns. It forms large rosettes of its finely divided pinnate leaves, and its colouring is good, the leaves being a pleasant sap green, and the flowers a pleasing yellow. It is very effective when self-sown in the chinks of a pavement or of stone steps, and also looks well in shady corners of the rock garden.

Verbena venosa has lived here for twenty years, but in severe winters has been reduced to the mother colony,

My Garden in Autumn and Winter

which finds a safe and happy home in the peach-house border, the nearest approach to the climate of Cornwall the garden affords in Winter. There it runs about freely underground, and also seeds itself and forms a nucleus for starting further colonies. After a succession of mild winters we achieve some brilliant patches of its rich purple flowers in the Eremurus bed. I have seen it brought on under glass and then bedded out for the Summer with very good effect, but I prefer that any plant that can be made to live out altogether should be left alone to grow as it pleases and show its true character. So this Verbena is treated as a hardy herbaceous plant. The deep purple of its blossoms is as rich as that produced by any outdoor plant of the season, and it is well worth a little care and thought to establish a good colony in some warm, well-drained bed. This season some self-sown and also some late planted out seedlings of *Lathyrus tingitanus* have been making a fine show. There are two forms of it, one has pink and crimson flowers and is known as Butterfly; but I prefer the other form, which is a deep purple-crimson, and if trained over a pea-stick and treated as one does Sweet Peas it produces a great quantity of its blossoms and has a well-bred, refined air about it that I greatly admire. Possibly it is due to the glaucous-grey foliage and the smooth shining appearance of the whole plant.

Francoa sonchifolia is hardier than the better known *F. racemosa*, the Bridal-wreath of cottage windows; but it is not quite so pretty, for though it has spikes of flowers almost as long as those of the other, they are flushed with pink and have large crimson spots on each petal instead of

66

Mid-September

being nearly white like those of *racemosa*. Still they are a
goodly sight when at their best, and they have done well
this year at the foot of the *Piptanthus nepalensis* in the pergola garden. This last-named shrub is full of seed pods
this season, and the contrast of their light yellowish green
with the very dark green leaves is most remarkable. The
flowering shrub that fills us with most pride, however, is
Feijoa Sellowiana, for it has not hitherto deigned to flower
here, although it had grown some five feet high and as
much through. Now it has borne a few blooms at a time
since mid-July, and though they are rather hidden away
under the round, grey-green leaves of the year's shoots,
they are showy enough if one parts the branches and catches
a sight of them. They remind me a little of those of a
Eucryphia, but the stamens and inner sides of the petals
are bright crimson. Very soon after the flowers open, the
outer edges of the petals curve inward until they meet, and
as they are white outwardly and they completely hide the
inner surface, the flower appears white with crimson stamens
tipped with brilliantly golden anthers. A large bush of this
plant, which flowered freely every year, was one of the things
I used to admire most in the late Mr. Gumbleton's garden
near Queenstown, and his success with it emboldened me
to try a plant in the open here. Its first Winter out, the
frost cut it to the ground, and more than once it has looked
very much scorched and the worse for wear after our
spring winds; but a few fir boughs have helped it along,
and two mild winters in succession have allowed it to grow
into the fine bush it now is, and at last to flower. I cannot
hope for the luscious, guava-like fruit to follow, for the

My Garden in Autumn and Winter

species has never, that I know of, borne any in England, even under glass. As it comes from Brazil, it is perhaps wonderful that it lives at all through our winters. My plant grows in front of a large stone pedestal that helps to protect it a little ; but I have planted a younger one against the precious south wall, for I fear greatly what ills a really severe winter will afflict it with when next we get one. *Feijoa* is noted as being the only Myrtaceous plant that has its stamens straight and upright in the bud. I rejoice in a plant that is original enough in its views to behave quite differently from all its kith and kin, so with the four-petalled *Rosa sericea, Actaea spicata,* the only berry-bearing Ranunculad, *Cucubalus baccifer,* which is noted for the same peculiarity among Caryophyllaceous plants, I treasure this unique habited *Feijoa.* I have never tried *Eucryphia cordata* here ; even my boldness in planting tender subjects failing me there, or perhaps it is only because no one has yet offered me a nice young plant, and I feel it would be wasteful to spend good money on one. *E. pinnatifolia* was so long in repaying my care with flowers that it perhaps discouraged me. The plant hates the lime in our soil and water, and it always has a yellower tint in its leaves than those that are really happy in sandy or peaty lands.

My specimen is in a bay of the rock garden, and quite ten years passed after its planting before the grilling it got, in the hot summer of 1911, stirred it to begin flowering, but since then it has given us an increasing number of its lovely white flowers each season. They are exquisite when newly opened, and when, as in St. John's Wort, the anthers are still reddish-orange, they contrast even more effectively

Mid-September

with the pure white of Eucryphia than the yellow of Hypericum. *Kirengeshoma palmata* has its home at the foot of this tree, and is rather dried and starved, but, as I cannot yet find a more suitable spot, it must stay there. It does just manage to flower, but is never the luxuriant, two-feet high plant I have seen in Ireland. It is a curious and beautiful object when a spike of its large, fleshy, yellow flowers rises above the light-green, handsome leaves. I have never seen the flowers as widely expanded as some of those in the figure in the *Botanical Magazine,* and believe artist's licence and a persuasive finger are responsible for this improvement on Nature. In any case, it is disappointing to find the flower one looked forward to seeing in fully expanded glory on the morrow, lying on the ground a ruin of fallen petals and stamens, when the day arrives. Its musical name is a compound of Japanese words, the native name for *Anemonopsis macrophylla,* with the prefix *ki* (yellow), a plan not quite in accordance with the strict botanists' views for the formation of generic names, but, all the same, the result is happier than it would have been had it been named after one of its discoverers and its habitat, for then it might have been *Yatabea* or *Yoshinagia ishizuchensis!*

CHAPTER V

Colchicums

THE Colchicums deserve a chapter to themselves—nay, a book, "if *you* had but the time and *I* had but the brain" to transpose the pronouns of the Butcher's snark-hunting speech. They form a large family, widely dispersed and most intricately jumbled and involved by the efforts of botanists and gardeners to sort them out and name them.

Mr. Baker's masterly papers on the Liliaceae include the family Colchicaceae, and it always amuses me to read the title of this particular section, "A Synopsis of Colchicaceae and the Aberrant tribes of Liliaceae." It gives one an impression of the irregular, wandering ways of wild nomads, and even a slight acquaintance with the Colchicums makes one feel they too might have been included among the other wayward wanderers. This paper was read before the Linnean Society in 1879, and is a model of careful collection of references and the results of examining herbarium material, and is still the last voice on the genus as a whole. But several new species and many varieties have arrived since its publication, and the cultivation of the genus has greatly increased of late owing to the beauty of some of the newer forms. There is room for a good monograph of the genus, on a wide basis, treating them

Colchicums

from a horticultural as well as a botanical point of view, as the living beauty of the flowers is hard to gauge from herbarium specimens. For the specimens are not easy to recognise and distinguish when several years have elapsed since they were dried, since the majority of them turn to a hideous drab shade of colouring. The absence of leaves at the flowering time in the case of the autumnal kinds makes them more of a puzzle, and it requires the devotion of half a lifetime, by some one possessing the rare combination of virtues that go to make an earnest botanist and good gardener, to the collecting and growing of the varieties, and then the other half of his sublunary existence to writing the needed monograph. Take, for instance, *C. alpinum,* for which Nyman quotes a list of localities that embraces the French, Swiss, and Italian Alps ; while Baker and the Abbé Coste tell us of a varietal form in Corsica and Sicily. With so wide a range one would imagine it would be difficult to dig plants in near Alpine regions without the trowel cutting into a few of its corms. I longed in vain to possess it for many years, and though I have bought everything I saw listed under its name, hope triumphing over experience, as a cynic said of a friend who married a second wife, I never got anything but a poor form of *C. autumnale* for it. When in the Alps myself in June I have delved like a mole after the deeply-buried corms of every narrow-leaved Colchicum I met with, and still I got nothing but *C. autumnale.* My anxious search for it infected Mr. Farrer, and he, who seldom looks at any plant from a subalpine meadow, suffered much in toilsome digging through tough grasses and transporting heavy

71

My Garden in Autumn and Winter

bundles of corms, alas, nothing worth and only *C. autumnale*.
Then one lucky day his wanderings brought him, late in
the season, over the Cenis, and behold the ground under
his feet was lilac with a fairy-like flower that could be
nothing else than *C. alpinum !* Its wee corms were but an
inch or so under the surface, and as easily collected as a
crowd round a broken-down motor, and if anyone has
seen the real thing, with its slender, rosy flowers in
August, and its narrow leaves, like those of seedling
Bluebells, in Spring, he could never again accept *C.
autumnale* for it. Why, then, its rarity in commerce ? I do
not say in gardens, for it may be a villain to cultivate. Once
one knows what to look for I expect it is only necessary
to sit down anywhere in a district where it occurs, and
dig holes promiscuously in the turf to pick out its corms
as freely as one might do with *Crocus nudiflorus* in the
Pyrenees. Mr. Farrer kindly sent me a postcard bidding
me meet him in London on his return, and receive a
bundle of this treasure, newly gathered, and in full beauty
of blossom. It seems to be the earliest of the family to
flower, and for planting among the choicest of dwarf
alpines, Gentians and Androscaces, it is a plant that
ought to be tried by everyone with a rock garden larger
than a pocket-handkerchief. I now find that a Colchicum
I bought, under the mysterious designation of "spec :
Serrota," for one mark, hoping it might be true *alpinum*, and
which first flowered this August, is not even a Colchicum,
but a form of *Merendera Bulbocodium*. If only some good
fairy could give the Colchicums a different fashion of
leaves, rushlike and standing stiffly erect for choice, they

72

Colchicums

would be delightful plants to pop in wherever a space could be found.

In Autumn the flowers are never out of place wherever they may appear, and one is inclined to fill up any bare spaces with further plantings, forgetting how much space will be monopolised by the leaves next Spring.

Most of the finest kinds require many square inches for the full development of their foliage, and unless allowed ample space their vigour will be impaired. These large leaves are certainly handsome when young, but in the Spring, even when at their best, they are disappointing to look at among the shoots of Lilies and Tulips, all of which promise good things later on, by the buds rising out of their centres. With a Colchicum it is otherwise, and one almost forgets how pleasing the flowers were, and is annoyed with the dull green seed pods that take on no bright colours as they ripen.

Then, in mid-June, these leaves begin to fade and collapse in an exceedingly aggravating and untidy fashion, and, flabby and yellow, are sad eyesores among the summer flowers. It is not good for the plants, however, to clear them away before they are quite dried up, and their stems no longer fleshy; and even when they have gone to the rubbish heap they leave bare patches that are not easily filled, because by that time it is too late to sow annuals.

I have tried many plants as a carpet for them, but most of them thicken too much, becoming of the Turkey carpet consistency and smothering the Colchicums, or else they turn the tables and their leaves, first as umbrellas

73

My Garden in Autumn and Winter

to keep off light and rain, and then as cold poultices of
fading and decaying masses, take all the *joie de vivre* out of
the poor carpet. The only plant that I have yet found good-
tempered enough to keep smiling under these depressing
circumstances is *Cotula squalida*, a creeping member of
the great order of Compositae. It carpets just as much
ground as its owner permits, and its glossy, bronze-green
leaves are as beautifully formed as the fronds of many a
fern. It is evergreen, very hardy, and makes a charmingly
refined piece of greenery deserving a more attractive name
than *squalida*. There is a little hillock in the rock garden
crowned with such a carpet in which a good form of *Colchicum autumnale* has grown quite happily for a dozen
years at least, and except for the extraction of a few of
the undesirable plants that sow themselves into it, and an
occasional tearing away of the Cotula where too thick and
ragged, and the annual clearing away of dead Colchicum
leaves, nothing has been done to it. Year in, year out, it
is good to look at, and is a bit of permanent planting
that never fails to please. I am now trying the larger
leaved *Cotula scariosa* under the largest Colchicums, such
as *speciosum*, hoping it may behave equally well. Its leaves
are wonderfully like those of *Ceterach officinarum*, the Scale
Fern, in shape, and turn a fine bronze colour in Winter ;
so if only it will stand the cold-poulticing of dying Colchicum leaves, it should become as universal an adjunct
to *C. speciosum* as mint sauce is to roast lamb. I have
two other Cotulas that might be used in a similar way,
so I am planning a marginal band of Colchicums for a
bed of shrubs to be carpeted with long stretches of varying

74

Colchicums

dimensions of the four Cotulas. *C. repens* is the plainest of the lot, so must only be allowed to cover a small space, but it is quite distinct from the others in its shade of brilliant light green, and will make a good contrast with *scariosa*. It hugs the ground rather tightly, and makes a dense mat of stems, but I think there is no fear but that the tough nose of a sprouting Colchicum will be able to pierce through it easily enough. The last one has many names in gardens, and may be *C. dioica* in one of its numerous forms. In appearance it comes between *scariosa* and *squalida*, but has greener leaves, that are rather fleshy, and more finely divided than those of *scariosa*.

Now, to review the autumn-flowering Colchicums. First of the large flowered kinds comes *C. Bornmulleri*, which is generally at its best early in September. It has a curious habit of opening nearly white and gradually deepening in colour until it is rosy-pink with a white eye ; but it often happens that portions of the flower remain permanently pale, giving them a piebald appearance that is not very pleasing. *C. byzantinum*, also known as *veratrifolium* from the great size of its leaves in Spring, generally comes next ; but its flowers are not built upon the ample plan of its leaves, and are scarcely larger than those of many good forms of *C. autumnale*, but I can always distinguish them, as *byzantinum* has a crimson stigma, and *autumnale* a white one. In Spring the leaves alone are a sufficient guide, those of *autumnale* being no more than two inches wide in the largest forms as compared with the five or six inches those of *byzantinum* can generally boast. It is a free-flowering species, though, and makes a good show when at its best.

75

My Garden in Autumn and Winter

There is a form with a narrow line of variegation round the leaves, but hardly distinct enough to make a fuss about, and its flowers are meanly formed, always look half-starved, and are of an unclean white in colour. *Speciosum* should be the next to thrust up, first a yellowish-green pair of bracts, and then from between them a fat bud of satiny texture, rosy, crimson, or pure white, according to the form it belongs to, and seeing either of them one realises the best of the Colchicums is before one. The perianth tube lengthens rapidly, and lifts a great flower up to the sunlight which opens out into something of the beautiful outline of a Tulip flower; but even more graceful on account of the gradual swelling out of the tube into the segments of the flower, instead of the blunt base (even square in a Darwin) that is generally seen in a Tulip. The perianth tube is generally of a brighter purple than the segments in *C. speciosum*, and is the only feature by which I can distinguish it from the plant sold as *C. giganteum*, in which the tube is greenish-yellow. It is now many years since I first saw the glorious white form of *C. speciosum*. It was in Messrs. Backhouse's Nursery at York, and there were then only three bulbs of it in existence, and they were worth their weight in banknotes. I next saw it at a Royal Horticultural Society's Show, a few in a pan, and still at a price only suitable for millionaires. But this most beautiful of all autumnal bulbous plants happily possesses a good constitution, and has increased so well that now a shilling will purchase one, and no garden in the temperate zone should be without it. The purity of its whiteness is as perfect as one can desire; the substance of the flower

76

Colchicum speciosum. (See p. 76.)

Colchicums

is almost as firm as a White Lily's petal, and the greenish tinge of the tube is just right to set off the purity of the rest. Some gardens do not suit it, it seems, and one hears of losses ; but with frequent lifting and fairly light soil in a position where it will not get broiled or baked in the hottest summer days, it ought to go on improving and increasing year by year. It must have been a happy day for the man who first discovered it in the seed bed, for apart from any visions of the monetary value of such a fine novelty he must have felt a glow of satisfaction and benevolence when realising what an amount of pleasure so beautiful and so hardy a plant would give to the lovers of beautiful flowers. I would rather have been the raiser of *C. speciosum album* than to have owned a Derby winner. Growing beside it at York, I saw another fine form, a deep crimson-purple one called *rubrum,* and a bulb came here soon afterwards ; whose descendants occupy some specially honoured positions in the garden, and are very brilliant and wonderful when in flower, glowing like garnets in the sunshine. The old type form is not to be despised, and I find it makes a good, bold edging for beds of large shrubs, as the leaves in a broad band are very handsome in Spring, and the large rosy flowers always welcome in Autumn. It seeds about pretty freely, but increases enormously by offsets, so that it is best to lift, divide, and replant the clumps and bands about every three or four years, otherwise they get too crowded, and as the old tunics are very tough they do not decay within a year of their super-annuation, and a mass of dry old skins chokes the corms, and prevents their growing to full size. If replanted often

77

My Garden in Autumn and Winter

it is surprising what enormous corms this species will make. Two rather uncommon species did very well on an upper-ledge of the rock garden last Autumn. They were planted under the shelter of a large bush of *Cydonia japonica*, that had occupied its position there for many years before that part of the rock garden grew up round it. As the ledge faces due south, and is so much over-hung by the Cydonia, you can imagine how hot and dry the position is, but it suited what I bought as *C. cilicicum*, whether it is right or no to call the plant by that name. It was rather longer in the segment than others I possess, and the flowers from different corms vary a good deal in the shade of rosy-lilac, but all lasted a long time, and were freely produced for over a month, being quite showy as late as Mid-November. *C. Decaisnei* was its neighbour there, and bore smaller flowers, but a great number to each bulb, between twenty and thirty of them, so you could hardly expect them to be very large. A great point in its favour was its lateness of flowering, as it only began when *cilicium* was waning. There are several Colchicums in which the flowers are tessellated with rich purple and pale lilac squares, but there is a terrible tangle of names and plants demanding patient working out. For if one tries to find agreement among the high authorities as to what are *C. variegatum*, *C. Parkinsonii*, *C. agrippinum* and *C. tessellatum* one begins to wonder whether it is the botanists or the plants that have been playing tricks. Of course one would like to feel it was quite right to follow Baker's arrangement, which has the approval of the *Kew Index*, and to believe that *Parkinsonii* is the same as

78

variegatum, while *agrippinum* and *tessellatum* are synony-
mous and form another distinct species.

So far that appears to fit in with my garden knowledge
of them, for I have for many years grown two quite
distinct forms. But when I want to be certain as to which
is which the trouble begins. For on turning to the litera-
ture of the subject I soon get puzzled. I like to look at
the figures my books provide as the first step. Therefore
I get down that indispensable book we so badly want a
new edition of, Pritzel's *Index Iconum Botanicarum.* It is
an index of all the plates of flowering plants in the more
important botanical books of the world, and, alas, it was
published in 1866, and therefore needs the addition of
thousands of figures published since that date. I have
tried to enter all the plates contained in the books of my
gardening library, and my interleaved copy is almost needing fresh interleaving, especially where certain families
such as Rhododendron or Iris appear in it. This plan
of interleaving, and trying to keep up to date, is but
another of the invaluable lessons taught me by Canon
Ellacombe. One year while he was abroad for six weeks
he most kindly lent me his copy of Pritzel, and I had to
work like a nigger during that period to get all his entries
copied into mine. I find by Pritzel I have figures in
Worster's *Alpine Plants* and Maund's *Botanic Garden,*
pretty plates both of them, but not very helpful. So I
go to the *Botanical Magazine,* and there I find the two
plants I grow very accurately represented, one as *variegatum* in 1807 drawn by Sydenham Edwards, the other
as *Parkinsonii* in 1874 by Fitch, and both differing widely

My Garden in Autumn and Winter

in many points. Then looking to see if Baker alludes to these plates I am all at sea, because he quotes both of the *Botanical Magazine* figures for one and the same plant, *C. variegatum, Linnaeus.*

I am entering into this Dr. Jekyll and Mr. Hyde sort of case rather fully because it is very representative of one of those that so often confronts the good gardener who wishes to be sure of the names of his plants. To him it seems quite a simple matter. He has two things so utterly distinct for garden purposes, that he can never himself be in doubt as to which is which, either when in flower or leaf. But he wishes to get more roots of the form that pleases him most, and, having ordered a hundred or two, finds he has landed himself with a fresh lot of the kind of which he already has too much. He may reason with himself, and conclude that if he gets the plant he doesn't wish for, as *Bloomingthingia Thisherei*, doubtless he will get the one he does want, under one of the other names, *B. totheronei* or *B. dontcherwishyermaygetitii* (true!). So he orders from the lists offering these attractive goods, and after another season he finds yet more large patches of his undesired old superfluity. Possibly he is then wrathfully disposed towards the innocent and honest nurserymen, and writes grumbling letters to all of them, and the matter is referred to someone who is supposed to be an expert on that genus. He gets letters from these nurserymen, each asking " Can you please tell us what is the *true Soandsoa Thingumbobii?* as a client of ours has questioned the plants we supplied him as such. The expert may know his two forms well—perhaps has grown each for twenty years—but quite forgets

Colchicums

which stock came from a friend's garden and which from
nurseries, home or foreign. So he turns to his books, as
he wishes to be exact and above question in his reply,
and here we pick up the thread of *Colchicum Parkinsonii*
once again. Supposing this to be the plant that our poor
conscientious expert is trying to sort out, we find him with
the two volumes of the *Botanical Magazine* and Baker's
Linnean Society Paper open before him, and he tries to
make out which figures and descriptions best fit the mental
picture of the plants that his memory conjures up. The
earlier figure, by Sydenham Edwards, shows a plant with
lilac flowers rather unevenly chequered with a darker shade
of purple lilac. "Yes," he says; "that I recognise as the
plant that flowers the earlier, holds its flowers up on higher
tubes, and I have always called it *C. variegatum*, and, moreover, the figure shows the long tube very well. I also
remember its leaves are taller and, I think, only very slightly
waved at the margins." He reads the description, and finds
no mention of waved margins. The later figure, by Fitch,
shows a shorter flower, with whiter ground colour and
more distinct purple tessellations, and a leaf with very
markedly waved margin. "My *C. Parkinsonii*," he says.
But Baker refers both these plates to Linnaeus' *C. variegatum!* To the bookshelf, then, for Linnaeus' *Species
Plantarum* (the first edition), to see what he says. Here
it is: "Species 3. Foliis undulatis patentibus"—and a
reference to the *Hortus Cliffortianus*. That great book
must then be got out and consulted, but in it Linnaeus
has no more to say. There is another reference given in
the *Species Plantarum* to Morison's *Historia*. Out it comes,

and he gets a step further by learning that the anthers of *C. variegatum* are purple. Purple anthers, and low-lying, waved leaves are such distinct characters of the plant with the well-defined tessellations, that there is no more doubt but that it is the one Linnaeus called *C. variegatum*, and Hooker called *Parkinsonii* in the *Botanical Magazine*. Therefore the name *Parkinsonii* must drop and become a mere synonym. But what is he to do with the other plant? It seems impossible that it is identical with *variegatum* as Baker declares by his reference to its excellent portrait by Sydenham Edwards. For, in that figure, it has *yellow* anthers and *purple* filaments and styles, and a *long* tube, while the other plant has *purple* anthers, *white* styles and filaments and a *short* tube. The investigator would like to believe them two distinct things, and follow the Kew *Hand-list* and Nyman's *Conspectus Florae Europaeae*, which is so wonderfully correct in its statements, both of which declare that *variegatum* and *Parkinsonii* are distinct species. It will not help him much to turn to Ascherson, for he is rather half-hearted and only alludes to the two as being "nearly related." So the expert must wait to deliver judgment until some new prophet arises, who is energetic enough to take the trouble to examine all the specimens of Colchicums in all the great herbariums. And after he has finished with the herbariums he must spend an Autumn or two in Greece and Italy to collect all the chequered ones that grow there. Then, with all the new knowledge and material this new Daniel come to judgment would have acquired, there might be a chance of finding out whether there is a plant to match

Colchicums

the one described by Herbert as *C. pulchrum*, which no one has seen since his day, which was 1846, and whether Sydenham Edwards was right in giving yellow anthers to the plant he drew. Even if plants are found to exactly fit all the descriptions given in Baker's classification of the chequered Colchicums, it would still seem that there was no place for the one figured by Edwards, with yellow anthers, and it would require a new description and name. I have an idea Baker's *C. agrippinum* ought to include it, perhaps as a variety with yellow anthers, for, except for the words "antheris purpureis" in his description, all the rest fits it well.

Hooker states in the *Botanical Magazine* for 1874, that Baker told him Edwards' figure represented "a larger species with less pronounced and coarser tessellation and having several leaves," and so differed from the plant of Fitch's drawing published then. So until the arrival of the Daniel above mentioned, and finding out what made Baker lump the yellow-anthered plant with *variegatum* instead of *agrippinum*, we must leave the riddle unanswered, and be ready to forgive both nurserymen and botanists for not being able to pronounce quite definitely in so complicated a case.

The largest of the tessellated Colchicums is *C. Sibthorpii*, a very fine thing indeed, as large as *C. speciosum* and later to flower. But, alas, it has a kink in its temper and refuses to be happy in cultivation in all the gardens and nurseries I know intimately. It has died out here, and the last two or three lots I purchased at high figures turned out to be *C. byzantinum*, and I found that the unfortunate nursery-

My Garden in Autumn and Winter

men had been as much taken in as I was by the appearance of the vast elephantine corms their collectors had sent them as the true thing. The true *C. Sibthorpei* did so well here at one time that I am very anxious to get it again to see if I cannot, by watchful and respectful care, make it happy enough to settle down and seed, for perhaps home-raised babes might have less touchy tempers.

Our native species *C. autumnale* is worth growing, though its flowers are rather narrow and fall over very easily, when compared with the finer members of the family. It is good for naturalising in grass where no cattle browse, but it is too poisonous to be encouraged in pastures. There is a pretty white form, and a striped one more curious than beautiful. And there is a very glorious double white one. It is known as *C. autumnale album plenum,* and if you get hold of the best pure white form of it, and it does well with you, you may call it one of the best flowers of Autumn, for its long, narrow white segments are beautiful for a much longer period than is usual with those of the single kinds. But there is a form that is less fully double, and not of a pure white, being just tinged with a lilac shade. It is pretty, and should not be burnt, but it ought to be sold at a much cheaper rate than the real beauty. There is also a double lilac form that is useful to possess, for it flowers later than the others, but is rather given to appearing with pied or half-white and half-rosy flowers if the weather is frosty at the time of their opening. Two other forms appear in lists, and I have grown both of them. That named *major* is simply *byzantinum ;* but *multiflorum* seems to be well named, and

84

Colchicums

produces a wonderful quantity of pale and small flowers for those who want them. *C. Stevenii* finishes up the season, often lasting into December. It is a queer little thing with flowers that are nearly white, very close to the ground, and so small that one would not trouble to look at them in June, but at their time of flowering anything with a blossom larger than a bee's knee is welcome. It is a pity the name of Meadow Saffron was ever given to the Colchicum, for it has helped to confuse it with the true Saffrons, the Crocuses. I must refer my readers to my Spring volume for the differences between the two; but will remind them that a Crocus is an Irid with only three stamens, while the Colchicum is a Liliaceous plant with six, as that is such an easy way of distinguishing them. The scientific name is said to be derived from Colchis in Asia Minor, where the genus is common. It was well described by Dioscorides, but was only known to the ancients as a poison. It was also called Ephemerum, because if it were eaten it killed the victim the same day. Another name was *Strangulatorium*, from the manner of the death it brought about. Parkinson tells us, "Some have called them also Filius ante Patrem, the Sonne before the Father, because (as they think) it giveth seed before the flower," and goes on to show that this is not true, and that it flowers in Autumn before its leaves appear, and the seeds follow with them. It was mentioned as a drug in the London *Pharmacopoeia* of 1618, but was not much valued before Baron Storck of Vienna and others at the end of the eighteenth century investigated its possibilities, and gave it the high position it has ever

My Garden in Autumn and Winter

since maintained as the great remedy for gout. Its power of easing the pain in this disease is said to be due to its powerful effect in checking the circulation, but it has a terribly lowering effect on the patient if used for any length of time.

It is curious to note how its medical reputation has grown, while that of the true Saffron has decreased, during the same period.

CHAPTER VI

Autumn Composites

As Autumn advances the great Natural Order Compositae, the largest order of flowering plants, supplies the greater number of tall and showy flowers in the garden. This Order contributes very few, and those chiefly dwarf and humble members, to the spring borders, Daisies and their near relations, and Felicia petiolaris if it has survived the Winter well, are the only ones that recur to my memory as coming into bloom early in Spring; but the numbers increase daily when summer heat returns, until Sunflowers of many kinds, Dahlias, Michaelmas Daisies, and Chrysanthemums hold the field. I will only mention one Sunflower of the many perennial species and varieties of Helianthus, and that because it is the latest to arrive at its full beauty, and one of the best when it has done so.

Dr. Lowe of Wimbledon gave it to me many years ago. He told me to call it *Helianthus laetiflorus*, and to believe it a true species, and I prefer to do so, and am a little annoyed when I am told it is only a form of *H. tuberosus*—the Jerusalem Artichoke. It certainly has slightly tuberous roots, curious, fleshy fingers and toes growing out of the base of the main stem, but exceedingly unlike the great fat tubers of the kitchen garden plant. I have noticed rather

My Garden in Autumn and Winter

a strange thing about these fleshy roots, namely that, in late Summer and Autumn they become infested by flocks of horrid white underground aphides and attendant black ants, but I have not yet discovered whether the ants come first and place their cows on this pasturage, or whether it is original sin in the aphides, and the ants only find them and make use of the discovery. The plant itself makes a handsome tall specimen, if thinned out or replanted, reaching some eight feet in height, and in October and sometimes right on into November, bears abundance of pale, clear yellow flowers, large enough to be showy, yet small enough to be graceful. The greatest of its charms, however, is due to the deep black of the stems. They are as dark as the ebony handle of a sable paint brush, and the contrast with the rich green leaves and daffodil-yellow flowers is delightful.

The name *laetiflorus* has unfortunately been used for a semi-double form of Helianthus (often wrongly called Harpalium), *H. rigidus*, but, so far as I can see without spending a month or two in herbariums or taking a journey to the Prairies, my black-stemmed plant may be the *H. laetiflorus* of Persoon, and therefore no other member of its family can have any right to use that name.

I should like to be strong-minded enough to dislike Dahlias and to shut the garden gate on one and all of them as a punishment to them and the raisers who have produced some of the horrors of modern garden nightmares. But as it would not make much stir in the world of Dahlias however tightly I barred it, and as I have a great affection for single Dahlias and all the true species I have been able to

Autumn Composites

get, the family is still admitted. I cannot believe I shall ever be converted to a taste for Collarette Dahlias. The crumpled little pieces of flower that form the frill cause an itching in my fingers to pick them all out to see what the flower would look like without them ; and latterly they have taken to themselves such appallingly virulent eye-jarring combinations of colour that I long to burn them, root and all. A screeching magenta Dahlia with a collarette of lemon yellow, or of a mixture of cerise and yellow, I think only fit to be grown in the garden of an asylum for the blind. Even the name annoys me ; it suggests a sham affair, a dickey or some lace abomination, a middle-class invention to transform useful work-a-day clothes into a semblance of those of afternoon leisure.

Then we have a new race of Pæony-flowered Dahlias that get larger and more violently glaring each season, and their poor stalks seem more and more unable to hold up the huge targets that grow out of them. They must be matchless for saving labour in decorating for Harvest Thanksgivings, one pumpkin with two Pæony Dahlias and one bud would be enough for the pulpit, and an extra large one would be all-sufficient for the font. I saw some magnificently grown last season, but so huge that I could not resist asking, in as innocent a tone as I could manage, whether they fried or stewed them, and if the latter, were they best with a white sauce or brown gravy.

Then I am not fond of Cactus Dahlias, and in this I find myself in disagreement with so many of my betters that I suspect I must be wrong, and that it is very likely because in our poor soil and crowded garden we cannot find room to

My Garden in Autumn and Winter

grow them well that I am prejudiced against them. I grew and liked their parent *Dahlia Juarezii* many years ago, but learnt from its ways that it is a family failing to smother up the flowers with coarse leaves, and this idea is firmly fixed in my mind, and I have still to be shown a large plant of a Cactus Dahlia that makes a good show of its flowers. Also, it worries me to see them growing year by year more spidery and twisted, and more like a Chrysanthemum or a sea anemone, and less and less like a Dahlia. But I grow one, a deep maroon purple, almost black in some lights, because I find it so good for cutting, free-flowering to begin with, lasting in beauty for several days, and making a delightful deep tone of colour on a flower table among either yellow, lilac, or pink massings of colour. It is J. H. Jackson, and if I could find a pure white and a clear yellow variety that would behave as well both when growing and cut, I should add them to my list of indispensables. I find some of the newer singles with medium-sized, round flowers and stiff stems are excellent for cutting. Snowdrop, white with a lemon-yellow ring towards the centre—Mrs. Joynson Hicks, orange with maroon eye, and Cardinal, rich crimson—are good (see plate). Peggy is a peculiarly lovely mixture of salmon-rose shaded with rosy-mauve, difficult both to describe and to believe in as beautiful without seeing how well all the shades blend. There is one table in the drawing-room here that has a Crown Derby bowl on it decorated with pink Roses and gold, and I like to surround it with vases of pink flowers. Sweet Peas are very effective there in their season, and later on pink Chrysanthemums, Penstemon Myddelton Gem (named after this garden as I gave it to Mr.

Autumn Composites

Wallace), and this Dahlia Peggy blend well together to make the rosy glow I like to see in that corner. This season I have planted two newer ones, a single called Sunrise, much like Peggy but of a deeper and warmer shade of rosy-red and a double decorative Dahlia named Delice, of a lovely shade of clear rose colour, and I am hoping they will both prove useful for my pink table.

We sowed a few seeds one season gathered from this round-flowered race of Dahlias, and among the results there came a very brilliant light yellow, with an additional ring of ray florets, not enough to make it look double or clumsy, but just sufficient to help it in substance and lasting power. So we discarded our older yellow and grow only this one. With Snowdrop and the double Cactus J. H. Jackson, each in its own vase, it makes a charming group on a table.

To my thinking the best scarlet among single Dahlias is a French variety called Aimée Barillet. The flowers are very brilliant in colour, and are made to appear even more so by the rich bronzy-purple tint of the leaves, and the almost black stems. I have noticed, too, in several seasons that a frost that has ruined all the other Dahlias has spared this one, as though its rich store of pigment acted as a protection against cold.

The old single white, White Queen, we still grow; but although its flowers are large and effective on the plant, they are not good for cutting, as they have weak stems, and the flowers hang over and are of a poor substance, so that they do not last long. The old maroon-purple Paragon I have given up to make room for a smaller

My Garden in Autumn and Winter

one called Winona, very charming for cutting. A Dahlia specialist will turn up his nose at my collection, no doubt, but if any one wishes for a good basketful of cut blooms three times a week, from August till the advent of the first sharp frost, and will try my nominees, I think he will not be disappointed.

[In reading this book I hope all will remember I have undertaken to write my experiences of *my* garden ; so, limited though they may be, no one must expect more of me, nor think me egotistical because I use the personal pronoun so often, both in the nominative and possessive cases.]

My favourite of all Dahlias is a true species, *D. Merckii*, or, as it is often called, *D. glabrata*. Its flowers are the smallest of any Dahlia I know, about the size of a florin ; but they are beautifully shaped, the ray florets wide, slightly curved inwards, and well poised on their slender stems. In colour they are a delicate lilac with a purplish disc, powdered with a ring of golden pollen. I also have a white form, but the lilac one is the better. It is very nearly hardy, and in a warm border it is fairly safe if planted deeply, even if left out without any protection ; it comes through the soil early in Summer, and begins to flower by the beginning of July.

The plant once called *Dahlia Zimapannii* but now known as *Bidens atrosanguinea* makes a good companion for *D. Merckii*, the flowers being about the same size, but as dark a maroon as can exist without being as black as your boot, which no one would desire for a Dahlia. Then I must not omit mention of the Green Dahlia, a very extraordinary monstrous form in which the flowers consist

92

Autumn Composites

of rosettes of green involucral bracts, looking like miniature Globe Artichokes. The terminal flowers on the stronger stems often come rather larger than those on side shoots, and in their old age lose their figures, and become hammer-headed, lopsided, and all sorts of queer shapes, and then disgrace themselves still further by producing a few crumpled crimson ray-florets among the green bracts. They get picked off as soon as I observe them, but they are interesting as showing the type of flower of which the Green Dahlia is a monstrous form.

One more Dahlia calls for mention, and it is really the finest of the whole family, but unfortunately cannot be grown along quickly enough to flower out of doors before the frosts come. It is *Dahlia imperialis*, the Tree Dahlia, which is such a wonderful feature at Christmastide in the gardens of the Riviera. There it sends up a stout stem like that of some great Bamboo and bears a crown of handsome light green, much divided leaves, and at last great bunches of pendant flowers, the ray florets of which are so long they seem to form an open bell. In colour they are pearly white just tinted with a suspicion of pink, and look as perfect as any flower I can recall against a clear blue sky. Here it must be grown in a pot and brought under glass with the indoor Chrysanthemums. Then it flowers during the November fogs, and lasts but a short way into December because of sunless skies and the way that green fly will attack it if the house is kept warm enough to make it really happy. In this garden the outdoor Chrysanthemums are crowded out of beds and the warm borders under walls they would like best, by

My Garden in Autumn and Winter

tender shrubs and delicate plants dearer to my botanical mind. So they are grown in rows in the kitchen garden. And how delightful it is to walk in among them on a sunny morning, flower scissors in hand, to fill a basket with golden-orange Horace Martin, white and cream Mme. Desgranges, and Goacher's Crimson. This last is wonderfully good for cutting; but then so is Bobby, a brown pompon of delightful habit and staying powers. Cecil Wells is the best brilliant yellow I have found; Espérance, a good white, and Harvest Home a useful variety in which there is a mingling of bronze and red that goes well with other colours.

Even after the frost has nipped all the others past recovery, I can often pick tall stems of an old variety I call Cottage Pink, because it is much grown in cottage gardens round here. It will open well in water even if the frost has been sharp enough to turn the foliage to bronze tints with here and there a touch of crimson, and this rich colouring sets off the delicate rose-pink flowers even better than the green leaves it retains in kinder seasons. It is always one of the last plants that I can cut tall sprays of flowers from in the open, in some seasons being quite presentable up to the middle of November. At this time its only tall rival in the beds is *Aster Tradescantii*, which a child once described very accurately as looking like Asparagus with Daisies stuck all over it. This Aster is a charmingly graceful species either out of doors or in the house, and even after really sharp frosts have destroyed all the flowers that were open, if cut and brought into a warm room the remaining buds will open fair and white. I

94

Autumn Composites

have noticed with pleasure the last few seasons that it is being grown for market purposes, and appears in the London flower shops in increasing quantities each year.

We must turn back now a couple of months or so and review the Asters, the Michaelmas Daisies. *A. Shortii*, a tall, lilac beauty, already mentioned, is one of the first to come and go. *A. puniceus pulcherrimus*, a stout-stemmed, hairy fellow with immense but rather washy lavender flowers is next, and also has too short a period of beauty, but is finer and lasts better if grown in a cool and moist spot. *A. acris* is a wonderful plant when well grown; which means that it must be divided every second year and replanted in well enriched soil. Then it makes a rounded bush about two and a half feet high, so well covered with its brilliant, bluish-lilac flowers that the leaves are hidden. As the ray florets are longer and narrower than in most Asters, and are arranged in a loose and irregular manner, the general effect is wonderfully soft and feathery, as the flowers intermingle and do not show their individual outlines. Butterflies love it and visit it on sunny days and add to its beauty, especially when the visitors are the Small Copper. There is a white form of it, a quaint dwarf thing only a few inches high, that is an attractive little inmate for the rock garden. A tall Aster, a garden variety called Arcturus, is a great favourite of mine, not only on account of its dark lilac flowers of an uncommon colour early in the Aster season, but also because it has nearly black stems, which greatly add to its beauty when in flower, and are good to look at even in July before the flower buds are

95

formed. It is about the third week in September that the Asters in the pergola garden are at their best, and if the Vines on the vine pergola are doing their duty that season and have coloured well, the contrasts of colour are beautiful on a sunny day. A row of the lovely rosy-pink Aster St. Egwyn crosses the front of one of the square beds, hiding up the plots of bare ground where the Daffodils reigned in the Spring. Though the colour of this delightful variety is charming at all times, it glows out with an extra charm just at sunset, and increases in beauty every minute until the light has faded almost away and all things begin to turn grey. Behind it grows the so-called double one, Beauty of Colwall. Only the terminal flowers that open first are really double, the next instalment being but semi-double, and the last to open on each spray having but one row of ray florets and an open, yellow disc. But its colour is good, a clear, cool lavender that is none too common among the newer Asters. I still grow one that I got from the late Mr. Wood of Kirkstall about twenty years ago, called Wood's semi-double, that is much like Beauty of Colwall in habit and colour, but is a long way behind it in the fulness of the first opened flowers. Robert Parker, Top Sawyer, and William Marshall are good strong growers of various shades of lavender, but are all eclipsed by that wonderful beauty from Aldenham, Climax, the largest flowered as well as the best coloured variety of this type of Aster. I still grow and prize an old form called *cyaneus*, which is generally in full beauty when others of this bluish-lavender shade are over. Another valuable seedling from Aldenham is The Hon. Edith Gibbs, one of the most graceful in habit

Autumn Composites

of all pale lilac Michaelmas Daisies. To get it at its best it requires either replanting or very severe thinning out each year; then it should produce stout stems three to four feet high, and a great cloud of lilac-grey blossoms on stalks thin as hairs and branching and spreading in all directions. The number of really good Asters that one can choose from nowadays is quite appalling, and I do not profess to keep up to date with the novelties, preferring to keep those that I have found do well here and maintain a succession of flowers.

Of the *Novae Angliae* section, the tall, hairy-leaved fellows with ray florets almost as thread-like and narrow as those of an Erigeron, I have learnt to love best Ryecroft Purple for a deep coloured one, Ryecroft Pink for a pale rosy shade, and Lil Fardel for a rich crimson; the flowers of this last are even larger and deeper in colour than those of Mrs. Raynor. It is wonderful how many flowers one stem of any of these will bear, and how many stems one ought to pull away in Spring to get the finest effects from those left. It looks sinful to waste some fifty strong shoots out of an old clump, and to leave only four or five standing with such large spaces between them. But when flowering time comes one finds a good many side shoots may be picked from such a clump, and yet the plant is one solid mass of flowers. Thirza is a pleasing, flesh-coloured variety, with small flowers and light habit. Coombe Fishacre rather stiffer, and of a deeper tone of pink, and Edward VII a dainty little thing with a foamy effect due to a confused habit of growth and small, thin flowers.

My Garden in Autumn and Winter

I have yet to find a really good, white Aster. Finchley White, and an unnamed one from Glasnevin, are my best thus far among large-flowered varieties, but both of them have the general fault of all white forms I know, they are only white for about two days, and then their disc florets turn brown and purple, and the general effect is dingy and tarnished. After all is said and done, though, one can hardly want a finer, white Composite for late Autumn than *Pyrethrum uliginosum*, whose stately stems reach a height of eight feet, and bear such large, white, and yellow flowers. It seems to have fallen into disfavour in many gardens of late, but has established itself very successfully in cottage gardens. We owe a vast debt of gratitude to the conservative instincts of our peasantry. Just think, for instance, how often it has happened that the weathercock of fashion has turned out the Chippendale chairs from the dining-room of the Hall first to some stable loft, and then to the cottages on the estate to be discovered and bought back half a century later. The same change of taste, or lapse and abeyance of good taste we might say, turned out the old Roses and herbaceous plants to make way for showier bedding sorts. Again, Cottage Tulips, rescued from cottage gardens, are clearly the throw-outs of various Tulip fanciers who discarded breeders that broke not, and even those that would not behave just as they wished, and their self-imposed rules decreed. Many a labourer in the gardens of such autocrats has said, "Whoi maester he do zay you do be teu long and teu dirty at the base, but oi loike 'ee, and my missus 'ud loike 'ee foine ; so come along o' me and see if a bit o' colour woan't look heartsome

Autumn Composites

under the washus window;" and perhaps fifty years later
a Barr or a Hartland has spotted a clump of some glowing
and graceful Tulip, and gladly purchased the stock from
the surprised tenant of that old cottage for what seemed
to him untold wealth for "they old Toolups what hes bin
theer, well, ever since Feyther first come into the cottage."
I have got many a hardy, sturdy treasure from cottage
gardens, besides *Pyrethrum uliginosum* and the pink Chrysanthemum, and anyone with a keen eye for a good plant
might do good work by keeping that eye open on cottage
plots. A really hardy, reliable plant of good habit is what
the cottage gardener wants, and it is after all not a bad
standard to set up for the larger garden, and a plant that
has thriven and been found worth growing for fifty years
in a cottage garden is certain to have many good qualities
in it. It is also much pleasanter to collect plants rather
than furniture among the cottage homes, because one feels
a cutting or root or two does not rob the owner of their
treasured possessions, whereas one cannot take a leg off
a Chippendale chair, or a spout off a Wedgwood teapot
to grow into perfect specimens.

There are some good white Asters, though, among the
small flowered varieties, and a plant I have had for over
twenty years as the typical *A. ericoides*, and which was
another of Dr. Lowe's precious gifts, is still the one I
like best. It grows four feet high when well treated, has
dark green leaves as small and closely set as those of an
Erica, which alone might account for the specific name;
but the masses of small white flowers are also, at a distance,
very suggestive of some kinds of white Heath, such as

99

My Garden in Autumn and Winter

Erica lusitanica or *E. arborea*. These small flowered types are not satisfactory for cutting, at least so far as I have tried them, flagging after a few hours unless cut very short and placed up to the neck in water. People tell me they find some of the *cordifolius* section last well in water, but I have met with no success in my endeavours to use them. They are so wonderfully graceful that I must try hot water, and all the dodges I can think of till I hit upon a successful one. In the borders the old form and the varieties named Diana and Isabel please me most, but because of their unfriendly habit of swooning when in the house, I have not acquired any of the newer varieties.

All of the *Amellus* section, on the contrary, are exceedingly sociable, and will smile at one on the dining-room table at the three chief meals of the day for more than a week, if they are cut while still young. A cut-glass bowl or wide-mouthed vase, filled as full as it can hold with two or three good forms in varying shades of blue-purple, is very good to look at, especially if the stems of the Asters are cut a good length. I like to fill four old champagne glasses for the corners of the table as well as the big bunch for centrepiece, and they generally hold a bunch of each of my newest and most precious sorts, or I fill two with Beauté Parfaite, a very large and deep-blue form, as good as any, and the other two, with that soft, rosy-lilac one, called Perry's Favourite, which looks almost a pink in colour unless you place it beside St. Egwyn or a La France Rose.

In the garden also the *Amellus* forms are hard to beat,

Autumn Composites

and if left alone even for several years deteriorate less than other Asters. An ancient clump is often a very fine sight, all the large flowers being packed so closely they form a level mass of bloom, and make a platform for the Admiral butterflies to alight on to suck their nectar. They enjoy sunny quarters, sufficient room to spread out in their natural way, and being so dwarf and shrubby in habit, they should never be staked. If I had room for it I should like a long, narrow border facing south in front of an old stone wall filled with every variety procurable of *Aster Amellus*. One might grow Spring bulbs under them, but nothing that flowers or wants room for leaves later than June. Then these Italian Starworts would find the space all their own, and would soon fill it; and if one could spare such a precious bit of ground all the Summer, it would be a joy indeed to visit it in September and onward for a month or more. I grow some of the best sorts in the rock garden, though, in spite of the amount of room they take up, and I and the butterflies enjoy them immensely. There is also a row of Asters in the kitchen garden to cut from, about half of which consists of *Amellus* varieties, and the plants are to be met with at corners where two paths meet, where a round-headed bush a foot in height and twice as much through fits in very pleasantly, and covers a patch of ground that is gay with some good Crocus in February.

There is a delightful little plant that is too seldom seen in gardens, and its name is *Aster purpurrimus* at shows, but I cannot find it in a book. It is not especially purple, as the name implies, but a very pleasing purplish-rose colour, and its charm mainly lies in its dwarf neat

My Garden in Autumn and Winter

habit, for it forms a wee branching specimen about eight inches high, smothered in a cloud of its pretty little flowers. It needs division every other year at least, or else it makes a woody root stock that ants seize upon in order to plant on it especially loathsome aphides, creatures of a mouldy blue-black appearance, that suck the life of the poor plant. Freshly divided plants do not appear to have the make of roots that is suitable for the ants' cowkeeping, and therefore escape.

When most of the Michaelmas Daisies are overblown *A. turbinellus* begins to open, and is especially valuable on this account; but even if it were to flower during the reign of the best varieties it would still be indispensable, for there is no other like it. It forms a rounded, bushy head of fine stems, thin as flower wire, and the flowers are very large for the thickness of the stalks, and of a most charming shade of mauve; it has another endearing quality in lasting well when cut. Nursery lists sometimes contain the name *A. turbinellus albus*, but so far as I have tested them it is a herbaceous Mrs. Harris. There is a hideous plant that does duty for her, as ugly as Betsy Prig, and, like Sairey Gamp, has too much crumb about her, having clumsy thick stalks; it is neither *turbinellus* nor white, a dowdy thing with unclean flowers. One with hairy leaves and quantities of small grey-blue flowers was given to me by Dr. Lowe, who used to say for want of a better name he called it blue *ericoides*. I make it out to be *A. amethystinus*, from Massachusetts; but, whatever it is, it is a very distinct one, and flowers late and long. *Aster trinervius*, as I grow it, just misses

102

Autumn Composites

being a useful plant, for it tries to flower as late as November, and generally gets so badly snubbed for its pluck by the Clerk of the Weather that the result is poor, but I can quite imagine that in the South of France it might make a good show with its large, handsome leaves and blue-purple flowers. Much the same fate overtakes *A. grandiflorus* in nine seasons out of ten, but if its large purple flowers succeed in opening they are as lovely as any the family can produce. If cut in the bud before very hard frosts have turned the leaves yellow they will open well in water, but this handsome plant is well worth growing in a pot, so that it may be brought into a house with the indoor Chrysanthemums, and then it should continue flowering almost up to Christmas.

I must not forget the Golden Rods, for Solidago belongs to the Composite order, and several of the species are handsome, late-flowering plants. My favourite is *S. Shortii*. Firstly, because it is generally at its best at the end of September and in the first weeks of October, when the other tall ones are over ; and secondly, because it has such a graceful habit. Tall, stiff stems grow up throughout the summer months, and then begin to branch out for some six inches of the upper part. The side shoots produced thus stand out at right angles from the main stem, and when they are laden with their small but numerous golden flowers, the tips arch downwards in very graceful curves that give the plant a look of dignity and distinction that is wanting in the early-flowering sorts.

103

CHAPTER VII

September's Farewell

THE last day of September is as the end of a period. With it passes away the feeling of security from frosts; and one must look anxiously at sky and thermometer each evening until all the succulents on the wall are safely housed, and all the cuttings of tender and doubtful plants have been secured. So I like to go round the garden and take a sort of farewell glance at plants that may be killed now any night, or, at any rate, cut down for this season; and also to notice what things are ready to take their place, and keep the garden full of interest after the calamity. Let us take an imaginary walk for this dual purpose. We must stop a moment in front of the house to admire the carpet of fallen Ivy blossom that covers the gravel under the large bush of golden-leaved Ivy just under one of the windows of the morning room. Many wasps and drone flies, and a still larger company of blue-bottle flies, are sucking away at the ovaries of many flowers from which the petals have already fallen, and their constant movement causes a shower of petals to fall as we watch. The Ivy blossom has opened earlier than usual this season, and there will not be much left for the time when frosts kill the other honey-producing flowers; I shall miss the pleasure of

September's Farewell

visiting it after dark with an acetylene lamp to see
whether I can pick up a rare moth or two among its
numerous nocturnal visitors. Moths do not go to Ivy
blossom much here until the counter attractions of sweetly-
scented flowers are gone. There is a delicious scent in
the air, blown to us from the tall spikes of *Humea elegans*
rising out of the Paul Crampel Pelargoniums in the two
beds on the front lawn, and I make a mental note to cut
those fragrant heads on the first day frost is feared, as they
give out a sweet incense-like perfume for months if stood
up in a large vase and allowed to dry. They look too
pretty, however, to be sacrificed just yet. The bed by the
dining-room windows is still full of flowers. *Salvia patens*
lives out there very satisfactorily if a few ashes are spread
over its crowns for the Winter, and its wonderful blue-
velvet flowers are as beautiful now as they have been all
the Summer. Even if they were not so lovely I should
grow the plant, because its large flowers show better than
those of any other Sage the wonderful mechanism by
which the anthers are bent down to wipe their pollen on
the back of a visiting bee. If you wish to see it for
yourself, take an ordinary lead pencil and push the pointed
end into the open mouth of the flower and downwards
towards the ovary and the honey just as a bee would
thrust in its tongue. You will then see the two anthers
bend down as if they knew what they were doing, and
touch the pencil about two inches from the point, and if it
is a young flower you have chosen, they will leave a
smudge of golden pollen on it. Now look for an older
flower, and you will be able to know it by seeing the stigma

hanging out from the hood, just about as far as your pencil's entrance caused the stamens to bend out. Push your pencil in again and you will find the stigma touches it just in the place where the pollen lies on it, and when the anthers are brought down to it by your pencil they are empty and shrivelled, their pollen having been carried away by bees on the previous day. Thus on its first day of opening, the anthers are rubbed on the backs of visiting bees ; and on the next, the stigma lengthens and hangs down far enough to receive pollen brought from a younger flower, and the cross-fertilisation of each flower is effected on its second day. If you wish to see the mechanism by which the anthers are bent down, cut away the hood until you lay bare the stamens as far as the point where they are joined to the corolla, and here you will notice they have slender white flying buttresses that keep them in place, and just in front, standing out into the passage way down the tube of the flower, are two white levers growing out from the filaments and blocking the mouth of the tube. Push your pencil in again and you can then see what happens. It strikes against these levers, and pushes them down with it, and as the buttresses hold the filaments in place, their upper portion is bent over from that point until the anthers touch the pencil, which should, of course, be the back of a bee. *Salvia Grahamii*, a good, hardy, shrubby species, is as bright with its scarlet flowers as *S. patens* is with blue ; they are much smaller, however, but make up for it by being very freely produced from May till severe frosts cause the buds to drop unopened.

Melianthus major is at its best now, and the huge

September's Farewell

bipinnate, glaucous leaves are wonderfully grey and tropical-looking for a plant that has lived out here for the last ten years. Next to it are large bushes of *Solanum aviculare* that you may not see there again. For the species is not hardy here, though it is in Cornwall, and the plants are rather troublesome to find house-room for in Winter. They make handsome bushes with dark green leaves, and flowers shaped like those of the Potato only larger and a little flatter, of a deep blue. They are followed by bright scarlet berries as large as a chaffinch's egg.

In the pergola garden several interesting plants are in flower. A large bush of *Ligustrum Quihoui*, a Chinese species, stands opposite the old brick pillar. It is one of the best of the Privets to plant where one wants a small tree, for it is graceful in habit, has good evergreen leaves, flowers later than most shrubs, and in mild winters some of the bunches of blossoms last fresh till after Christmas.

Clematis Durandii has been flowering throughout the Summer, but is still a fine sight. It is a hybrid of *C. integrifolia* crossed with *C. lanuginosa*, and was raised by the firm of Durand Frères, who sent it out under the name of *C. semperflorens*, which well describes its bountiful ways. The flowers are larger than those of *C. integrifolia* and of a deeper shade of blue, but have inherited much of the metallic sheen as well as the pendant position of those of their mother. It seems happy here, scrambling up among the stems of Roses on the pergola posts. Dr. Lowe's Crimson *Rosa chinensis* is as bright and full of

My Garden in Autumn and Winter

flower as it was at any time during the last three months, its single flowers glowing like rubies if you get them between you and the sun.

Phygelius capensis, too, makes a good show, with its large bunches of Penstemon-like flowers of a peculiar brick-red colour with a greenish-yellow throat. Here it grows as a herbaceous plant, and gets cut down by design or by frost some time during each winter. But in warmer gardens it grows into a tall bush; in Ireland I have seen high walls covered with it, and there it is a fine sight when full of flower. I tried it once here on a wall, but it was not a very sunny one that I could afford it, and it did no good there.

The grass border, by the pond, begins to look rather brown, so many of its occupants having gone to seed. *Oryzopsis miliacea* is the only one that feels young enough to send up new flowering shoots, that look all the fresher and fairer from the contrast their elderly matronly neighbours afford. *Stipa Calamagrostis* has learnt how to grow old gracefully, and the pale fawn-coloured heads are very effective now.

The pond edge is bright with the delicate light green of the semi-transparent, juicy leaves of *Impatiens fulva*, which sows itself rather too freely among the other waterside plants. It is easily pulled up, though, having a wonderfully slight rooting system. The flowers are a good tawny orange, that goes well with its pale leaves, and the seed pods explode and shoot out the seeds as is the habit of these annual Balsams. The last of the Nymphæas to look happy is the faithful James Brydon, that still opens

Autumn tints round the Pond. (See p 108.)

September's Farewell

half a dozen of its fresh, round, rosy flowers every day
that the sun shines on them.

It is perhaps in the rock garden that there is most to be
seen that is not a legacy of Summer but the gift of Autumn,
Acidanthera bicolor, a beautiful bulbous plant from the Cape,
has managed to flower before the frosts come this season,
and opens one or two at a time of its large, white flowers
flushed with lavender and spotted with rich purple. They
are rather like those of a Gladiolus, but more open, and held
away from the stem on a curved tube that gives them a
peculiarly graceful effect. *Brassica insularis* is just beginning to bloom, and though it is but the wild Cabbage of
Corsica, is a very fine plant. It makes a stout stem in its
first year, bearing large grey-green leaves, very similar to
those of any coarse growing Cabbage, and my friends have
made fun of both me and the Brassica all through the
Summer, declaring the great plants reminded them of Mrs.
Wiggs or boiled caterpillars, and wondering at my giving
up so much of the precious rock garden to such a culinary
crop. But now that the large white flowers are open
like those of some magnified single Stock, and scenting
the air with their fragrance, visitors are quite respectful,
and ask whatever that magnificent plant can be. Severe
frosts spoil the flowers that are open, but it is marvellous
to notice how bravely the young buds struggle on and
manage to open during mild spells, even in the depth of
Winter. If well treated it should grow eight feet high,
and branch freely. I have seen it grown under glass,
and a really fine sight ; and if it were better known,
it would be highly prized as a decorative plant for

My Garden in Autumn and Winter

conservatories in Winter. *Convolvulus Cneorum* is in full flower, the pink buds and large, white blossoms very beautiful among its silver leaves which shine like satin. Two rather large bushes of it grow among a carpet of the beautiful, lilac-flowered *Convolvulus mauritanicus*, and now that both are in full flower that part of the rock garden is worth lingering over for some time every morning, when the sun shines, and causes all the flowers of these two species to open out to their fullest. There is a brilliant tuft of crimson in the uppermost bed of the fish-hatchery moraine, provided by the third flowering of *Polygonum sphaerostachyum*. Just now it looks more lovely than ever before, for it has lately had a new carpet spread over its roots and round its feet—a carpet of brilliant emerald green composed of an interwoven mass of the creeping stems of *Mazus reptans*, a wonderfully pretty Japanese plant that has only lately found its way into most gardens. In Spring it is covered with lilac flowers with yellow crests, rather like those of a Linaria in shape. I rather fear a severe winter would cripple, if it did not kill it, so although it has passed through the last mild one without a check we are keeping a panful under cover, for it is far too lovely a thing to be lost, if care can save it. A very interesting and curious plant is flowering for the first time here. It is *Zingiber Mioga*, a hardy member of the Ginger family. Mr. Elwes tells me he found it in dense woods in Japan, growing two feet or more high. But here it has found a home at the foot of the southern bank of the last new strip of rock garden, as I feared it might not be hardy. As it has done so well there, and is increasing rapidly, I

September's Farewell

shall act on my newly-gained knowledge and take a portion to cooler quarters, as the handsome sword-like leaves now reach no more than one foot.

The flowers are produced on separate shoots, only rise a few inches from the ground, and are of a pale straw-colour, more curious than beautiful. I learn from that delightful book, *The Useful Plants of Japan*, that these flowers with their bracts are collected in Summer and Autumn by the Japanese and eaten either raw or boiled, and that they have an aromatic odour and a slight acid taste. So perhaps some day I may have a salade à la Japonaise composed of them. That the old leaves, when twisted and kneaded, are used for making saddles is another surprising bit of information given by this book. Several other flowers are used by the Japanese either as salads or boiled. Several species of Hemerocallis, Brassica, and Pæony, as well as *Pyrethrum sinense* and *Gardenia florida*, provide flowers for these uses; while those of double Cherries and *Cymbidium virens*, preserved in salt, are used for drinking like tea.

Dianthus fruticosus, close beside the Ginger, is in full flower, and I think would justify Sibthorpe's high praise of it if only we had known its habits better and given it a higher position on the bank. For the long flower-ing stems are all produced from the lower portion of the round-headed, grey-leaved bush, and fall on to the gravel path, and their brilliant cerise flowers lose a good deal of their effect thereby. There are younger plants on a higher ledge, though, that should make a better show when they are as large as the old one, as they are hanging over blocks of grey Kentish-rag, that will suit their complexion better than the red gravel path. I owe this fine plant to Mr. Bartholomew of Reading, who is so energetic in introducing new and rare plants. He was fired by the glowing words of praise in Sibthorpe's *Flora Graeca*, and managed to get seeds of it, and kindly gave me some of the young plants they produced. I can quite imagine that, growing out of a rocky cliff in Greece, an old specimen with hundreds of the brilliant flowers open would be a fine sight. The first one that flowered here was of rather too blue a pink to entirely please me, but one of the younger plants has flowers of a warmer shade; so that it seems likely that seedlings and careful selection might help us to a more beautiful form. Anyway, it is a fine plant, and useful for flowering so late in the season. I have another late flowering Dianthus that I think must be a form of *D. gallicus*. Dr. Lowe first gave it to me, and I afterwards found it myself growing wild on the sand dunes near Biarritz. It is rather a straggly, wild-growing plant, and its flowers are of a truly cruel purplish-magenta, but so numerous, so prettily fringed, and so resistant of wind and cold, that a plant of it is very cheery and welcome so late in the season. *Chelidonium Franchetianum* I have praised before, but it must be mentioned here again as it is so especially beautiful in late Autumn. Its clear yellow flowers do not last very long, but they are so freely replaced by younger ones that the plant has an air of Spring about it, not too frequent among those that have already flowered for several months. *Desmodium penduliflorum* is the name most familiar to many of us, but *Lespedeza bicolor* is the

September's Farewell

correct one for a very beautiful plant. In warmer climates it should become shrubby, but here it gets cut to the ground in most Winters. Even then it sends up strong shoots some four to six feet high, which arch over in September with the weight of their flower buds, and towards the end of the month make as fine a show as any shrub in the garden. The general effect may be described as that of a rich purple Laburnum, the long branches of pea-shaped flowers hanging from the axil of almost every leaf. If grown on an upper portion of a rocky bank and allowed to wave out as it chooses, a good specimen is really a magnificent sight so long as the weather remains kindly disposed; but rough winds and rain are apt to knock the flowers about in a pitiable manner.

Anemone japonica is a plant I should like to grow every known form of, even some of the very double ones, but space forbids, so I have limited myself to a few. It is one of those plants that when first introduced to Britain was treated as a greenhouse plant, and instructions for so growing it may be found in old gardening books, of the date of Mrs. Loudon's. Also, like so many introductions from China or Japan of that date, it was a garden form that came, a semi-double, crude pink one, still with us, but one of the least desirable. It is only within the last few years that the really wild type has arrived. It is a charming plant, perfectly single, of a soft tone of pink, with neat habit, round flowers about two and a half inches across, and one of the best of the many plants that have poured into our gardens lately from the Chinese province of Hupeh. It was at first called *Anemone hupehensis*, but is now generally re-

113   H

My Garden in Autumn and Winter

garded as a wild form of *A. japonica*. I like it as well as
any of the larger forms, for it has the look of a species
about it, and a wonderful substance in the flowers. Then
there is the beautiful old white form, formerly known as
Honorine Joubert, and a plant one should allow to natu-
ralise itself among shrubs and in cool, half-shaded borders
as much as it likes, for it will give nearly three months'
display of its well shaped pure-white flowers, which have
the most lovely of golden centres, both for form and
colour, of any flower I can think of except *Rosa bracteata*.
The pale pink form known as *Anemone japonica elegans* is
not quite so well formed, but it makes a pleasing companion
for the white. I consider the best of the newer forms is that
called Queen Charlotte, a very large, bold, pink flower, semi-
double, and of a delightfully warm shade of pink. It has
taken possession of rather more of the lower shaded portion
of the rock garden than I desired, but it is so lovely
that I cannot bring myself to root any of it out until I can
find a corner where I may make a fresh planting. Unfortunately, none of them last very well when cut, unless individual flowers are cut short, and placed up to their necks
in water. At least so I have found, but I must confess I
have not tried many of my favourite dodges for making
cut flowers last with them, and perhaps a jug of hot water
carried to the plant, as is my custom with Shirley Poppies,
might help matters. I have tried the newer, semi-double
white ones, but have not learnt to love them so well as the
old single form, the simplicity of outline and graceful
habit of which are quite good enough for any flower
intended for this world and not for the meads of Asphodel.

September's Farewell

One form I grow chiefly on account of its foliage. It is well named var. *crispifolia*, and when it is at its best has the appearance of some unusually fine form of Parsley rather than of a Japanese Anemone. But it seems to take a long time to get settled, and not until it is vigorous and well established does it produce the curiously frilled and fringed leaves that are its chief attraction. The flowers are large and pink, and generally borne on rather short stalks. I have planted it in the piece of garden given over to plants with curious habits and malformations, and which from the eccentricities of its inmates has been called the Lunatic Asylum. It is a little too shady for this plant to show off to the best advantage, and if it remains plain leaved, and refuses to put on frills, as Huck Finn's father would express it, it must be certified as sane and moved to a sunnier bed. The great family of Ranunculaceous plants which provides such a wealth of flowers for early Spring and Summer fails to help us much in the Autumn, and would hardly be represented but for this Anemone, a Hellebore or two, certain species of Clematis, and *Adonis autumnalis*, whose crimson flowers among leaves like those of Fennel or Mayweed are very beautiful. Some of the Clematises really belong to Summer, but are generous enough to go on doling out a few flowers in little bursts of liberality long after their main display is over. One such, a large florists' form (whose label the seagulls removed to play boats with on the river, so that I have long since forgotten its name), gives us three successive flowerings. The first, in May, consists of double flowers, but in the second, in July, and the

115

My Garden in Autumn and Winter

third, in late September, the flowers are single. This third *floraison* may be seen in the illustration facing page 108.

The plant covers one of two terra-cotta vases that stand on either side of the entrance to the Pergola garden. They are fine handsome vases, but spoilt to my taste by a too elaborate scheme of ornamentation. They have panels of deer reaching up to eat bunches of acorns and Oak-leaves. These last are as large as life and twice as natural, but the deer are so small that the acorns bear the proportions of vast pumpkins compared with the size of their mouths.

Further, the handles of the vases are fashioned to represent Oak boughs, bark and all, and have a sharp angle in them that makes them resemble arms with bent elbows, and the poor vases look as though they have bad headaches and are holding their hands to their temples. That is why I like the Clematis to smother one, and am always trying to induce another plant to do the same for the left-hand vase.

So far some unkind fate has always overtaken that plant. Clematises have succeeded one another as rapidly as Presidents of Mexico, and have perished untimely of that sudden, blasting disease that overtakes the family so often, and our ancestors would have accounted for, quite as satisfactorily perhaps as we with all our knowledge can, had they deemed them "overlooked."

A plant of *Pyracantha angustifolia* grew to a fine specimen, only to be killed outright by frost, though another in a colder part of the garden was spared. I hope you recognise the plant we knew as *Cotoneaster angustifolia* now I have placed it under its authoritatively determined name, namely, *Pyra-*

116

September's Farewell

cantha angustifolia. So now, as the picture shows, this ill-fated spot is at present tenantless, and the deer are terribly obvious, but fortunately the elbowed handle being in full face does not worry the eye. The worst of large vases such as these (they stand five feet high), is the difficulty of finding suitable plants to fill them permanently. Agaves would do in a kinder climate. Yuccas, our best substitutes, are not over happy in pots here, and *Eryngium Lasseauxii,* which was a great success for two seasons, was killed by frost in the third, suffering more severely up there where the frost could get to its roots through the pot, than it did in the open ground. I think Tree Ivies have solved the problem though, and a silver variegated one in the left-hand vase, and a golden one in the other, have increased in beauty every season for the last five years.

Clematis viticella in many forms, and especially the beautiful white one, will frequently keep up a good succession of flowers till the really cold nights come. But there are others that only commence to flower now, and one of the best is *C. Jouiniana.* It is said to be a hybrid of *C. vitalba* and *Davidiana,* and if so it is curious that it should bloom so much later than either of its parents. I should not have been surprised if *C. grata* had been named as one parent, as, but for its greater vigour and more rampant habit, it bears a great resemblance to some forms of that plant. I have a *C. Jouiniana* here that is making itself at home in the arms of a variegated Holly, is mounting a yard or two each year, and will, I expect, soon reach the top. The flowers are freely borne, and are white

117

My Garden in Autumn and Winter

with a slight greyish tinge on the backs of the sepals.
Then later still comes *C. paniculata,* sometimes even after
frost has destroyed most flowers. There is a very fine
form of this at Bitton with large waxy white flowers, but
though I have often tried, at different seasons and in
different ways, I have always failed to root cuttings. So I
have only got the usual form of the nurseries. It has
handsome, almost evergreen leaves, and is a rampant
grower, blossoming freely when it has become well established. The flowers are much like those of our wild
Traveller's Joy in size and shape, but are more fleshy and
of a greenish-white. It is one of the first shrubby plants
to bud out into new leaf in early Spring, often racing the
Honeysuckles, Elders, and *Spiraea sorbifolia,* all of which
bring us signs of Spring in the time of Winter.

Later still in the year *C. balearica* carries on the
succession. It dries up here when the drought sets in,
and looks as though it were about to die, but reclothes
itself with young leaves during the Autumn, and in the
end of November produces pale emerald-green buds, that
contrast delightfully with the leaves, which by then have
become a rich shining green. If the weather keeps mild
these buds open into small bells of very quiet colouring, a
mixture of grey-green and cream-colour. There is a good
figure of it in Wilkomm's *Illustrations of the Spanish Flora,*
but it shows rather larger and whiter flowers than I ever
get here. It is best to regard it merely as a local form of
C. cirrhosa, but it is very distinct as a garden plant, flowering in the end of the year instead of the early Spring for
one thing, and its flowers lack the red spots that in some

September's Farewell

of the best forms of *C. cirrhosa* add so greatly to the beauty
of the inside of the flower. My plant of *C. balearica* trails
over the balustrade of the steps by the pond, and has a
very dry and overhung position, and I cannot think of any
other plant that would put up with such a back seat of a
position with equal good humour and look so attractive
from September to June. *C. cirrhosa* has smothered up a
tall specimen of *Pyrus Niedzwetzkyana* and is now ambi-
tious of treating the Hollies behind it in the same way. It
is a pleasing way, so I feel disinclined to interfere.

The first Hellebore flower of Autumn is always borne
by an early-flowering form of the Christmas Rose, *Helleborus niger praecox*, which generally begins flowering in
the end of September. Its large white flowers are so
lovely that in spite of its unseasonableness I should like to
have more than the one clump that has not increased very
much, though it has lived in a cosy corner of the rock
garden for many years. I have another form that came
to me as a seedling from the wooded hill-side above
Menaggio, or Cadenabbia, I forget which, and is one of
the best I have ever seen. Such round, perfectly-shaped
flowers as it produces throughout November and sometimes in late October are none too plentiful just then.
Coming so early before the cruel frosts, the flowers are
borne on tall stalks and are as clean and perfect as
though they had been grown under glass. So many have
admired this beauty that I have chopped into it rather
recklessly to satisfy the cravings of some of its admirers,
and for the last two seasons it has sulked a bit. I must
turn miserly over it, and refuse more divisions, and advise

My Garden in Autumn and Winter

instead an autumnal visit to the Italian Lakes and the collection of good early forms in the woods. This last Autumn brought the first flowering of a batch of seedlings given to me in their infancy as *H. lividus*. I could see they were not the true plant, that flowered once in Trinity College Gardens, Dublin, was drawn for the *Botanical Magazine*, and then died, for its leaves are veined with a pale green pattern in a remarkable and unmistakable manner, while these babes were wholly and dully green. They did not look exactly like the plant known as *H. corsicus* or *argutifolius* in gardens, which many high authorities refer to *lividus*, but surely in ignorance of the true plant of that name. So I had been anxiously awaiting this flowering. Had the sepals been dove-coloured, flushed with mauve and pink, like those of the *Botanical Magazine* plate, I should have been obliged to give up my views about those distinctly veined leaves and believe *H. lividus* might vary in that respect. The open flowers were of a lovely shade of emerald green, and just like those of *argutifolius*, only they opened in the end of November, and *H. lividus* prefers February for its flowering, and also they were larger and finer altogether than any green-flowered Hellebore I had been used to. Look at the accompanying portrait of them, taken in December, when they had been open for several weeks, and some, as the photograph shows, had already dropped their anthers and petalloid nectaries.

You will see how great is the length of the leaflets compared with their width, and also how much more glossy they are than those of ordinary *H. argutifolius*, and if you

Helleborus argutifolius.   (See p 120.)

September's Farewell

know the older plant as well as I do, will certainly agree that this is a very fine form of it, even if it is not deserving of higher rank as a named variety. The contrast between the emerald-green flowers and deep Holly-green leaves has not come out so distinctly as I hoped it might, chiefly owing to the gloss and patches of high light that make the leaves appear lighter than in nature. This group of half a dozen plants was a beautiful object throughout the whole Winter, and it seemed quite contented with what many plants might have considered a too shady and overhung position, as the very large old trees of *Cornus mas* rob that border of light and air, as well as moisture. Our native green-flowered Hellebores belong to the Spring, according to their flowering season, but the commoner species, *H. foetidus,* is so handsome all the year round, and especially when the central bud of the flower-shoot begins to break away from the palm-like crown of black-green leaves, that I must here insert a plea for its wider cultivation.

It has the darkest green leaves of any low-growing plant that I can recall, and they are so beautifully cut up into long tapering fingers that their interlacing mass is a wonderfully telling object, especially among such plants as *Megasea* and *Funkias,* whose large entire leaves make a striking contrast with the elaborate design of the Bearsbreach. Also it is such a good tempered plant that it will grow almost anywhere, even under a Yew. It is worthy of a good open place here and there all the same, and will then reward you by forming a grand specimen. I have great hopes of a panful of seedlings raised from some pods

My Garden in Autumn and Winter

I gathered among the rocks where *Primula Allionii* and *Lilium pomponium* grow wild and happily in the Valley of the Roja. It struck me as a far more beautiful form than I was accustomed to, the leaves more finely divided, the whole plant more vigorous and stately, and the flower heads wonderful indeed for size and number of blossoms. It may be that such a warm favourable home helps not a little to improve its appearance, but I was glad to find the same glorious thing very plentiful in the Valley of the Vesubie, and reaching up into regions where snow and frosts must be severe. Yet these plants in the higher woods and bare roads were finer and larger than any of those in the sheltered valleys below. Even Mr. Farrer's fastidious eye was attracted by it in the Roja, and his trowel jerked out seedlings with the dexterous rapidity that astounds me so much when I watch him at work among some high alpine of exceptional glory of form. Some day then I hope to astonish my garden visitors with a planting of a dozen or so of *Helleborus foetidus* each a yard across, their leafy, lower halves dark as night and their heads of flowers above, a clear yellow-green like that of a midsummer sky after nearly all sunset colour has faded and only the cool light is left. The larger and stronger of these young hopefuls have been planted out and are already showing a marked superiority over the ordinary form that has always sown itself rather too freely in this garden.

CHAPTER VIII

The Rarer Crocuses

I SHOULD not be doing my duty to the genus Crocus, the family above all others that is treated really seriously and to our very best in this garden, if I did not write about those members of it that are rare in cultivation. They may be rare for one of two reasons, either they are plentiful and cheap to buy but not easy to grow successfully in British gardens and so are not often renewed, or else they are not in general cultivation, never having been collected in appreciable numbers. But I fear if a plant is beautiful and has been introduced for more than a decade and yet remains rare in good gardens, this must mean that it has an evil trait or two in its horticultural character, is as feeble as Mrs. Dombey at making an effort, as hard to please as Mrs. Gummidge, or as wilfully negligent of the nourishment provided for it as Augustus the Soup-hater.

Among the Crocuses one finds several whose delicacy is the outcome of misfortune rather than fault. They belong to climates dry and sunny in the winter months, and their best efforts at cheerfulness here are snubbed into failure by our unkind Winters.

Others would be safe frozen hard or under snow, but cannot arrange matters to suit our alternations of muggy

My Garden in Autumn and Winter

damp days with periods of sharp frosts. They are for the most part so lovely and so welcome during the dull months that where a cold frame can be spared for them few plants can give so much pleasure during the darkest and dullest days of the year. When their needs are thoroughly learnt by a season or two of careful watching under cover, many of them may be planted out in special positions in the rock garden, or under the shelter of other plants or walls, in sunny beds. Others can be helped through their troubles by the kindly shelter of a glass during especially evil periods.

Crocus Scharojanii is a rare one. It fetches the high price for a Crocus of 1s. 9d. a corm, and until Mr. Van Tubergen sent a collector for it in 1902 it was not possible to purchase it. Even then it seemed at first a hopeless guest, but I will let Mr. Hoog tell the story by quoting from a letter he kindly wrote to me about it. He writes :

"I think I may be congratulated on having at last secured this much-desired plant. My man spent five weeks in hunting it up, as it could not be found in the spots cited by Ruprecht and Maw. The Mount Oschen, which is most difficult of access, is completely clothed with almost impenetrable bushes and trees, and the man searched it all over, as also neighbouring peaks, but without success. The whole thing was a complete failure, and a costly one too. Happily I knew of another locality, also in North-Western Caucasus, and there my man found it in abundance. Unfortunately when at last he came there most of the bulbs had done blooming and were fruiting, and it was useless to

The Rarer Crocuses

tear those up as the small corms were totally exhausted. Nevertheless on northern slopes he managed to collect a few hundred bulbs that had not yet started, and these have arrived here to-day in very good condition."

That was good news indeed for Crocus lovers. Even better for this particular one was another paragraph of the letter saying dried specimens and living roots were on their way to me as a kind gift from their fortunate introducer. No wonder *C. Scharojanii* is still rare. That letter teaches us not only that it is difficult and costly to collect, but, being an inhabitant of shaded bush-clad mountain-sides, the conditions it craves are difficult to provide for it here. The worst lesson of all is that it is a plant with *small* corms, exhausting itself by fruiting. Shade or cool conditions might be arranged for, but take my word for it that all Crocuses with *small* corms, that is to say with corms having a diameter of less than half an inch, are likely to prove difficult to grow, will exhaust themselves if they fruit, and be disinclined to make offsets in any circumstances. It was many years before I was able to make this glorious Crocus comfortable. Shady, bush-planted slopes of the rock garden will keep it alive, but it will not be vigorous enough to flower every season. The shady front of the frame so much appreciated by *C. byzantinus,* another woodland species, does not suit this one. I tried it among my precious, collected forms of *Primula pedemontana* and *P. Bowlesii* in the piped moraine, and there in the half-shaded end, in rather more peaty soil than fills the rest of that sandy moraine bed, it has flowered well for three seasons in succession, and sent up such strong leaves this Summer that I shall be bitterly

125

My Garden in Autumn and Winter

disappointed if the usual effect of writing of a garden success overtakes me and my plant fails to grow when next its season of reappearance arrives. The flowers appear at intervals throughout August and September, and are of such a glowing orange that even if they came in Spring they would be remarkable among golden Crocuses. As the first Crocus of the season they are of course doubly welcome. The leaves appear later than those of any other species, in some seasons they do not spear through before the end of April. They are distinct from those of any other Crocus, except the closely allied *C. vallicola*, in having the keel as wide as the blade and sufficiently grooved down its centre to give the appearance of a four-winged leaf ; more like that of an Iris of the *reticulata* section than of a Crocus. These leaves should be retained by the plant until the next season's flowers appear, but even in the coolest, most shaded spots I have never yet succeeded in keeping them from drying off and disappearing in the hot dry days of late June. *C. vallicola*, alas, has not approved of all my efforts to please it, and has died out here. I believe it is nowhere in cultivation except at Glasnevin, where a potful of its precious corms forms one of the greatest treasures of that wondrous storehouse of floral wealth called the Frameyard.

How many happy mornings have I spent among those frames ! and how many rare or new plants have I seen for the first time there, and how deeply ashamed I should be of the long lists of desiderata I have made after seeing them, were it not that those lists have always been so kindly received, and their contents so generously added to my

The Rarer Crocuses

treasures before I had found time to realise and repent of
my greediness. I wish *C. vallicola* could be reintroduced
in quantity, for it is possible that the latter-day energies in
gardening resulting in moraine beds, underground pipes,
or cunning mixtures of soils, might induce it to multiply
and replenish the earth. It is a beautiful thing, the most
delicate shade of cream-colour imaginable, with a light
veining of lilac lines at the throat externally, and internally
two wonderfully brilliant golden spots in the throat of each
segment, like gold studs, and which show through the
delicate substance of the flower. Twice I have seen the
flower, and once I possessed a root, of a most lovely lemon
yellow variety that seems unknown to science. It may be
a hybrid between *C. Scharojanii* and *vallicola*, but whatever
it is, a good clump of it in full flower would be one of the
loveliest things a garden could show. My own corm lived
for three years and flowered twice, but made no offsets
and died without seeding; all I now possess are two
dried flowers and a water-colour drawing, and many
years have passed without any fresh collection of its
roots.

C. karduchorum has been known in herbaria ever since
its discovery by Theodore Kotschky in 1859, yet it was only
in 1910 that it was introduced to cultivation and flowered
here. It is a lovely flower, very much like that of *C. zonatus*,
but of a darker and bluer lilac, much more richly veined,
and with a pure white throat, without a trace of the golden
zone of *zonatus*. It would be a great addition to the
flowers of early Autumn if only it were not as mad as a
March hare.

My Garden in Autumn and Winter

There may be method in its madness, but so far I have
only discovered the madness and have missed the method.
Its mania is this, when the corms start to grow in early
Autumn, instead of the shoot starting off at a right angle
from the top of the flat corm, it turns over to one side and
so, unless you lift the corm and plant it on its side, the
shoot travels along underground and produces its flowers
there, only to perish buried alive, and to be followed by
anæmic blanched leaves that rot away unless one digs
down for them and lifts them out into the light and air.
Can it grow on perpendicular cliffs when at home in
Kurdistan? But were this so one would think it would
be happy on steep slopes of the rock garden. Those I
have tried there still insisted on burrowing downhill like
a mole. I must try sloping slates round the corm to catch
the shoot and lead it out to the light of day. For I do not
like to be beaten by a mad Crocus and to be unable to
prescribe a remedy for those who write to me describing
the same strange behaviour in their gardens.

C. olbanus is a new importation lately collected in the
East, and appears to be a near relation, if not simply a
variety, of *C. sativus*, and not far removed from the forms
classed as *var. Elwesianus*, from which it differs chiefly in
the narrowing of all its parts. The leaves are the narrowest
I know in a Crocus, but when viewed through a lens are
distinctly ciliated along their edges, as is the way of all
forms of *C. sativus* and *hadriaticus*, and of those only. The
narrow segments of the flower give it a very peculiar look,
but of course detract from its beauty. As it seems no
more robust than the other earlier forms of *C. sativus*, I

think I may boldly prophesy that it will continue to be a rare species in our gardens.

C. ochroleucus is seldom met with, but it increases wonderfully in light warm soil, as the corms bud off all round into little bulbils like pills. It flowers very late in the season, generally in November, and is hardy enough to stand out of doors in a fairly protected spot. I have two forms of it, one a poor little wretch, pallid and thin, its stigmata colourless, and the orange of its throat reduced to straw-coloured spots. If it were not so amiable in flowering, and keeping neat and clean through even a November fog, it might not have been allowed such cosy nooks as it occupies in the rock garden.

The other form was one I picked out among some corms collected by Egger of Joppa. It is twice as large as the other, of a good substance, and purely white except for the rich, orange-coloured throat and the stigmata. Even then it is not so large and lovely as the one shown in Maw's plate, and as he has not flattered any other Crocus, except perhaps *C. Malyi,* I am always hoping that some day I may get hold of as fine a thing as he figured.

C. Tournefortii has been represented by Maw as a dowdy little grey thing with a brilliantly orange stigmata, and his plate fails to do it justice, for it is one of the most dainty, clean-looking beauties among all the lilac ones. It has a peculiar clearness of colouring, a soft rosy-lilac, like that of the sky on a very fine evening just as it ceases to be blue and begins to think of turning pink. The whole flower is of such a uniform tint, so lightly veined, and opens out so flat that it has very little shading about it and

My Garden in Autumn and Winter

strikes the eye at once as being a cool self lilac. It increases well here and in favourable seasons is very beautiful in the rock garden in the end of October, but I have often heard complaints of its being rather tender and even being killed outright in a severe Winter. Therefore I always keep a reserve of corms in the Crocus frame, and rather a large reserve too, for not only do I love it greatly, but also it must be owned that with all its perfections it has one fault. Once it opens out widely it never makes the slightest attempt to close again, as most other Crocuses do, even for a passing cloud. *Ç. sativus*, as I have already mentioned, is foolish in this respect; but as it flowers earlier in the season it is not so liable to be ruined by a cold or wet spell as poor silly trusting *C. Tournefortii*. Its flowers are a sad sight after rain or frost, becoming transparent where wetted, and even falling to rags after a heavy shower. In the frame a dozen or so blossoms all open wide is a great treat in October. The scarlet stigmata and white anthers give a most beautiful finish to its delicate colouring; so lovely and easily grown a Crocus does not deserve to be so rare as it is. If the gardening world did but realise the value of *C. laevigatus*, and the fact that each Autumn the environs of Athens must be starred with its blossoms of many varying shades and patterns, it would not remain such a rarity in rock gardens. It seldom flowers before November, and in sheltered corners will go on bravely until Christmas, and in some seasons until the first blooms of *C. chrysanthus*, *Korolkowii*, and *Imperati* have heralded in the spring-flowering section. I came across its leaves while crawling about on my hands and knees

130

The Rarer Crocuses

collecting *Cyclamen graecum* and *Anemone hortensis graeca* seedlings in the middle of March, both on the road to Eleusis and in the opposite direction near Kephissia, and I dug up a goodly number of corms, though of course they were not in flower and I had to chance what forms I should get. All of those I brought home proved to have the ground colour white, and most of them were feathered and veined with crimson or a soft shade of brown-madder, but no two quite alike. Three of them, however, were without feathering, and pure white but for a suffusion of soft yellow up the centre of each of the outer segments. They have done well here, and now I have a good stock of this pretty white one, and have sent a good many into the gardens of other Crocus lovers. When I collected them, like all Crocuses found growing wild, they had the remains of the tunics of many previous years adhering to the very small corms, and they presented a strange appearance, for in this species the tunic is strongly coriaceous, more so than in any other Crocus. In very robust specimens I have found it almost as strong as a thin nut-shell. This stout coat splits at the bottom into a series of vandykes as the corm swells and stretches it, and no one who has once seen it could ever mistake a corm of *C. laevigatus* for that of any other plant. I peeled the tunics off these wild corms very carefully and counted the number, and was astonished to find in many cases no fewer than fifteen, showing that those corms were at least fifteen years old, and had not increased by division during that period. The majority of those sold by the nurserymen have the ground colour lilac and are not so variable in the range of featherings as my

My Garden in Autumn and Winter

collected forms proved to be, but the lilac ones are very lovely, and as all of them possess the true essence-of-spring scent, they are worth a little fussing over in order to grow them well.

The late Herr Max Leichtlin very kindly sent me two very fine forms. One he had grown as *C. Boryi,* but its tunic and feathered flowers and upright stigmata proclaim it a form of *C. laevigatus,* and a very fine one too. For it is twice as large as any other form I have seen, and it is very robust and free in growth and flower. I have always called it *C. laevigatus major,* and I see that Mr. Tom Smith lists it under that name. I know he has the true thing for I sent him some corms one year when mine had been extra prolific, and I felt extra generous, but why he places it and the two others I sent him, *albus* and *Fontenayi,* among the spring-flowering species, I can no more tell than the writer of the "Bab Ballads" could tell why the gentleman who illustrated the ballads gave Mr. Blake a cocked hat. I do indeed hope they flower in Ireland as well as they do here, but it looks as though they had not yet proclaimed themselves as late autumn and winter bloomers.

The *C. laevigatus Fontenayi* mentioned above was the other that came from Max Leichtlin, and he told me he received it with that name from Professor Heldreich of Athens. It is a very pretty thing, with a soft lilac ground colour, but the outer surface of the three outer segments pale buff and beautifully feathered with rich crimson, so that it has a great look of *C. Imperati* or *C. corsicus* about it, but can be recognised at a glance as *C. laevigatus* by the

132

The Rarer Crocuses

snow-white anthers. It is the latest form to flower, and is generally the one that provides the last flowers belonging to an autumnal species in the New Year. Of course it is best when grown in a frame on account of this habit of winter flowering, but in the rock garden, in a sheltered nook and provided with a sheet of glass while it is in flower, many a fragrant blossom can be picked from it to bring indoors and delight one's eyes and nose on dull December days. My neighbour, Mr. Hubert Edelsten, who is almost as mad about Crocuses as I am, having caught the disease from me and my Crocus frames, was fortunate in purchasing a very round-flowered, robust form of *C. laevigatus* some seasons ago, and has kindly presented me with some corms that have now grown into fine clumps both in the frame and rock garden. It is perhaps the most beautiful of all the forms as it has more substance in the flowers than any other, and the featherings are also heavy and handsome. It is near to the var. *Fontenayi*, but flowers earlier, and is different in shape and general effect, more like *C. chrysanthus* in shape and *C. minimus* in colouring. What splendid work someone with a quick eye for good forms could do, if he were an energetic pedestrian and could roam about Greece in the Autumn and Winter, and collect Crocuses of all sorts and post them to me as fast as he collected them. There must be many a lovely form there wasting its beauty on the unappreciative goats and lizards.

C. hyemalis is plentiful in Palestine, and especially so round about Bethlehem, and as it is a winter-flowering species it is pleasant to think that when the shepherds heard the first Christmas carol in the fields, the turf was very likely starred with the delicate white flowers of this sweetly-scented Crocus. Maw figures the type form of it as having yellow anthers, and states that it is common round Jerusalem and on the Campo di Pastori at Bethlehem. But although I have several times received supplies of it from friends in Palestine, and one kind friend looked over hundreds when in flower, hoping to find a yellow-anthered one, all I have seen or can hear of now, are the forms with black anthers that Maw calls var. *Foxii*, and describes as coming from Der Diwan, near Jericho. It would be a very curious case if the roots sent to Maw were the last yellow-anthered ones found in Palestine. It is largely collected and imported into this country, and whenever I see it shown I carefully examine it for yellow anthers, but have not as yet been rewarded by the sight of one, all being the dusky-anthered form, var. *Foxii*. I cannot keep it alive long out of doors, and it is none too happy in the frames, even though I give it the place of honour right at the back where it catches every ray of sunlight our Winter provides, and gets well baked in Summer. It is a very pretty species, of especially graceful shape, due to its pointed segments. It is white with a rich orange-coloured throat, and varies a good deal in the amount of purple markings on the outer ,segments. *C. vitellinus* is another Syrian species, brilliantly orange and very sweetly scented, and it flowers throughout December, both in the frame and rock garden. It has been very difficult to procure the true plant lately as the collectors have sent home for it a spring-flowering plant some authors consider

The centre of the Terrace. (See p. 134.)

The Rarer Crocuses

to be a form of it, *C. graveolens*, but a most inferior plant, dull yellow, spring-flowering, and, as I have stated in the Spring volume, a most offensive little rascal on account of its power of spoiling a sweet spring day with its abominable reek of black beetles. The true *C. vitellinus* is well worth growing, and one of the species that carries on the Crocus season through its dullest winter weeks, and often keeps up a show till the first of the spring species is ready to relieve guard.

I have derived so much enjoyment from struggling with the rare and difficult Crocuses, that I do not hesitate to advise others to make attempts to grow them. Certain species may always remain rare, but I believe if some of them could be induced to seed and were raised from home-grown seeds, half of their perversity of nature would disappear and a more vigorous race would be obtained. I find my seedlings of *C. laevigatus* are inclined to flower rather earlier than their parents, and are certainly more vigorous, and some day I hope to have sturdy stocks of most of the rarer ones that will help to turn them into common Crocuses in all gardens where a really refined and beautiful flower is truly loved.

CHAPTER IX

Before the Frost

In this part of England we often get a sharp frost or two early in October. Clear sunny days with the wind in the north-east give us warning that the mats must be spread nightly over the beds of succulents and other tender plants that we wish to save and take in for the Winter. Then a milder spell may return, and we can enjoy the fulness of the garden, the mixture of summer bedding and the fore-runners of autumnal tints alongside each other. The un-certainty of its continuance from day to day makes me feel that I must be in the garden as much as possible throughout the daylight hours to observe and enjoy every detail of this culmination of the year's growth, before the fatal Nasturtium and Dahlia slaying frost robs me of half its beauty. With a sense of farewell till another season, as when leaving a favourite mountain peak at the close of a botanical raid on its floral treasures, I stand on the river bank by the beds of the terrace and inhale the scent of the Heliotrope beds, then I half close my eyes to look through my eyelashes at the blaze of scarlet in a large bed of *Salvia splendens* (Pride of Zurich). This may seem rather childish to a reader of sterner make, but I advise such an one to try it and find out whether he too will not

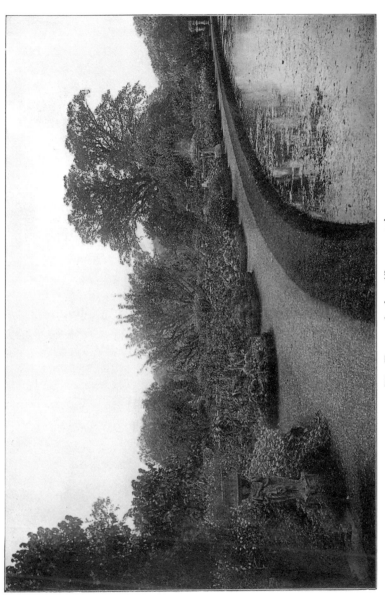

The Terrace beds. (See p. 137.)

Before the Frost

thrill to the sensation of satisfaction such a wealth of scarlet glow can produce on his colour senses. Just the magnificent colour without the details, almost as exhilarating to me as certain sunsets in clear cloudless skies that I have seen on the Norfolk Broads, or the deep ultramarine blue of the Mediterranean below and the clear turquoise of the sky above, when out of sight of land and the world seems nothing but blueness.

Next I gather a basketful of the double Marguerite *Mrs. Sander*, making no impression on the solid whiteness of the bed, and wish such a wealth of flowers could last for a few weeks longer. It adds to the present pleasure to call up the picture of these beds as they will look when all this colour and growth have gone, and the beds are flat again, the brown soil covering dormant Tulip bulbs, and their neat box edgings the only bit of growing greenness. The succulents that fill some of these beds are at their very best at the moment when we have to decide that it is prudent to uproot them and carry them under cover. But they have had a long season in which to please us in these terrace beds (see plate), so we ought to have had our fill of their beauty by now, and there are many other plants peculiar to these weeks of young October that are worth looking at and cannot be enjoyed at other times of the year.

The first place should be given to *Saxifraga Fortunei*, for not only is it as beautiful as any member of its good-looking family, but it does so well in shady corners, among ferns, or where Bloodroot and *Anemone nemorosa* have long since retired below ground, and which, but for this fine white

My Garden in Autumn and Winter

flower, would be uninteresting spots at this season. One must make the most of it, too, when it is really good, for the first sharp frost will turn it into pulp, and it is not in every season that it manages to get its flowers open, being only too often cut down just as it is ready to give us of its best. It belongs to the group known as the Diptera, that is, the two-winged Saxifrages, because the plants included in it have petals of unequal length, and in some species, as in *S. sarmentosa* for instance, the familiar old Mother of Thousands of cottage windows, two petals are nearly four times as long as the other three. In *S. Fortunei,* however, it is only the lowermost petal that is long. It has remarkably handsome leaves, rounded in outline, but divided into lobes. They are very leathery, and of a deep rich green, with the look of some unusually round-leaved Begonia about them.

I have a rather interesting and curious form in which the leaves are bronze shaded with yellow-green; they have bright crimson under-sides, and I am fond of twisting a leaf or two so that they get caught by others, and are held upside down and show off their beautiful red linings. What a pity it is we cannot teach certain plants to twist their petioles as the Alstroemerias always do, and so wear their leaves upside down. *Carduus heterophyllus,* for instance, has a brilliantly silvery under-surface to its leaves, but scarcely ever shows them unless a nasty buffeting wind is blowing, the sort that makes you hold your hat on, or keep your head on one side to prevent its blowing off; the hat, I mean, not the head. In that stress of weather one cannot fully enjoy the leaves of

Saxifraga Fortunei. (See p. 139.)

Before the Frost

a Thistle, however white. The variety in colouring of the under-sides of leaves is, so far as I know, mostly unexplained. It is wonderfully common among plants from New Zealand. Turn over a branch of *Olearia Haastii* or *Corokia Cotoneaster* and you will be astonished at the contrast it makes with an unturned one. It is well known that seedling Cinerarias can be sorted out into the range of colours—red, blue, or white—of their future flowers as soon as they have leaves large enough to show the colours of the hairs that clothe their under-sides, and which always coincide, more or less, in colour with that of their flowers. Gardeners are accustomed to pot up so many blue, so many red or white, relying on this characteristic, but I cannot believe the plant evolved it simply and solely to assist the gardener in obtaining a varied range of colours in his Cinerarias. I cannot tell you then why most plants of *Saxifraga Fortunei* have plain green leaves and this eccentric one lines them with red. The flower stems push up rapidly when once they have risen above the leaves, and if grown in good soil they should reach to a foot or more in height and bear hundreds of the beautiful white flowers. A good plant is shown in the illustration facing page 138. As it is rather slow work multiplying this plant merely by division, I thought I would try if I could get seed by lifting one when in blossom and potting it up. The plan succeeded admirably, and we raised a panful of youngsters, and the plant shown in the photograph was once one of them. A hard frost kills every atom of the plant that is left above ground so thoroughly, turning it to a horrid mess of jelly and squash, that it is remarkable there is any life left in the root-stock.

139

My Garden in Autumn and Winter

Hitherto I have found they have been none the worse for the sudden check and have reappeared quite happily with the Spring. *S. cortusaefolia* is an inferior plant to *S. Fortunei* so far as looks go, having less bold, lighter green leaves, and thinner heads of smaller flowers. However it possesses one merit that I value, it flowers quite three weeks earlier than *S. Fortunei* and so generally manages to finish up its very youngest bud before the nipping frost catches it, and in seasons when *S. Fortunei* is late and gets caught before it is at its best we are glad to have had the lesser plant so good. I have grown *S. sarmentosa* out of doors for many years, and have tried it in many different parts of the garden, but only in one has it been really happy for long. That is at the foot of a low bank facing north on the opposite side of the walk to the Cactus bank. There it has flourished for fifteen years and has filled every bit of soil among the stones, flowering freely in June and July, and at other times making a charming bit of colour with its red veined leaves. Though seldom seen out of doors and considered tender, it is well worth a trial in a place similar to the one I have described.

Another plant that is always cut down when at its best is the Jalap, *Ipomoea Purga*, a very beautiful member of the Convolvulus family. It is a native of the Mexican Andes, where it grows in shady woods, in deep vegetable soil, and enjoys a climate that includes daily rains and a temperature of 60° to 70° F. in its programme of events. It is marvellous then that the plant should be able to exist in the open air here. Though it is not safe to leave all our plants out through the Winter, as is possible in some

Before the Frost

Gloucestershire and Sussex gardens, I have had good success in favourable seasons with some plants at the foot of a wall. We always lift our most venerable plant when the frost has ruined the beauty of its growth, and store it away dry, to be potted and started in gentle heat in Spring. Treated thus, it is in flower many weeks before those left to the mercies of Winter. This petted old specimen has a vast tuber shaped like a huge bullock's heart, that grows larger each season, so that it may soon resemble that of a Dinosaur and require a tub instead of a pot. The purple stem and deep green Convolvulus-like leaves soon cover a great expanse of wall, wherever they can find something to twine round. Strings run from nail to nail suit them best, and when their limits are reached long sprays of side shoots fall downwards from them. In September the rich crimson-violet flowers begin to open every morning, to fade away and roll up into pulpy twists as juicy as a squashed Mulberry, before the evening.

It is a lovely sight on the old grey stone wall as I have seen it at Bitton, and also on the soft ochre of the stone of the beautiful old house at Gravetye. Here it has only red bricks to clamber up, but is so lavish with leaves that it furnishes itself with a harmonious background for its flaunting flowers. It is one of the plants, and the true and most valued of them, that produces the medicinal Jalap, the chief ingredient of the black draught of the days of strenuous purging remedies, and is euphemistically termed a brisk cathartic in a book of high authority. I well remember when the panacea for all ills in children, servants, or villagers, under the direction of this household, consisted

My Garden in Autumn and Winter

of a blue pill and a black draught. Not only was this combination of potent medicines prescribed, but it was always provided if the victim would accept it, and I remember the case of the head gardener's wife which appeared peculiarly obstinate and unresponsive to the treatment until it transpired that her husband had placed the pills in his waistcoat pocket, and there they had mingled with the seeds of some precious strain of Sweet Pea he had gathered, and for two nights running it had been *Lathyrus odoratus* seeds and not a few grains of calomel that the poor old lady had trustfully swallowed. As I never hear of Jalap nowadays as a medicine, I shall not slice and dry any of my tubers for home use. But I really might try to turn an honest penny by disposing of the bark of portions of a sturdy young tree of *Rhamnus Purshiana*, the source of Cascara sagrada, the modern substitute for Jalap. I cannot afford to sacrifice a scrap of any of my clumps of *Podophyllums* for medicinal purposes, for both in Spring with their lovely waxy flowers, white in most, but salmon-pink in *P. Emodi majus*, the best of the lot, and in Summer for fine foliage, and yet again in early Autumn for the huge egg-shaped scarlet fruits, few plants can equal them in their distinct beauty, which combines charm of colouring with strange and bold outline.

Crinum Moorei must also be visited and admired. It is the boldest and largest species I can keep alive in the open ground here, and one of the parents of the hardier and smaller *C. Powellii. C. Moorei* is easily recognised by its wide leaves, which have a waved margin unlike that of any other species with any claim to hardiness. If a sheltered spot could be given to it, under a south wall of a greenhouse for choice, it would be one of the finest of out-door flowering plants, but hitherto I have not been able to spare it any site quite so favourable, and my best plants are in one of the Iris beds under the old Yews by the riverside, and they need a good mound of ashes over their crowns during Winter to keep them agoing. They generally give me three or four heads of flowers in October, and the pendulous, widely-opening flowers are grand if they happen to be fortunate in timing their appearance during a spell of mild weather.

The form I grow outside is the white one, but I have the rose-coloured as a pot specimen, and also a very large flowered form, flushed with pink, that was given me by my old friend the late Mr. Gumbleton, who prized it highly. It is known as var. *platypetalum*, and when I can divide it I hope to try a piece outside, as the flowers possess more substance than those of the white form, and substance is sometimes an indication of greater hardiness. Mr. Elwes has kindly given me a plant of his variety with magnificently variegated foliage, a seedling of the original plant, which doubles its interest in showing that the variegation can be inherited. It so often happens that the offspring of a variegated plant are either wholly without chorophyl or entirely green, most probably due to the fact that the ovules had arisen from cells of the ovary which were either entirely white or green. This Crinum, and the variegated forms of *Barbarea vulgaris*, a golden-spangled form of *Potentilla fragarioides*, certain races of Kales, and the new silver-variegated Tom Thumb Nasturtium, are some

My Garden in Autumn and Winter

of the rare instances that have come under my notice of variegated foliage being transmittable, and the seedlings being healthy and like their parents.

Many years ago I planted a bulb of *Crinum Moorei album* in a square bed in the conservatory here, and that is evidently the treatment that suits it best, for it has now increased to over a dozen enormous bulbs, and many smaller ones; it grows over five feet high, and sends up wonderful stems of flower heads that overtop the leaves by a couple of feet.

It generally flowers from the middle of September till well into late October, and is really a magnificent sight when at its best, and before I cut some of its stems, which I generally do for the Harvest Thanksgiving on the first Sunday in October. They look so well, with Agapanthus and Belladonna Lilies in a setting of red leaves of Virginian Creeper. The Crinum's flowers are more of a certainty though than the Belladonna's, for this plant is a fickle jade here, and unless the sun has wooed her with unusual ardour throughout the Summer, she grants no favours in buds and blossoms in the following Autumn. In planning out a new, or replanting an old garden, one of the first considerations should be the ear-marking of existing, or the arranging of future positions, suitable for the cultivation of *Amaryllis Belladonna*. In all but the most exceptionally well-favoured gardens of the British Isles, this means a border at the foot of a south wall, and especially in front of a greenhouse of some kind where hot pipes inside the wall add to the warmth outside. When every available site has been

Before the Frost

noted, if it were in my power to order the next step, I should say plant half the spaces with Belladonna Lilies, and the rest with *Iris unguicularis.* Plant both well and generously for permanency, and wait a year or so in patience for your reward, and then you may reasonably expect it for yourself and for your children after you. Both of these plants, when once established, are best left alone unless they push themselves out of the ground by increasing faster than their space permits. Even then, removal of the uppermost supernumeraries is easily accomplished without disturbance of the rest.

I know a garden in the south of Ireland, where a dry sunny bank has been planted with hundreds of bulbs of Belladonna Lily, and I have seldom seen a more lovely picture than the mass of their soft, rose-coloured flowers on their purple stems, with here and there the deep brown-madder shaded with crimson of the younger spikes whose spathes are as yet unopened, and the whole mass of colour backed by grey-leaved shrubs. What I suffered in the way of pins and needles one September day, while I sat on my heels like a Turk, to paint a little sketch of them seen from their own level! I cannot imitate the Irish display here, nor yet grow the plants as edgings to paths as I saw them at Tresco, but every now and then we get a good season, and a plentiful flowering along the southern side of the conservatory and the peach-house, and I hope soon to have a good display from a row planted two years ago along the unheated greenhouse, for in spite of its possessing no hot pipes inside, the wall catches a good deal of sun, and the ground slopes away so rapidly that it ought to help matters at ripening-off time. This new row is of the form known as the Straffan variety, which, I believe, is an early-flowering form with a very deep purple stem, and taller than any other, but it is many years since I have seen it in flower.

The two varieties I think best, so far as the colour of the flowers is concerned, are those sold under the varietal names of *rosea perfecta* and *speciosa purpurea*. Why does this plant suffer so from double-barrelled varietal names? There is also a *spectabilis bicolor* form of it listed from time to time. After so lovely a combination of names as *Amaryllis Belladonna* affords, it is rather a shock to think of a form being known familiarly as *spectabilis bicolor*. Anyway you should try the two first, and see what a lovely way they have of flushing a deeper and richer pink every hour of their floral life till they expire in a finish of crimson. At the foot of the rock garden grows a plant of the wonderful form known as the Kew variety, a mysterious creature of whose origin many stories are afloat. Even New Zealand has been given as one of the places where a cross between *Brunsvigia Josephinae* and *Amaryllis Belladonna* resulted in this remarkable plant.

It seems possible that the cross has been made more than once, and the offspring should bear the name of *A. Parkeri*. I believe I have the same plant in a pot, and that it came to me as a Nerine from the Cape, and I look to the simultaneous flowering of both my specimens to decide the question. It is some years since I have seen the real Kew variety or my pot plant in flower, having generally been away from home when it favoured us with a spike, but I think my memory is right in assuring me that the most remarkable difference between them and ordinary Belladonna Lilies is the flush of apricot orange in the throat of the Kew variety. The Belladonna Lily is the only plant now admitted in the genus Amaryllis, but popular usage bestows that name in a most confusing way, especially when used in nursery catalogues, for the distinct genera Crinum, Brunsvigia, Sternbergia, Hippeastrum, Nerine, Vallota, Sprekelia, Lycoris, and Zephyranthes. Brunsvigia is the only one of these genera that I have not tried to grow some member of out of doors. *Vallota purpurea* did so well for three seasons that I planted several clumps in different places for trial, and then came a wet Autumn and cold Winter that killed the whole lot so remorselessly that I have never ventured on another trial. *Sprekelia formosissima* lives in warm and dry quarters, but seldom gathers up enough strength to flower. *Lycoris squamigera* is about as hardy as the Belladonna Lilies, and flowers in the same seasons that stir them up to generosity. Its flowers are not nearly so beautiful, being shaped as in some Nerines, with the perianth segments arranged in a fan at the upper portion of the flower, and leaving a gap at the lower part, the centre of which is occupied by the stamens Again, the pink of the flowers is shot or shaded with a dull, leaden, lilac shade that intensifies as they age, and gives the head a faded, dusty look. It is an interesting looking plant, however, and if not grown by the side of its fairer cousin, is worthy of a good place. *Hippeastrum brachyandrum* has lived out in the peach-house border for many years, but like the others is only roused up to flower in exceptionally favourable seasons. This form is not the best, however, being a washy pale pink even to the base of the tube, and I am told it is probably one of a set of hybrids raised at Kew. I now have a potful of the true plant, in which the flower shades from a pure rose-colour at the tips of the segments to a rich claret-crimson at the throat of the tube. It is one of many precious gifts with which Mr. Bartholomew, of Reading, has enriched me and my garden, and as he introduced this beautiful plant into cultivation, the bulbs he gave me have a double value in my eyes.

Sternbergias are the most easily managed of these false claimants of the name of Amaryllis, and the best is a form of *S. lutea* known as var. *angustifolia*. The first bulb I possessed was given to me more than twenty years ago by Mr. Robin, in whose garden near Bishop's Teignton, in Devonshire, I first saw and fell in love with it. I well remember his long row, a band some eight inches wide in the front of a narrow border, and the beauty of its daffodil-yellow flowers and glossy, dark-green leaves. As with most of my newest and rarest plants, I started this treasure in the peach-house border, where it grew and gradually increased into a large clump. When a cousin was stationed with his regiment in Malta, I worried him to dig up Crocuses for me, and, as usually happens with amateur Crocus collectors, the first box of bulbs he kindly got for me contained no Crocus at all, only Crocus-like plants. But as it held a fine supply of this best of Sternbergias, I felt I had no reason for complaint.

From these two sources I have been able to stock the garden rather plentifully with it, and also to give away a

good many bulbs. It requires a very open sunny spot to
flower well, and is best left alone for three or four years,
and then lifted and divided, as by that time the bulbs get
jammed into one another after the fashion of tinned
sardines. The season before the need of lifting is apparent
is the one to see a clump. Then there should be a mass of
bright yellow flowers just overtopping the young leaves,
and they will last in beauty, fresh buds keeping up the succession, for over a fortnight.

The typical form of *S. lutea* has much wider leaves, but
I do not consider that they are as effective as the narrow
ones, looking almost too heavy for the flowers, which are
much more sparingly produced than in the narrow-leaved
form. So its chief value in the garden consists in my
being able to point out how much wiser it is to grow the
var. *angustifolia* whenever it is procurable, which generally
ends in a request for a few of my bulbs.

S. macrantha is, I believe, still alive here, and puts up a
leaf or two in Spring, but as I cannot induce it to give me
any of its great leafless flowers in Autumn, like dwarf
yellow Tulips in their full wide outline, I am not much in
love with my bulbs, for the species is not worth its place as
a foliage plant.

Parochetus communis on the contrary would be worth
growing, even though it never flowered, for the sake of
its pale green trifoliate leaves. Each leaflet is ornamented
with a charming little patch of colour, which varies a good
deal, according to the age of a leaf, and the amount of
exposure to sunlight it has obtained. The brightest of
these look as though they had been painted with crimson-

lake, and generally in two very neat parallel crescents on each leaflet. But the shape of these markings varies as much as the colouring. In some the crescent is divided into two, making a mark something like a pair of eyebrows that meet in the centre, or the conventional figure children use to represent flying birds. In some leaves the space between the crimson marks is filled with a band of grey, and when the upper mark is almost purple, as though painted first when there was a plenty of paint in the brush, and the lower one lighter, you have the most effective pattern the plant achieves. Sometimes old leaves will turn yellow, with very brilliant bands of red on them, while the young leaves begin life with the grey mark only, and go through every stage imaginable of the evolution of red edging till they achieve a deep crimson. So that on one plant you can find a marvellous variety of patterns and colours. Parochetus is so much like a Clover in general appearance that one expects to find round heads of small flowers on it, and is astonished the first time the large blue, pea-like flowers are discovered. They generally appear singly along the stems, but in very strongly grown plants in pairs, and are of as lovely a shade of pale blue as the flowers of *Ipomoea rubro-coerulea*, and though not so large are longer lived. The finest planting of Parochetus I have ever seen was a mass growing by the side of the running stream in Mr. Walpole's lovely garden at Mount Usher, near Wicklow. There it found just what it loves, rich vegetable soil, a mild climate, and abundance of moisture. It had even strayed from the bank into the water, and formed a mat of stems whose painted leaves

Before the Frost

and flowers, of as deep a blue as an Italian sky, hid the water from which they rose, but were kept in constant motion by its ripples. Here the Shamrock Pea has to lurk in shady moist corners of the rock garden to keep cool in Summer and to be sheltered in Winter, for only when growing with its roots under a stone can I keep it alive in a cruel Cistus-killing winter. Dr. Lowe gave me my first cutting of it, and made me promise I would pronounce its name correctly, *par-ochytus*, and never *parrokeet-us*, because it is *para*, alongside, *ochetos*, a brook; if you remember that and have been to Mount Usher you know where to plant it, and can put your knowledge into action if you have got the brook and the plant.

Another thing that delights me in Parochetus is the way the leaflets fold together for their night's sleep. The two outer ones fold together upwards like a butterfly's wings, but before this happens the middle one takes a half twist to the side and then is lifted back between the other two until they are all packed away as flat as a piece of folded paper, and only their edges are exposed to the cold night sky, so that the leaf may be protected from the danger of too great loss of heat through radiation. This method of folding is also common among the Melilots, but differs from that employed by Clovers. A Trifolium leaf gets ready for bed by first closing the two outer leaflets upwards in a similar manner to the Melilots and Parochetus, but as the leaflets approach each other they begin to sink over backwards towards the petiole and generally end by touching it. In this position they hang with their tips pointing downwards, instead of upwards as in Parochetus. Furthermore, the third and central leaflet bends upwards and backwards towards the closed pair until it ends by assuming a half-closed position and so forming a regular little span roof above them, its under-side exposed to the zenith. With species of Oxalis the rule is that the leaflets should sink downwards till their tips touch the petiole, and as in most species the blade of the leaflet is too wide to fit in without folding, each one closes to form an angle of 120°. Then the under-surfaces of two adjacent leaflets are closely pressed against each other, and a leaf viewed from above presents the aspect of three radii at angles of 120°, which are formed of the adpressed outer edges of the leaflets. A model of this can be made with three books, each opened three-quarters of the way towards flatness, and stood up on end on a table and pushed together till their backs touch in the centre. This nocturnal attitude of the Oxalis family is, I believe, peculiar among trifoliate plants. It is very remarkable in one called the Bats' Wing Wood Sorrel, *Oxalis vespertilionis*, in which each of the leaflets is divided at the tip of the midrib and prolonged into two long, forked swallow-tails. In their sleeping posture these leaves have been thought to resemble bats' wings, and hence their English name. It is a plant that soon becomes one of the most undesirable of weeds in a warm border, but is so quaint in leaf structure that it is worth a place in some out-of-the-way corner. In some seasons it has been very effective in the dry bare ground under the old Cedar. It is worth anyone's while to go round the garden of a night with a good acetylene bicycle lamp to observe the night postures of

Before the Frost

leaves, and I expect it would come as a surprise to many to find what a great number of familiar plants have entirely altered their outlines after dark. *Tropaeolum majus* has a pleasing habit of bending the upper part of the petiole so as to bring the shield-shaped leaf over sideways and present only one edge to the zenith in place of the flat upper-surface. Some Lupins erect half their leaflets and depress the others to assume a similar position to that of the Nasturtium leaves, but others depress all the leaflets in the same way as an Oxalis.

Many plants with long, pinnate leaves not only close the pinnae upwards or downwards, but raise or depress the petiole as well, and the whole aspect of the plant is changed. It is an interesting study and worth following up, to note further differences. It would be wise to read the chapters on the subject in Darwin's *Movements of Plants*, one of the most interesting of his books to the gardener, but the scarcest and most difficult to obtain. He invented the word nyctitropic for these nocturnal movements, and gives the answer to the questions how and why they are performed in such concise language that I cannot do better than quote the passages. First then for *How:* " The nyctitropic movements of leaves, leaflets, and petioles are affected in two different ways : firstly by alternately increased growth on their opposite sides, preceded by increased turgescence of the cells ; and secondly by means of a pulvinus or aggregate of small cells, generally destitute of chlorophyll, which become alternately more turgescent on nearly opposite sides—and this turgescence is not followed by growth except during the early age of the plant." That

My Garden in Autumn and Winter

is clear enough if we remember that turgescence is the condition of being distended to the full with liquid, like an india-rubber hot-water bottle when filled till it is fat and hard. If you could imagine a tea-tray balanced on several such bottles, and then those on one side filled to turgescence, while those on the opposite side were left empty and flabby, the tray would certainly be tipped over on to the side of the flabby bottles.

Then for *Why?* to which Darwin answers: "Generally the position which the leaves occupy at night indicates with sufficient clearness that the benefit thus derived is the protection of their upper-surfaces from radiation into the open sky, and in many cases the mutual protection of all the parts from cold by their being brought into close approximation."

Down in the rock garden there is always sure to be a good store of flowers so long as there is an absence of really sharp frosts by night and plenty of sunshine by day, so that mid-October is generally rather a good time to see it. No doubt it would be better if many of the alpines flowering now would but reserve their buds till Spring. But if once they are restless and wakeful in Autumn instead of going off for their winter sleep nothing is gained by picking off the buds, and one might as well enjoy a few stray blooms in October on the bird-in-the-hand principle.

Gentiana verna is a regular sinner in this way, and this year some very extraordinary violet-purple and pale mauve-coloured forms I collected in the Tyrol are making quite a show. These latter are very much the same colour as the common Periwinkle, and are not so beautiful as the better

154

Before the Frost

known blue forms. They looked so wonderful in the alpine grass far away in the Val Magiassone, where they were the commonest form and blue ones rare, that I could not resist bringing some of them home, feeling pretty certain that I should not be likely to find myself up there again in a hurry.

Ranunculus bilobus, from another Tyrolean hillside, has refused to go to sleep and is as excitable as a naughty child who runs away from nurse at bedtime. So full of flowers and buds are the plants that I fear it presages a restless night and an awakening in Spring in a condition of sulks, feeling tired out and good for nothing. I like to see an alpine plant close itself up into a good fat bud in Autumn, and then there is no need to worry over its leaves turning yellow or even disappearing altogether in some plants. All the Erodiums are sitting up late this season, and *E. corsicum* is still gay with its rosy, crimson-veined flowers in a cosy nook by some steps where a Helianthemum holds itself over the wee plant's head like a large umbrella.

Campanula garganica, var. *W. H. Paine,* is flowering for the third time, and as bright as ever. It is a very delightful addition to our choice Campanulas, its colour being of a much brighter violet-blue than any other form I know, and in addition it possesses a beautifully clear, white eye that shows up the violet petals.

Pentstemon puniceus has been in flower ever since June, with the exception of a short interval following what I then regarded as a deplorable accident, but now believe has saved the life of the plant. I have but one, and that was given to me as a seedling, and I would not trust it out-

My Garden in Autumn and Winter

side for the Winter, so it passed the time cosily in a pot in a frame. It was planted out in April, rather a lanky, hobble-dehoy specimen shooting up into a flower spike. When the flowers were at their best I broke the whole spike off while weeding out some hateful Equisetum growing just behind it, and as I was hoping for seeds I told myself what I thought of such clumsy ways. A week later, how-ever, the plant began to shoot out several fine strong shoots which soon developed into long flower spikes, and though I have been mighty careful not to smash them again, never a seed have they set, but constant successions of scarlet, tubular blossoms have followed one another ever since. It is a lovely thing, the soft scarlet flowers contrasting so exquisitely with the blue-green leaves.

Felicia abyssinica is still a mass of pale mauve daisies raised on light stalks over the feathery foliage, but the first frost will kill it.

Gerbera Jamesonii, planted among the Cactuses, has four flowers open and many buds that will get no chance.

Linum maritimum is full of its small, orange-yellow flowers, but as it is a two-year-old plant and looks un-healthily woody, this extra autumnal display is most likely a last effort, and, as is usual with an old plant here, the Winter will kill it.

Phyteuma campanuloides is not a common plant in gardens, yet once get it in and let it seed, and you will not easily eject it. It is a fine thing for making a show of colour late in the season though. It bears tall and very narrow spikes of purple, starry flowers in August, and when they have turned to seeds, or better still have been

Before the Frost

cut out by a watchful owner, the side shoots develop and run up, and the second flowering is more effective than the first, as, though the spikes are shorter, they are so much more numerous. It makes a huge root-stock, and is a wonderfully good-tempered thing, settling down in any position and refusing to die, however much you pull its head off, and nothing short of digging down a foot or two to extract the entire root will dethrone it.

Reseda alba has a good effect when grown among it. This tall, white Mignonette is only a biennial, but very hardy, and almost as persistent in flowering as the Phyteuma itself, if only it can find a fairly open spot to develop a good wide rosette of its pretty divided leaves before it shoots upwards.

Aster Linosyris, Goldilocks, has seeded itself about, and the self-sown plants, in chinks of rocks on the north side, are much stronger than any I planted, and also bloom later, so that their yellow, rayless flowers are quite a feature of the rock garden now when such bright, yellow flowers are rather scarce.

CHAPTER X

Autumnal Tints

MANY people feel there is a quality of sadness in the tints of Autumn, however beautiful they may be. They associate them doubtless with decay or death and the passing of time, the end of another Summer's flowers and fruits, and the approach of bare colourless Winter once again. It is true that the glorious colouring of a leaf shows that the end of its work is approaching, and that the death of the individual is at hand; but on looking a little deeper and thinking on a larger scale, we should realise that every gradation from brilliant green, the symbol of active chlorophyll, through yellow and tawny shades to flaming orange or scarlet, is a sign that all is working well for the community, of which each leaf is but an individual member. With a daily decreasing supply of sunlight and heat, the roots become less active and less sap reaches the cells of the leaf. Consequently the outer cells of the leaves become less and less charged with sap and cease to absorb carbonic acid gas from the air.

The chlorophyll granules are no longer needed to act as analytical chemists and kitchen-maids, dividing the carbon and oxygen and preparing the former for the plant's meals, but pushing the oxygen into the plant's air-cells to go back

Autumnal Tints

into the atmosphere for animals to breathe again. These clever little servants have worked hard throughout the hours of daylight and now deserve a holiday, so along with the other chemical constituents of the cells that are valuable to the plant, they pass out of the leaves to be stored away in dormant buds, stems, and roots until the activities of the next Spring's awakening shall call them back to work. Thus it comes about that the leaf-cells gradually get emptied of all but a few useless chemical substances. These, in the absence of sap, crystallize and reflect to our eyes the wonderful colourings of Autumn. Tints of yellow are the most common, but a certain number of plants contain much anthocyanine and flame out in scarlet and crimson. Even the fall of the leaf, if accomplished in its own destined way, carries with it a message of hope, and evidence that ripened wood and healthy buds are left behind, well prepared for their winter rest and next year's renascence. It is a curious contrast with our behaviour, this denuding themselves of their coverings for Winter. One would at first sight imagine plants suited for climates with severe Winters should retain their foliage, even if dead and brown, as a protection. But a moment's thought should teach us that a tree laden with large leaves could not bear the weight of a heavy snowfall in consequence of the greater surface that would hold it. Also the rough winds would tear off a certain number of the leaves and broken tissues would be the result, causing wasting of precious sap and stores of chemicals, and leaving open gates for the entrance of fungoid foes. Large-leaved, evergreen plants are the inhabitants of lands with mild winters. Bays and

My Garden in Autumn and Winter

Laurels and Aucubas suffer sadly here in really bad Winters.
I can remember two seasons in which our Bay-trees were
cut to the ground. The hardier Rhododendrons save their
lives by their habit of emptying the leaves of sap just as
during a drought, so that they droop downwards and their
edges roll inwards and afford little lodgment for snow,
and present but a small surface to the clear frosty sky.
The Holly is the largest leaved of our native evergreen
trees, and we all know how stiff and unbending the stems
of Hollies are and what a load of snow they can bear without mishap. If you want a tough stick that will not easily
break in spite of being long and thin, choose one of Holly.
I learnt that from the old naturalist, George Tate, with
whom I used to roam the New Forest in my days of active
entomologising. He always had a long holly-stick or two
for the purpose of larva-beating, and more than one of them
passed into my possession and proved a useful instrument
with which to thrash strong boughs in order to scatter the
caterpillars collected there for dinner-parties, that they
might fall into my beating tray, along with earwigs, spiders,
and creeping things innumerable.

The hardy Palm, *Trachycarpus excelsus*, is the only instance I can recall of a really hardy evergreen plant with
very large leaves, but then it is so marvellously prepared
for resisting intense cold by the sevenfold layers of strong
fibres that wrap its stem like a fur coat. At the top of
each layer there is an opening like that of a pocket, and
it is possible to slip one's hand down into it, and to feel
the thickness of other layers forming the back and front
of the pocket. These wrappings of fibre cover the whole

length of the stem, and are so tough that they seem as fresh and waterproof at the base of the stem as they are at the crown in a twenty-year-old palm. Then again I have often watched the snow gathering on the great leaves and weighting them till they bend down more and more, and at length hang so vertically that the slightest jerk from a breath of wind causes the snow to move, and it all slides off ; the leaf rises up to its normal position and begins to collect a further supply, only to be shot off in the same way. Pines and Firs, Yew and Box are the typical evergreen trees of a cold climate. The skins of their leaves are too tough to be burst by frozen juices, and their tenuity allows snow and winds to pass through them without causing trouble.

The leaves of deciduous trees prepare themselves very fully for their fall, first, as I have stated, by emptying themselves of all useful constituents that can be conveyed into the stems. Then the cells at the junction of the leaf stalk with the stem undergo a change. The cell walls of a good many of them disappear, leaving a hollow between the end of the petiole or leaf-stalk, and the stem from which it grew. The cells that are left on the stem side of this hollow are then filled up with a substance similar to that of the bark, and are ready to form the outer surface after the leaf has fallen. By the time this has been accomplished and this *separating layer*, as it is called, is formed, the leaf has but a very slight attachment to the stem, and a rough wind may blow it away, or, as often happens, the first sharp frost will freeze the moisture in the hollow between petiole and stem, and its expansion

will push the leaf off, but so long as the ice remains un-
melted it will prevent it from falling. That is why the first
sharp frost is so often followed, as soon as the air gets
warmer, or the sunshine falls on a tree, by a simultaneous
fall of a great number of leaves, even on a perfectly still
day. One can easily see that this must be of use to a tree
in wild conditions, for if the leaves fall in this manner they
are not carried far away by winds, and most of them lie
and rot round the roots of the tree; they give back to the
earth much of their food substances, to be gathered up
once again by the roots for building up another generation of leaves. So an Autumn of brilliant tints, and a
peaceful fall of leaves following the earlier frosts, should be
looked upon as good and true signs of ripened wood and
promise for the future, and if only it were not so fleeting,
here to-day and gone in the night, the glory of autumnal
tints would be as joyous as that afforded by any of the
seasons. But only too frequently just when it is approaching its best and fullest pageantry a squall of heavy rain,
lasting perhaps less than half an hour, a frost of anything
over six degrees, or a sudden change of wind, may turn a
scarlet pyramid of fire into bare black bones. One
November day I received a telegram, in fulfilment of a kind
promise, bidding me hasten next day to Westonbirt to see
the autumnal tints, as they were at their best and might go
any minute. I rushed off and was in time, and that afternoon and next morning enjoyed a feast of beauty that far
surpasses anything I had ever imagined possible in old
England. But then Sir George Holford, and his father
before him, have planted most cleverly and successfully

Autumnal Tints

all that they could find that would produce the best autumn colouring. Also I think there must be something in the air and exposure of that part of Gloucestershire that favours the production of rich colours, for I have never seen elsewhere Japanese Maples of such absolutely Pelargonium Paul Crampel scarlets and *Linum grandiflorum* crimsons, nor Tulip-trees and Norway Maples of such Daffodil yellows. Nor have other people such huge old specimens of many of these good things, nor such generous plantings in groups, backed by Atlantic Cedars, or grand specimen Cypresses. I carried away a wonderful vision of beauty to live in my memory, which, I think, is all the more precious because, when next we met, Sir George told me it was but a few hours after I left him in that fairy land of colour, that a storm of rain and wind swept over the hills and robbed him of all the best of the display. In this garden we get a good deal of coloration in most seasons, but more often scattered over a long period rather than altogether "simultuous," as an old gardener once expressed it.

This last season brought some mysterious influence to bear on several of my vines. I had been inclined to complain of many of them because their leaves remained green until sharp frosts cut them, and they fell, a dingy, dishonoured mass of tarnished reputations, the colour of an overboiled Brussels-sprout. Last Autumn an old *Vitis Coignetiae* that had never before got beyond the golden bronze of a new penny, astonished me by turning a rich purple in early September, and then proceeded to produce semi-transparent patches of the rich crimson I associate with carbuncles among gems and

My Garden in Autumn and Winter

currant jelly among jams, wherever the sunshine fell on an exposed portion of leaf. For several weeks I made an afternoon pilgrimage daily to this pillar of fire, to stand with it between me and the westering sun, to catch the full glow of its tones of reds, growing more and more scarlet every day, and reminding me of Burne-Jones' wonderful window in Birmingham Cathedral.

V. armata soon after caught the same passion for colour, and flared and flamed so that I wished I had not cut off so many of its straggling sprays that Summer. *V. Thompsonii* followed, and for the first time ended its season in the garb of a Scarlet Ibis. But in the light of later events I can only account for their unwonted roseate hues by believing that some horrible fungus was at work among their roots. For when Spring came and it was time for their new leaves, these three Vines were found to be as dead as Rameses and as dry as his mummy. The Claret vine beside them, though not quite so dazzlingly brilliant, was better than ever, and that says a good deal, and has been faithfully purple and woolly in its many leaves this Summer. An old Snowy Mespilus, *Amelanchier canadensis*, is always one of the first trees to colour, and goes through a long series of tints. The leaves take on an edging of bronze as early as August, and this deepens to red, and spreads to the veins as the weeks slip by, until the greater part of the leaf is crimson, and then the remaining portions light up with yellow and orange shades, but then never more than two or three days of gorgeous beauty elapse before some ill wind lays it all out on the lawn, to be swept up and carried away in a wheelbarrow.

Silver Elm and Deciduous Cypress. (See p. 165.)

Autumnal Tints

I have no old Maiden-hair tree here, I am sorry to say, but only a youngster who has suffered much by having been planted before I had found a suitable place for it, and so has had to put up with a move when improvements called for it. It is not a very promising specimen, but I must do it the justice to state it colours every season with such success that it makes up for having twice lost its leader and a consequently crooked stem. This season it began as usual by colouring at the edges of the leaves first, and when it had outlined every one with pure gold, it remained in that stage, as if conscious of its beautiful effect, for more than a week before it assumed its final dress of pure amber. Few trees turn such a transparent clear yellow as *Ginkgo biloba* does here, for the old Tulip-tree had to be felled many years ago to allow the Cedar to stretch out its long limbs to the south. There are two very fine Tulip-trees on an outlying portion of the estate, but, alas, I cannot move them now. The tall Silver Elm shown in the picture opposite page 164 turns to the fine gold of its family in some Novembers, but it is altogether a tricky, unreliable creature. In some seasons it is an absolutely silver pillar from top to toe, with more than half of every leaf pure milky white.

Another year it will hardly show the variegation, and in yet another it may be spangled, with minute silver specks all over the leaves, but with no large pure white markings. I believe it is in the seasons that it is greenest that it turns the finest autumnal yellow. Mr. Elwes tells me this is a very fine specimen of a variegated Elm, and should have been figured for his great book if he had seen it in time, and also that it is unusual in being on its own roots, whereas most of them are grafted. This one suckers up all over the lawn and in the adjacent flower beds, and reproduces all its vagaries of variegation in the persons of its offspring. The tree next to it on the right is the grand old *Taxodium distichum* planted by my great-grandmother, which I have mentioned in my Spring volume. If you have very good eyesight or a passable lens, you may be able to make out that a small cousin of mine in a sailor suit is standing by my side just beneath it, and that will give you some idea of its height. It colours as finely as anything in the garden, first getting touched with yellow that deepens to orange, but ending off with a wonderful shade of deep red brown, the like of which I can only recall in a fox or a Hereford ox. Perhaps Indian red is the nearest thing in paints to its fullest and deepest colouring. It generally keeps its leaves on for a long period after they have turned colour, and is often the latest of the brightly-coloured trees to lose them. And what a mess it does make if a high wind blows its feathery leaves all over the lawn and flower beds, giving these last the appearance of having been mulched with cocoanut fibre.

The most brilliant bit of scarlet I get in the Autumn is supplied by a starved little plant of *Rhus cotinoides*, that grows on the slope of the hollow lawn, in gravelly poor soil, and as though that were not enough to have to put up with, it is only a free use of my secateurs that prevents its being smothered by a large bush of its commoner relation, *Rhus Cotinus*. The two were planted a good distance apart, but the Venetian Sumach has grown so much more

The hollow Lawn.   (See p. 166.)

quickly that it has surrounded the lesser and rarer plant, which appears through a hole I clip for it out of the *R. Cotinus*. Another much larger, healthier, and happier plant of *R. cotinoides* that I have in fatter ground never colours so well as the starveling, so dear are the uses of adversity. It flares up long before the Venetian Sumach begins to colour, and when the sun shines through its semi-transparent leaves rivals any scarlet Pelargonium. The *R. Cotinus* would have been cast away long ago but for its value when coloured in Autumn, for it is one of those inferior forms that produce a poor wig in Summer. In buying *R. Cotinus* you should always see your plant bearing its fluffy wig, and be assured that it is both dense in its fluff and brilliant in colour, for bad forms exist far too commonly in gardens. Yet among the thousands I have seen wild on the shores of Lago di Garda, and the lower ranges of the Maritime Alps, I have never seen one that was not far more brilliant, even in June, than most of our garden specimens. Where then do all these bad ones come from ? I think they are permanently evil forms, for I have often seen them by the side of a good one in a bed, and have been told the one is always bad and the other always fluffy and virtuous. This again proves it is no question of climate. There is a good form known as *R. Cotinus*, var. *atropurpurea*, that has a deeply coloured wig, but it is not so brilliant as the orange-scarlet ones I have seen growing wild, and, so far as gardens are concerned, only at Glasnevin. My old dowdy-wigged one does manage its affairs well, though, at colouring time. It begins to turn a transparent yellow that reminds one of a ripening Golden drop plum, as its first stage ; then it shows what it can do, by allowing one whole branch to take on orange and scarlet markings on its leaves, while a neighbouring one will prefer bronze and purple markings. Other leaves will turn to a fine rose-colour that is freely shaded with a bluish-mauve, unlike the colouring of any other leaf I know. This wonderful variety of tints all on the one bush, but arranged in masses on its different sides, makes it such a precious possession for a fortnight or more, depending on the leniency of Æolus in keeping his winds away from it, that I forgive its lack of wig and allow it to spread out more widely every year. I have noticed that the forms that bear the best wigs seldom produce a sound seed, but the indifferent ones bear many flattened seeds on their poor attempts at fluff.

In some seasons the standard Wistarias colour finely to shades of yellow and orange, and their leaves hang on till very late, but the old *W. sinensis* on the house remains green until frosts wither the leaves, and they fall with an appearance of immaturity and unwillingness. The hardy Orange, *Ægle sepiaria*, very nearly rivals the Ginkgo in the quality of its autumnal gold. The latter, in this garden, is like the great ivory throne of Solomon in being overlaid with the *best* gold, but Ægle has very little alloy in its gilding. The brilliant green of its stems and immense thorns makes a lovely setting for the brilliant trifoliate leaves when they are at their yellowest, and if it has been a favourable season for the setting of fruit, and here and there one catches a glimpse of an orange, either green and velvety, or already ripe and the colour of an apricot, one

Autumnal Tints

feels this is a plant worthy of a good position, inasmuch as it pays rent quarterly in both beauty and interest.

All the three hybrid Citranges, its American children, are much more like their fathers in evergreenness, and even the one called Morton, which is most inclined to a fall of leaf in Winter, does not take the trouble to arrange a coloured and glorious exit for its cast-off leaves. Another grand patch of yellow gold is given by *Apocynum androsaemifolium*, a coarse weedy plant that has too high an opinion of its own value, desiring to fill a whole range of the rock garden that is allotted to more deserving occupants. In Spring and early Summer I ruthlessly tear up its red-stemmed shoots, and not until they are full of the small waxy white flowers do I begin to respect their right to live. For they are interesting from possessing a curious power of catching flies by their tongues. So far as I can see, it is only a cruel punishment, a vindictive sentence passed on weakly-built flies who have not sufficient strength to pull apart the anthers and carry off pollen to another flower, as the dead fly is of no use to the plant. The mechanism by which these wretched insects are imprisoned is very remarkable, but so small that one needs a good lens, a needle, and much patience to see it all for oneself. Perhaps you will rest contented to take my word for it, as I have peeped and probed and seen it. The anthers are arrow shaped, and form a cone, their tips appearing to be welded together, but if they are poked at with a needle, it is found that they can be parted at the tips, but are joined to a sticky, green, egg-shaped body which is the capitate end of the style. It is divided by a ring into an upper and a lower portion, the latter being the actual stigma. The anthers are fused with this ring at about half their length, so that a chamber is formed, the walls of which are the upper halves of the five anthers, and its floor the top of the green egg. Into this chamber the pollen falls, and is unable to reach the stigma. Between the filaments are five nectaries which secrete honey. A fly inserts its proboscis in the wide aperture at the base of the anthers, searching for nectar, but in trying to withdraw it almost always pulls it up into the narrow slit just below the place where anthers and stigma are fused, and then unless it is a very powerful insect the tongue gets caught, its enlarged end prevents its withdrawal, and the poor creature hangs there till it dies. A stronger insect can break the fusion, and then its tongue not only leaves behind any pollen gained from a previously visited flower, but, passing on into the pollen chamber, carries away a fresh load for the next flower it visits. I have never yet seen seed pods form on my plants, but almost at any time, when it is in flower, many wretched flies may be found hanging by their tongues. So it seems that the right kind of visitor does not appear here, and the plant commits all these cruel murders in vain. Its beauty begins with its yellow autumnal dress, which when it is really well developed makes a glorious bit of colour, together with the red stems. It is rather more fitted for the wild garden than the rock garden, however, and I am always hoping to find a more suitable home for it, where it can spread freely and do no harm to worthier neighbours.

Populus Bolleana turns golden in a favourable season,

and has a fine parcel-gilt effect, on account of the white felted lining of the leaves. This beautiful Poplar is not planted as much as it deserves. It is a very fast growing tree, and soon makes a good specimen, and at all times of year is a striking feature in the landscape. Although not quite so fastigiate in habit as the Lombardy Poplar, yet it makes a good pillar, and the additional charm of its iron-grey, silver-lined leaves should not be forgotten when planning a planting of trees. Poplars are so useful as screens to shut out unsightly distant views, that it is often forgotten how beautiful a single specimen is in the land-scape. Most views are improved by the addition of a great towering Poplar trunk, or even a group of three. What minarets are to an Eastern city, and a campanile to an Italian one, a good Poplar should be to a grove of mixed trees. It must be confessed that they have very hungry roots, but they make partial amends for their rob-beries by their lack of spreading boughs, thus allowing the rain to fall on lesser plants grouped round them. Within the last five years I have planted both a *P. Bolleana* and a real Lombardy Poplar in the garden, and I greatly enjoy watching them shooting up above their neighbours and getting more beautiful every season.

A few Roses give a contribution to the Autumn tints. *R. nitida* is the brightest of them, and turns a fiery crimson. *R. rugosa* and *R. lucida* both favour yellow as a rule, but sometimes the latter species gets a splash or two of orange and red in it, and its brilliant scarlet hips add to the effect.

There is no need for me to praise the two common Virginian creepers, either on tree trunks or on the house,

My Garden in Autumn and Winter

for both are well enough known ; but precious few people know that *Ampelopsis Veitchii* is not the correct name for the smaller self-clinging plant. Once upon a time it was merged in the great vine family as *Vitis inconstans*, but now that it is again fashionable and permissible to rescue certain genera from the general lumping under Vitis, we can follow the views of Planchon and group those of the family with sticky adherent tips to their tendrils, and inflorescences without tendrils, and so forth, in the genus Parthenocissus, and this well-known plant becomes *P. tricuspidata*. But I must say a word or two for *P. muralis*, also known as *Ampelopsis Engelmannii*, as a wonderfully good plant on a house. It clings of itself when young, but is all the better for a fastening here and there when its stems get woody. The leaves are much like those of the common Virginian Creeper, *P. quinquefolia*, only smaller and more elegant, and its wonderful show of crimson and scarlet in Autumn is unequalled by any. *P. St. Pauli* is rather like it, and is mounting up the terminal pillar of the new wall, clinging splendidly, but so far has not troubled to colour at all before the frost has brought its leaves off. That may be because it is still young and is growing on the north side.

Vitis Henryi has covered a pillar in the pergola, and generally manages to give us a week of fiery scarlet leaves, with the grey marking characteristic of the plant still visible in the centre of each leaflet. I was told it preferred a north wall, and produced handsomer leaves in such a position. So I struck a shoot and planted it against the wall to see what would happen. For three seasons it has

The back of the New Wall.   (See p. 172.)

Autumnal Tints

refused to climb straight up where I wish it to go, but will grow off in a slanting fashion towards the east, and will not stop growing in time to get hardened for the Winter. So much of it gets killed back annually, and it would take the lifetime of Methuselah to get it to the top of the wall at such a rate.

Many years ago we bought at a sale some very attractive-looking pot plants labelled *Ampelopsis Hoggii*. One of these was planted on the wall at the back of the conservatory, and soon covered it, and was a beautiful thing to look at, with large trifoliate rich green leaves that turned orange and scarlet in Autumn, and never needed a nail, clinging by root-lets like those of Ivy. Then, alas, we found it was the dreadfully dangerous Poison Ivy, *Rhus toxicodendron*, but I hoped all would be well if I warned all the gardeners never to touch it or trim it without gloves. Two bad cases of poisoning from cutting it occurred, and so I cut it through at the root one Winter and cleared it off, and thought that was the end of it. But little pieces of stem have forced their way under the roof of the conservatory, and, in spite of an annual clearing out, two or three shoots manage to appear each season, and would soon cover the wall again if left alone.

Japanese Maples are none too happy here as a rule, partly, I believe, owing to their being all grafted. I have an idea that grafted plants are not so suitable for a very dry and hot garden as for a cooler and moister one. Perhaps the junction of host and scion gets too dry and sap does not pass freely enough. Anyway I lose a great many grafted plants here that other folks seem to grow well enough. My largest tree of *Acer palmatum atropur-*

pureum lost more than three-quarters of its branches one
Summer, and almost all the remaining ones the next. So I
have a very scrubby bit in its place, and I miss its rich
crimson and scarlet in Autumn. Now I am much delighted
with the free growth of the plain, uncoloured, wild form of
A. palmatum, which is making quite a nice little tree after
only four years here. At present it is rather fitful in its
ways of colouring, the leaves mostly falling green, but here
and there amongst them we get a few as scarlet as any
Pelargonium petal could aspire to be. I hope great things
of it when a bit older, as some of the most scarlet of all the
leaves I saw at Westonbirt were on trees of this plain
green form.

Two species of Cotoneaster colour well, the lovely *C.
horizontalis* for one. This is one of the most obliging of all
plants for making a fine specimen either for growing perpen-
dicularly or horizontally. Plant it in open ground and it will
grow out flat and will make a wonderful spreading specimen
no more than a foot high. Again, if you trim it in, it will
grow up higher and higher, layer above layer, until it forms
quite a tall bush. And yet again, if planted against a wall,
it will press its shoots against it as closely as though they
had been nailed there, or will certainly rise to a height of
six feet, and very possibly clothe a wall to a much greater
height with a little training and fastening. Its leaves fall
off in late Winter, but turn to a wonderfully rich crimson
before their fall, and if it is well set with its scarlet berries,
the effect is absolutely dazzling on a sunny day, and the
crimson and scarlet shades blend better than one would
expect. *C. adpressa* is rather like *C. horizontalis*, but it grows

Autumnal Tints

close to the ground, and turns to a fine bronzy-purple that is very effective near the grey-leaved plants it has for its neighbours in the bed by the house. Some of these are at their best late in the Autumn. The leaves of *Kniphofia Tysonii* for instance are then very large, and of a wonderfully steely shade of blue. *Othonnopsis cheirifolia* sprawling down the bank with *Cineraria maritima* and *Centaurea Clementii* are as good and silvery as they have been all the Summer, and *Melianthus major* behind them makes such grand fern-like leaves late in the year that it seems cruel Winter should come and spoil them. Funkias provide wonderful patches of transparent orange and yellow leaves even when grown in shady corners. *Atropa Belladonna* I only allow to grow in the centre of beds, far in out of the reach of anyone who might be tempted to pluck and eat its luscious-looking berries, so black and shiny they look like some giant's boot buttons. It generally needs looking for in the Summer among the brighter-coloured flowers of its neighbours, but in late Autumn it is so flaunting in a suit of yellow satin that it is exceedingly conspicuous among the latest of the Asters.

Rheum Emodi has long inhabited the rock garden, but although it is Himalayan in origin, and bears the name of a great mountain, it is no alpine plant in appearance. Its stout stems run up nine feet or more when happy, and its immense oval, entire leaves may measure four feet by nearly a yard. It was put into its present position fifteen years ago, as one would send an invalid to a convalescent home, for it had refused to be happy and healthy in two borders that we thought it would beautify. It picked up strength at once after this last move, and has done so well that, though what was then an empty bank of newly-built rock work, is sorely needed for many dozens of rock plants, I have not the heart to displace the Rhubarb until I shall have successfully established a specimen elsewhere that rivals it in beauty. Pieces we have taken off have not so far brought about this possibility. The leaves and bracts of the flower stems first, and then afterwards some of the more up-standing radical leaves, take on a glorious range of crimson and scarlet shades in Autumn, and with the sunlight through them, are so magnificent even from a distance that the great clump pays us well for the space it occupies in Summer. As it appears very late in Spring, I find Wood Anemones, Daffodils, and many Violets are quite happy for a yard or two round its centre, and do not resent its leaves as a roof over them from June onwards.

Stephanandra Tanakiae, although graceful in habit, with its long arching growths, with good red stems in their first year, and bunches of Spiraea-like flowers the next season, is not a wildly exciting shrub until Autumn chal-lenges it to make a show and justify its existence. Then it responds with an offering of orange and red leaves that rivals the effect of many of the deciduous Azaleas.

Eucryphia pinnatifolia, in spite of its tough shining leaves that look so much as though they should be ever-green, decks itself out in many bright shades of yellow and tawny orange before it casts off its clothing, like Saint Elizabeth of Hungary, to lead a quiet, sober life of brown-stemmed dullness for the next six months.

Autumnal Tints

The *Osmunda* by the pond gets tipped with coppery orange on its highest fronds first, and then the colouring spreads downwards till it is a tawny brown all over, and remains of a warm russet tint all through the Winter.

The *Canadian Rice* turns to a wonderful tint of creamy yellow that is very beautiful, rising out of the dark water and contrasting with the red-brown of the common Reed.

Thus just before the first sharp frost and as long as rough winds permit, the garden entirely changes its aspect, brilliant patches of colour appearing sometimes where least expected, for that is one of the charms of autumnal tints, they vary so much from year to year, and even though one or two, that are generally to be relied upon, fail one, some startling novelty is certain to appear in an old friend we should never have suspected of such giddiness as appearing in fancy dress after all the years we have known it as sombre as a Quaker.

CHAPTER XI

After the Frost

THE Roman numerals at the head of this chapter warn me
that the time has come to turn my attention to the unwelcome presence of Winter in the garden. I dislike cold
weather and its effects so much that I am very loth to
cease writing of the staunch and faithful floral veterans,
remnants of the glory of Summer and Autumn, that still
carry on their brighter traditions under daily increasing
difficulties as sunshine and heat fail them, and with the
certainty of a final catastrophe ahead, when the frost at
last shall end the struggle. The task at first sight resembles that of the biographer who has to chronicle the
latter years of some veteran who outlived his usefulness
and the friends of his younger and active days. One by
one they disappear from the history, and all that is left is
an account of failing powers, and the increasing influence
of sickness and pain. A faithful biographer may be
obliged to deal fully with such a phase if it throws light
on history or the character of his hero. But considering
that such a fate is common to almost all gardens in
England, I feel the destruction of summer bedding and the
depressing influence of a raw November afternoon are
experiences any reader may recall to mind for himself, and

After the Frost

I am free to treat this garden in a different manner, trying only to record the brighter side, the beauties that appear in spite of, or actually on account of, the effects of cruel frost. To continue the simile of a biography, the record shall be chiefly of the sterling traits of a noble character such as are only perfected by the brave endurance of adversity and disease, just as a touch of frost brings out the colour in the bark of the Dogwoods and Willows, and improves the flavour and crispness of Celery.

We will suppose then that a sharp frost of some ten or more degrees has visited us in mid-October, the Dahlias have been wheeled away, black and lifeless ruins, but very useful to bury deeply in ground that is being prepared for planting, as there is much in them to make for cool conditions and a store of food, in starved and extra dry corners. The garden looks rather bare when the wreckage has been cleared away, but what remains looks all the better for the clear stage. If it so happens that the clearance comes before S. Luke's Little Summer commences on the eighteenth of October, many of the Asters, *Helianthus laetiflorus*, Colchicums, and Crocuses will be among the principal actors, but I must not write of them again, only of late comers that have had no mention hitherto. Many will be plants that have flowered for months, but can stand a certain amount of frost without feeling snubbed.

Erigeron mucronatus and *Borago laxiflora* are two rock-garden weeds that I pull up in handfuls during the Summer and treat with marked respect after the frost. The white juvenile, pink middle-aged, and crimson elderly flowers of the Erigeron are often beautiful well into December. The

My Garden in Autumn and Winter

exquisitely soft turquoise blue of the Borago's bells has earned it the name of Fairy Borage; if only the blossoms grew from a rosette about the size of a Ramondia's, and on stems of about three inches, it would be one of the most cherished of plants, and if it were unpleasantly stuck-up and fastidious as to position and soil, people would construct special moraines or morasses for it. It sows itself by hundreds, waxes fat, and sprawls over a yard or more, and bears flowers by fifties on long branching stems. When the first few appear and the stems are not very long, one says, "What a gem, I must have a lot more of it." When a month later the leaves have lengthened and grown coarse, and the flowers are mixing with those of choice Campanulas in a neighbouring bay, one says, "Out you must come." Then in November a pink bud or two, and the dainty, sky-blue open flowers poised on their thin stalks, peep out among reddening Epimedium leaves, or hanging over a green mossy rock, and one asks, "Why did I not leave more of you to cheer up these late and empty days?" So take my advice, let *B. laxiflora* sow itself into shady corners and crevices, snub it moderately in the days of garden luxuriance by cutting back its too ambitiously wandering stems, and then a fresh supply will be at your service when other plants fail. *Salvia Grahamii* among shrubby things recovers wonderfully after the frost if a few days of good weather give it a chance, and will be ablaze with its crimson flowers, as sweetly scented and fresh to look at as it was in June.

Caryopteris Mastacantha is tender by repute, but has lived here for many years among the Irises under the Yews by

After the Frost

the river, the two oldest bushes being two cuttings I struck over twenty years ago from a branch I brought away from a Devonshire garden. It looks almost like a Ceanothus when covered with its lavender-blue flowers, and is a very valuable small shrub for a dry spot, and in some seasons, after the Dahlias have been killed by frost, it goes on serene and happy, a source of immense joy to the blue-bottle flies, and a rival to the blossom of the Ivies. It is surprising how many plants that are none too hardy, and often get cut to the ground by Spring frosts, take but little notice of quite sharp ones in Autumn if sunny days follow. *Passiflora coerulea Constance Elliott* is one, and on the new wall will go on producing perfect flowers, white as ivory, long after the common and hardy Bindweed has shrivelled.

Also *Eupatorium Weinmannianum* and *Solanum jasminoides*, though their open flowers get tarnished by sharp frost, will be a mass of pure white in response to a sunny day or two. Then there are still more precious plants that regularly flower in late October and early November, and are special features of these weeks only. One must not expect them to be very large or very showy, but all the same one may look for a quiet beauty in them. *Liriope graminifolia* can be relied upon, wherever a well-drained place can be spared it, to produce its long spikes of purple flowers among the grassy, evergreen leaves. The blossoms are small, but of a good purple, and set so closely on the spikes that they somewhat resemble a Grape Hyacinth. It is often grown in greenhouses, both in its plain green and variegated forms, but is hardy enough for most gardens.

My Garden in Autumn and Winter

The variegated form, however, generally falls a prey to slugs if I plant it out here. The cream-coloured stripes on the leaves render it an especial delicacy, and they enjoy it as much as we do the blanched Asparagus and Seakale. The plant is often labelled *Ophiopogon Jaburan*, and has been figured under the name of *O. spicatus* in the *Botanical Magazine* and elsewhere, but Nicholson declares these figures are Liriope. *Funkia tardiflora* is, unfortunately, a very rare plant, and very difficult to procure true, all save one that have come to me under the name being either forms of *F. lancifolia* or *F. Sieboldiana*. It is, however, a very distinct plant, and the small leaves are much more glossy and sharply pointed than in any other Funkia. When the spikes of pale lavender flowers are open in November one wishes it were possible to plant a good mass of it, but it is the slowest old tortoise in the world in the advance it makes towards replenishing the earth. My plant has dwelt in the rock garden for ten years, and has owned a most desirable residence in an exceedingly select neighbourhood, as house agents would call it, all cold winds cut off by large stones behind it, and for neighbours the very élite of the Cyclamen world such as *C. africanum, pseud-ibericum, libanoticum,* and *Coum,* surely it ought to puff with pride and spread about like butter on a hot plate. Once only in all this long time have I felt justified by the possession of three crowns to the plant, in cutting off one to give to one of the best and most generous of gardeners. It was a great pleasure to me to do so, but the plant seemed to say, if that is what you do with my offsets, you may whistle for another. Flowering so late no seeds are formed, so it is

After the Frost

likely to remain among the number of rare plants for many a long day. The waste places of Southern Europe, from Gibraltar to Brindisi and Rome to Naples, at least according to my own experience, are brightened in Winter by *Calendula arvensis*, a very variable but always cheerful little Marigold. Though it becomes rather coarse if grown in rich soil, in stony parts of the rock garden it makes a neat plant, and bears its bright orange flowers, ranging from the size of a silver penny to that of a shilling, sometimes throughout a mild winter, but generally up to Christmas. I prefer it in its smallest forms, especially a very minute one that grows on the walls of the Colosseum in Rome, and a plant or two in a crevice in a region of the rock garden devoted to Sempervivums and Sedums, will make a delightful picture. This again is a plant that needs Summer snubbing, as otherwise it becomes lanky and seeds far too freely, but a young plant or two, or older ones cut well back, are very precious, after the frost. The name Calendula was given to the genus in recognition of its perpetual blooming throughout the year and providing flowers for each of the calends. I always collect seeds of the smallest forms when I meet with it growing wild, but it seems they are not so hardy or vigorous as the larger races, for I generally get more than I want of rather coarse forms, and never enough of the real Lilliputian.

Correa magnifica is one of the successes on the new wall up to now, but of course a really severe Winter may alter matters, for it is an Australian plant. Mr. Gumbleton gave it to me many years ago, telling me it was said to be the hardiest of them all, and did well in the open in Cornwall.

My Garden in Autumn and Winter

As it made a very lanky pot plant, and its flowers are not
my idea of magnificence, being greenish-white and none
too large, I thought it had better take its chance out on the
wall, anyway until space was required for something
better. It has done so well there, and covered it with neat
evergreen growth, and flowers so freely from October to
May, and is so interesting in mid-winter, that I hope it
may long occupy its allotted space. The greenish flowers
look much better out of doors among their dark green
leaves and against the red brick wall, than in a conservatory
among more showy plants. They are very elegant in
shape, delightful little bells with stamens hanging from
their mouths, and even in times of fairly sharp frost, that
is to say ten degrees or so, it is only the fully open and
most exposed flowers that get spoilt, the buds escaping
unhurt to replace them when kinder weather returns. It
should make a very useful plant to train on a sheltered
wall of a house, as it is so very neat in habit. Close by it
grows a bush of *Camellia Sasanqua*, which I believe to be
the wild type, as it. is quite single, and the petals well
formed. This one is pure white, I am glad to say, for
many varieties are known, pink, striped, and also semi-
double, and these latter are more often met with than the
more beautiful single forms. Its flowers are not made
the most of by the plant, as they hang at the ends of the
shoots and are rather hidden by the leaves, as they grow
in the axils and have such short necks. This no doubt
protects them from bad weather, but in the present lowly
stature of my plant, one has to lift up a branch to see
the flowers well. They are very pretty when cut though,

After the Frost

and placed in a vase so that they look at you from under the leaves. It seems kind to cut them and bring them into a warm room, as they appear from late October till after Christmas. It is very closely related to the Tea Plant, of course, and it is said that its flowers are used to mix with tea to add fragrance to it. This use is not mentioned in the *Useful Plants of Japan*, however, but it is included in that book on account of an oil being expressed from its seeds, which is chiefly used for burning in lamps.

Not many of the broad-leaved, shrubby Veronicas are hardy enough to survive our Winters, so I am greatly delighted with two that I brought from Bitton because they had proved perfectly hardy there. Both of them have passed safely through more than one of our ill-tempered Winters. A sudden snap of north-east wind and dry cold in March is what nips up the tender Veronicas here. One of these has the inappropriate name of *V. lobelioides*, and is not a bit like any Lobelia I have ever seen. It forms a shapely, rounded low bush, and flowers vigorously in July, and if the seed heads are clipped off a second crop of flowers is borne in October and November. I think these late flowers are even prettier than the first, as the buds and newly-opened flowers are a good rose-colour and fade to a purer white than in the Summer, so that the spikes are very prettily shaded. The individual flowers are large for the size of the spikes. The other's name of *La Seduisante* is more fitting. It is a larger grower, rather on the coarse side perhaps, and needs careful pruning to keep it in shape, or else it gets too wide and spreading with bare stems towards the centre. So I shorten a bough or two from time to time, and

185

their stumps break out into dense clean growths and flower about twelve months after the operation of amputation is performed. The flower spikes are of a good length, and a bright crimson pink, and it generally happens that some of the trimmed branches give an offering of flowers in the end of the year. *V. Veitchii* is undoubtedly the largest and best of the blue-flowered Veronicas, but I have not thoroughly tested its hardiness. In Cornwall it is magnificent when in full flower ; but here I have grown it only as pot specimens. They stand out during eight months of the year, and are carried into the shelter house in the middle of the new wall for the other four. If the seed pods are removed they will try to flower from August on to Christmas at least. Cuttings I have given away have done well in western gardens, so I have now planted out one of my old specimens to take its chance on the southern side of the old Yews. *Hamamelis virginica* is not the showiest of plants as regards flowers, but it can do wonders when it likes in the way of autumnal tints, and adds to this a habit of beginning to flower before the leaves fall, and continuing to open flowers throughout the Winter. These are not so showy as those of the Japanese species, which flower in the early months of the year, but are very well worth having during the garden's silly season. They are yellow, and of the same make as those of other Winter Hazels, rather like a spider with yellow legs formed of the narrow threadlike petals. The curious habit of winter flowering and of bearing ripening fruit at the same time suggested to Linnaeus the construction of the generic name from the Greek *hama* and *melon, with* and *fruit.* Among the new plants from China there is a useful

After the Frost

evergreen for growing in shady places where nothing else half as exciting could be expected to grow. It is *Sarcococca ruscifolia*, that is to say, being translated, the *fleshy berry with Butcher's Broom leaves*. I thought I would give its shade-enduring powers a thorough test, and have planted it at the foot of an old Scots Pine, where it is also overhung by a Barberry-tree. It has turned a bare spot into a charming clump of greenery, and adds to its interest by bearing queer little green flowers in the Winter months, but the fleshy berries that sound so attractive have not yet appeared. I possess another member of this genus, which I believe to be *S. Hookeriana*, though it was bought for *S. pruniformis*. Its pleasant sprays of long narrow evergreen leaves suggest the growth of a Lily or Solomon's Seal, and it also flowers in Winter, but as the genus Sarcococca belongs to the order Euphorbiaceae, one must not be disappointed at the greenness and insignificance of their flowers. *Prunus Miqueliana* is the most sensational discovery made lately of a really beautiful winter-flowering shrub or small tree. Although introduced in 1888, and a few good-sized trees exist in this country, it is not at all well known, and its origin is somewhat mysterious. The fact that it has semi-double flowers seems to suggest that it is of garden origin, perhaps a form of *P. subhirtella*. It came from Japan too, that land of many garden forms of Cherries. Before the leaves fall in Autumn, flower buds appear on many of the shoots, and they open a few at a time from the middle of November until the young leaves appear in Spring together with a somewhat more general attempt at flowering. My plants hitherto have only borne dowdy pendant pinkish

187

My Garden in Autumn and Winter

blossoms in this Spring crop, and the first time I saw them I feared some worthless plant had come instead of the one I wanted. But the next Autumn brought the pretty pearly-white, semi-double blossoms I had been so delighted with, when sprays in full bloom were shown before the Floral Committee of the R.H.S. one December day. It appears a fast grower, and I should think would be a very useful thing to plant for cutting in Winter, as the buds would open well in water, judging from a few I brought into the house. They look wonderfully delicate and out of season on a December day out in the garden, but are none the less welcome when other flowers are so rare. It is a great pleasure to feel there is something yielding flowers even at that season, and something to look for and pick all the year round, so anything that flowers from about the second week in December till the end of January should find a place in every garden. This Prunus for one, and *Lonicera fragrantissima* for another, its small white flowers being so deliciously sweetly scented.

Iris unguicularis of course is the best of all, and has often given me a large bunch of flowers for Christmas, but I said so much of it in the Spring volume, I must not praise it further. *Crocus laevigatus* and *C. vitellinus* keep the Crocus pot a-boiling till *C. chrysanthus* and *C. Imperati* are ready to sizzle.

"Sambo," said the master, "take off the pot before it boils over." "Pot no boil, Massa," said Sambo the cook. "Take it off, I tell you ; I can hear it boil," said Massa. "I tell you it no boil, Massa, for I spit in he and he no sizzle." And I have always wondered whether Massa's hunger was keen enough to provide a sufficiently good sauce for such a meal.

After the Frost

Snowdrops again should provide a flower or two from the appearance of *Galanthus Olgae* in October until the forms of *G. nivalis* come with a rush in February for Candlemas Day. For *G. Rachelae* should bridge the gap in November until *G. cilicicus* is ready to take its turn and last until *G. byzantinus* begins. Last Autumn and Winter I had a fine show of this useful wild hybrid, having planted a good many freshly-imported bulbs, which always bloom extra early in their first season. They were very lovely through November and well into December, and were especially pretty where they rose through a group of a *Viola cornuta* of a wonderfully everblooming variety, and which was cheerful through the whole of last Winter. The Snowdrops and Viola had for next-door neighbours some self-sown *Primula malacoides*, that began to bloom in September and kept up a succession right on for the next ten months, until their babes were beginning to show in green patches of tiny seed leaves round them. Of course every now and then a sharp frost destroyed all the fully-opened blossoms, but it was not long before others expanded. It is a good plan to plant out any old plants of this Primula in Spring when they are getting too lanky for the greenhouse. Choose a cool half-shaded spot, such as ferns are happy in, and with luck you will have a self-sown colony that, if only you can defend them from slugs, ought to give you great pleasure in late Autumn and early Spring, even if not right through an open Winter.

Chimonanthus fragrans is indispensable, and should be planted in any garden large enough to hold two plants.

Iris unguicularis should be the first, and Chimonanthus the second, but it is very strange that one so seldom meets with a really good tree of it. People have delusions about its tastes and temper, and firmly believe that nothing less horticulturally luxurious than a position on a south wall, that would be good enough to grow fine peaches, would do for Chimonanthus, and the majority of people prefer peaches. I believe this arises from the fact that the Winter Sweet takes a few years to settle down in any position and does not attempt to flower until it has made a certain amount of old wood, and as the foliage is not very lovely or exciting, two or three seasons of barren winter twigs induce the owner to tear it up and plant something more showy. Of course it does appreciate a place against a sunny wall, but I find it has done quite well enough here without it. I had a pot plant that looked so sickly and shabby I prescribed a period of convalescence in the kitchen garden for it. It was planted behind a large pyramid Pear-tree, a greenhouse to the east of it, but exposed to the north, and the Pear stands on its southern side. It grew away freely, and as I am always hard up for a sunny bit of wall it was left in its retirement longer than I had intended, and after three years was so big that I funked moving it, and now I am glad I did, for it has been covered with bloom every season so far, since it first felt old enough to behave like a grown-up. It is the variety known as *grandiflora*, in which the flowers are rather larger than in the type, and are of a brighter colour, quite a fair yellow, instead of the transparent drab of the older plant. They are not valuable for colour effect though, but to please the nose and not the eye. A tea-cup saucer, with a

After the Frost

little water in it, is the best receptacle for flowers picked off the twigs, as they can be packed closely in until one has a solid mass of them, and the scent is delicious and fills even a large room. Later in the season, when there are not many buds to open, the twigs and sprays can be cut, and are pretty in a quiet refined way, arranged in old tall champagne glasses with sprays of Garrya catkins, and a relief from the Chrysanthemums, perpetual Carnations, and Poinsettias that one meets everywhere before forced Daffodils take the field.

Last Christmas the garden went mad, Summer plants refused to go to bed, and Spring flowers woke up far too early. But it was pleasantly unusual to go and pick strange companions for the vases. I unearthed some old purple glass finger-bowls from a downstairs china cupboard, the asylum for aged survivors of sets of glass and china whose companions have fallen victims to the accidents of daily use and washings, and that awful original sin of all crockery—" Came to bits in me 'ands, mum "—and these imperially coloured survivors are sources of great joy to me when filled with Violets or other purple or lilac flowers. In the dead time of Winter they are often vacant, and are put on a shelf in the store-room, as in sunless weeks our frame Violets go on strike. This last Winter I kept them going with pickings of Tufted Pansies, Maggie Mott, and Kitty Bell especially, and for several weeks I mixed among them spikes of flower of the Winter Heliotrope, *Petasites fragrans*, which was as early as the Pansies were late, and the cool grey effect of the Coltsfoot was charming among the Pansies, and the scent was delicious. *Jasminum nudiflorum* is too well known to need praising, but it is not often enough planted. It makes quite a pleasing bush if trained round three central sticks and cut back each Spring after flowering, and then allowed to push out new growths in every direction. These make better shoots for cutting than those one can get from plants trained on walls, and are generally rather later in flower, and therefore very useful. A good bunch of foot-long sprays mixed with the catkins of Hazel and Alder make delightful centre vases for the dinner-table, and I enjoy watching the lengthening of the catkins in the warm room, and almost every bud of the Jasmine will open into a clean, bright flower. I must not omit the Glastonbury Thorn, a young tree of which, close to the house, generally provides a bunch or two of flower buds at any rate, and sometimes open flowers, to pick and mix with the Holly and Mistletoe of the dinner-table vases for Christmas Day. *Eucalyptus cordata* and *E. pulverulenta* form their flower buds in Summer, and begin to open them from October onwards, and during a mild Season will continue a brave show of their golden-fringed rosettes on fine days, even till Spring. They also are useful to cut, the blue-grey leaves and creamy-yellow blossoms look very pretty, though not showy, stood in a room away from other flowers. I like to be able to watch the opening of the flowers at close quarters, first the lifting of the beautifully constructed little lid that covers the unrolled host of stamens, and which is recorded in the name Eucalyptus, *well covered*. Then the unrolling of the stamens takes a couple of days to produce the fully opened flowers. *Vinca difformis* tries its best to

192

After the Frost

supply flowers all through the Winter, but lack of sunshine
spoils its efforts. I have seen it used as a bedding plant in
Italy, and it produced a mass of pale lavender flowers in
the latter part of January. At Bitton, grown under a
spreading Pine, it is a charming sight all through the
Winter. Here it is only in spells of fine weather that it is
worth picking, but it has not as good a position as might
be. I feel sure it would be a plant worth trial; planted
at the foot of a south wall, and potted up and brought
into a cool house, I know it has proved a great success.
It seems very doubtful whether this grey-flowering
Periwinkle is a form of *Vinca media*, and whether the
deep purple-blue Italian plant, sometimes called *acutiflora*,
is only another form of the same thing, so I stick to the
name Canon Ellacombe gave me with the plant until
someone shall make all the books agree about this member
of the family, for at present all is confusion. Anyway, this
grey fellow is the only one that is a regular and persistent
winter flowerer, and with it must end my list of flowers
that come after the frost.

CHAPTER XII

Evergreens

PTELEA TRIFOLIATA, the Weeping Willow, and Paul's Purple Peach are the last deciduous trees of this garden to shed their leaves. The Ptelea starts into growth late, so it seems fair it should provide us with a late fall to make up for it, or, perhaps, looked at from the plant's point of view, it should be allowed extra time to enjoy and use its leaves, like the twenty minutes allowed for the carver for a large family, at meal times. The other two are among the earliest of all trees to start work in Spring, so it is very praiseworthy of them to go on so long. All three trees were full of leaves on December 10th last Winter; the Peach had flowered freely in March and early April with the Almonds, and the Willow is always the first tree hereabouts to look golden-green from a distance with newly opening leaf buds. When all the leaves are down and swept up, one realises the debt the gardener owes to evergreens. This garden is well endowed with them. The fine old Yews along the river have been there some three centuries, and never look better than during the winter months. When the weather is too abominable for any other garden work I put on an old coat and take a scrubbing-brush and

Evergreens

work away under the shelter of their umbrella-like heads, and get warm and pleasantly tired by the good exercise derived from scrubbing their stems. I learnt this form of Winter sport for gardeners at Glasnevin. The first time I visited Ireland was late in September, and climatic conditions were similar to those Thackeray described in saying there was only one shower of rain during his visit, but it began before he got there and was going on when he left. So I first saw Glasnevin on a drizzling day, and was attracted by a row of glowing red-stemmed trees that showed up from a great distance. " Whatever are those trees ? " I asked ; " surely not *Arbutus Andrachne,* for their heads are not like it." "They are Yews, the row called Addison's Yews," was the Director's reply. I thought they must be some scarlet-stemmed forms of Irish Yew then, but was assured it was nothing but a continued application of scrubbing-brushes and elbow grease that produced those glowing trunks, and that they improved in colour every year under the treatment. So I have adopted it here, and though at first it meant the flaking off of a good deal of dead and scaly old bark before I got to the smooth red living skin, it proved fascinating work for bad weather, and by degrees I have scrubbed the stems of this row as high as I can reach when standing on a chair. The trees seem to like it, and, I believe, grow better for it, especially where the trunk is formed of clustered columns, for just in the crack where two columns join the layers of bark get pinched between the swelling columns and must press against the living wood with great force. It has dislodged a vast horde of spiders and wood-lice, of course, but my feelings are not very tender towards them. The result is certainly good, especially on a damp day when the smooth stems are bedewed, or after a good wetting rain, and they are of a most surprisingly beautiful rich crimson colour, but some trees seem by nature of a finer colour than others, and they are always those with the smoothest stems. I do not believe anyone can know what an absorbing and fascinating job is the peeling of an old Yew-tree. The scaling off of the loose flakes first, then peeling off large flat pieces and leaving the smooth surface below, and the pleasure grows as one gradually reveals the real outline of the trunk. But the best bit of all is the final brushing over, when the colour turns from that of the lean of a rather dry ham to a rich warm crimson under the scrubbing-brush.

After the first season's removal of several layers of dead bark, not much peeling is needed ; the loose flakes will come away while the trunk is being brushed, and the deepest colour of all comes out on a layer of bark that has been scrubbed for three successive seasons.

The Bamboo bed runs at right angles from the old Yews and forms the western boundary of the hollow lawn that was once a pond. Unfortunately it is on the top of the slope instead of the bottom, and so although the Bamboos look well up there, the bed dries out terribly in hot summers and the growth of its occupants is stunted thereby. Bamboos are for the most part shallow-rooting things, but they love a cool layer of leafy soil

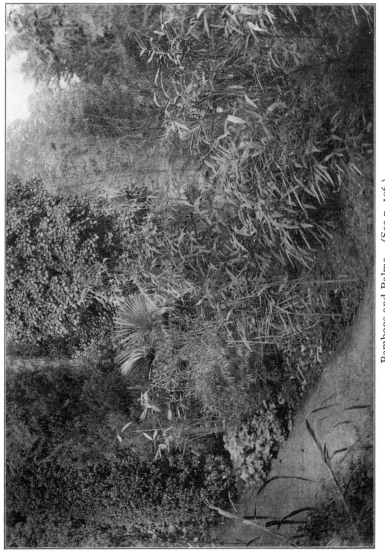

Bamboos and Palms. (See p. 196.)

Evergreens

to run about in, so a hollow in a wood, just deep enough
to be cool and moist but not actually wet, suits them
best. I own I erred in being too much of an optimist
when I planned the planting of this ridge with Bamboos
and Palms, and they have not grown to the dimensions
I hoped for, but all the same I have no more suitable place
in the garden, and I do not believe any other evergreen
plant would have produced so good an effect there as
these poor half-starved Bamboos. The illustration facing
page 196 shows the back of the bed, but was taken within
a year of the replanting that had become necessary on
account of the tangle having got too thick, so it does not
do justice to their usual appearance. The picture shows
about half the length of the main planting, and behind
the Cypresses and the great tower of Ivy on the old Pine,
which block up the view at the left of the picture, there
is another band of them almost as large. Only one of
the Palms can be seen, as the others are nearer the lawn
side of the bed.

I see the photograph was taken in the end of October,
because the band of Colchicum that edges the walk had
almost finished blossoming, only one flower being left
standing, and I remember they were planted late, and
were unusually late in flowering that season. Bamboos
are at their best here from October to March, and their
fresh glistening foliage is very welcome at a time when
so many other plants are bare or looking bedraggled.
The only one that looks a little bare and scrubby in
the winter months is *Arundinaria nitida*, the plant that
occupies the centre of the picture, and is the tallest but

My Garden in Autumn and Winter

smallest leaved of those shown. This old clump was the sole one in the bed I did not move in the last general post, and that because it looked so handsome and hearty I thought it best to leave well alone. Thus it happens that it is the only Bamboo in the bed that has not lost its tallest growths. As Winter sets in *A. nitida* drops about half its leaves, and the long canes look rather naked, but it makes up for this winter *déshabille* by being the first of all Bamboos to break out into fresh growth in Spring, when its dainty little green leaves are charming signs of the times. As it is perhaps the hardiest, and is so wonderfully graceful in habit and will grow in almost any position, but better perhaps in partial shade than in full sun, it should be in every garden. The slender shoots reach a height of about ten feet here, and in their first season bear but few leaves. Each one will, if all goes well with it, live for five or more seasons, and as in each succeeding year increasing numbers of branchlets spring out from the nodes of the main stem, the culm is weighted more and more until it bends out from the main clump and arches over in a most graceful curve, forming a shower of delicate greenery. For this reason *A. nitida* should not be crowded up among other plants, but, where possible, allowed plenty of space to arch out over dwarfer forms. I have planted it under a Yew-tree and it has done well. I have another plant quite in the open, that has spread into a large mass, but has not produced such long canes as those planted in shade, and therefore is not quite so graceful, while on hot days the leaves of this exposed specimen roll up so tightly that they lose much of their

198

Evergreens

beauty, until a cloud or evening cools the air and they can open out again. If I might only grow one Bamboo I should choose *A. nitida*, it has so many good qualities, for besides those I have mentioned, of hardiness and graceful habit, it is a tufted grower, spreading out rather slowly at first, but, of course, after some years with a larger circumference the annual supply of new canes round the old clump carries it outwards at a much faster rate; it is no runner, and so, as we have proved here, may be left alone for a dozen years or more, and will still go on increasing in beauty as well as size.

Somewhat similar in general appearance, at least from a distance, is a mysterious species, which, from the doubt as to its original home, Lord Redesdale named *A. anceps*. It is not hardy everywhere, and, alas, only moderately so here, having been twice cut to the ground. On the coast of Norfolk it seems indestructible, but in many inland gardens people complain that it is tender. I have here the actual plant that does so well in Norfolk, or I might have supposed mine was not such a hardy form. I have another planting that I believe is also *A. anceps*, that came from another source, that fine Irish garden, Hamwood, where it grows into magnificent jungles of great height. The late Mr. Hamilton told me it was quite hardy there, when he gave me the plants that have formed my clumps. Here this form gets very badly damaged in all but the mildest Winters, and has never been able to show its true character of very tall growths bent over by the weight of its brilliantly green leaves. At a distance *A. anceps* looks like a very fine piece of *nitida*, but

199

My Garden in Autumn and Winter

when one is close enough to notice its manner of growth the widely running habit shows it to be *anceps*. A stretch of it can be seen in the photograph, just to the front of the Palm, but it was made up out of small pieces cut out of the big clump behind the Ivy pillar, and they were too young to show their habit. By now they are arching out over the gravel walk. *A. Hindsii*, var. *graminea*, is a good hardy one, and has a distinct appearance due to the great length of its narrow, deep green leaves. It is rather stiff in habit and runs out a little, though not enough to be interfering and disagreeable for its neighbours, but just enough to make it easy to dig off a piece for a friend or another position in the garden. *A. Simonii* has been banished from this gathering along with *Phyllostachys Boryana* and *P. Henonis*, and all three for the same reason—they flowered. Once a Bamboo takes to flowering the habit is as incurable as that of drunkenness in a human being. I have cut them down to the ground on detecting the first symptoms of the vice. Promising new shoots soon appeared, rather thin perhaps, but looking as though all would be well; but no sooner had they furnished themselves with a few leaves than the hateful oat-like spikes began to appear, and the old root had to go to the bonfire. A flowering Bamboo is a hideous sight, here at least. First it loses its leaves, then the flower spikelets turn a dull grey-green and go a shade browner each day, and directly the seeds have formed and become milky inside, the impertinent London sparrows out in the country for their Summer holidays, hop-picking or corn-stealing or whatever they call it, flock

Evergreens

to the stems and pick them bare. Of course the day may
come when all the plants of *A. nitida* or *anceps* in Britain
will take to flowering, as other species have done, but as I
look at my waving clumps I hope it may still be far distant
if it means the death of the plant in their case, as it does in
most others. *Phyllostachys aurea* is the only species that I
have known to indulge in a mild bout of flowering, and
then pull itself together when it has had enough of it. It
seems as though it signs the pledge, or joins the Blue
Ribbon Army, or its vegetable equivalent, and refrains
from further excess, and settles down as a good sober
old plant again.

P. flexuosa is a good tufty-habited species, but the
canes never reach a greater length than six feet here,
and they bend outwards so freely that the plant only forms
a low rounded mass. It is said to be capable of flowering
and seeding in a fairly thorough manner, and afterwards to
recover itself and throw up fresh leafy shoots. *Arundinaria
japonica*, the *Metake* of the Japanese, fills in spaces among
the lighter growing ones in my planting, but it is not one
of my favourites, for it always has a heavy and sombre
appearance, and unless it is divided and replanted, or its
two-year-old shoots thinned out, it soon looks rather
shabby. *A. Falconeri* and *nobilis,* that are so beautiful in
Cornwall and Ireland, get cut to the ground in most years
here, and so never arrive at a stage of full beauty out of
doors. *Bambusa palmata* is one of the most useful wherever it can be allowed space to run as it likes. It has the
largest leaves of any that we can grow, strong ones being
over a foot long and three inches wide, and they grow in

a group of three or more, giving the plant a fine palm-like effect. The culms reach to six or seven feet in height when doing well, and branch freely in their second, third, and even succeeding years, but the best effect is obtained by thinning out the older shoots, or cutting them down halfway to make room for younger ones. It is a villain for running, the rhizome pushing through most things, gravel paths included, and no wonder, for it has a point as sharp as a bayonet. As it is so easily pulled up, or discouraged by being cut down, it does no great harm, but it is as well to remember its wandering ways when planting it. Its near ally, *B. Veitchii*, has never done well here, evidently the climate is too dry for it. It is a dwarf counterpart of *B. palmata*, but has an interesting trick of acquiring a band of faded tissue as a margin to each leaf in Winter, that gives it a variegated appearance that is very striking. *B. Ragamowskii*, also known as *B. tessellata*, is said to produce even larger leaves than *palmata*, but has never done so here, but probably requires a damper home and better feeding. Therefore I advise the use of *B. palmata* if a reliable, sturdy, large-leaved Bamboo is wanted, one that will settle down and enjoy life on plain fare and a restricted allowance of drinks. The largest clump here is in the lower portion of the rock garden, and grows on a bank composed of little else than coarse gravel that was dug out in making a small pond just below it. I feel sure no other plant would behave so handsomely in such a position, and look so well for the greater part of the year. *Saxifraga peltata* does almost as well as the Bamboo on the same bank, but then it is on the lower slope and so at

Evergreens

the water's edge, and is saved from the trials of thirst. The Saxifrage, of course, is deciduous and is bare all through the Winter, and the highest honours must go to the Bamboo During Summer and Autumn the contrast of the palm-like Bamboo foliage with the great round lotus-like leaves of the Saxifrage is wonderfully fine, and suggestive of a flora from warmer lands. The grouping is completed by a colony of *Myrrhis odorata*, the fresh green leaves of which, like those of a giant Oak Fern, look all the more delicate for their stiff and heavy neighbours just behind, and a big clump of *Senecio Clivorum* with its leathery green leaves in front. Some people say that Bamboos should always be planted by themselves, as they are so distinct in appearance from other plants, but I have planted several in among shrubs or herbaceous plants for the sake of contrast, and have always enjoyed the effect produced. *Phyllostachys aurea* is one of the best as an isolated specimen, being stiff and upright in habit and no runner. *P. viridiglaucescens* makes a good companion if two are wanted within shouting distance of each other, as it is distinct enough in shade of green, and has a more arching manner of growth. I have these two at the back of a herbaceous bed, and rising out of a sea of Alstroemerias in Summer, and groups of Crown Imperials for Spring, and I think they improve the effect of that end of the bed at all seasons. Then again, the dwarf *Bambusa pygmaea* is simply charming as a carpet among specimen shrubs. The beds in front of this house are very difficult to plant effectively, being cut up by areas, gratings, and foundations till there is but little planting space, and that little is so thoroughly

drained that only the most long-suffering plants can
live there.

In spite of all these difficulties, one of these beds looks
well all the year round, and especially in the Winter; so
it may prove helpful to others, who possess similar spaces
that prove difficult to plant effectively, if I give a list of
its occupants.

First in importance come three specimen Tree Ivies,
the largest of which is a spreading bush of a golden-leaved
variety, about four feet in width, but kept low by pinching
out the topmost growths, as it stands under one of the
windows. Further back and between two windows there
is a round-headed standard of a very pretty variety, with
such good silver variegation that it affords a delightful
contrast with the other two. The third Ivy is always deep
green as to foliage, a bush of the golden-fruited Ivy of the
South of Europe. This bush is also kept low by trimming
off aspiring shoots. In the shadiest corner grows a fine
specimen of *Nandina domestica*, graceful as a Bamboo, and
in front is a queer-looking round-headed specimen that I
have evolved from the small form of the cut-leaved Bramble.
This plant is generally seen as a sprawling tangle, rooting
at its tips wherever the ends of its long shoots touch ground,
and needing much trimming and uprooting to keep it in
bounds. I thought I would try if I could make a standard
of it, so I tied up three or four shoots of one in the rock
garden, cutting away all others; then I shortened side
growths till a head was formed, and after fifteen years it
has grown into a bush that looks more like a good cut-
leaved Japanese Maple than a Bramble. I liked it so much

Evergreens

that I planted another in front of the morning-room window, where it would be under my eye and hand, and by training it up an iron stake and continually turning the tips of its growths into the centre of the tangle, it has been compelled to form a round ball of intertwined growth, covered with the prettily cut leaves, and is a very attractive object at all times, even in Winter when it is rather bare of leaves, as the thorny stems are so intricately intertwined. The effect of these specimen plants is immensely helped by a thick green carpet of *B. pygmaea*, about eight inches in height, and so thick that no weeds have a chance of growing among it. I like to cut down a portion of this carpet every Spring so as to keep it low and thick and clear of old leaves and stems. If this is done in April, just before the new leaves are produced, it is only for a fortnight that it looks at all bare, as the young shoots appear very rapidly. *Arundinaria auricoma* is another Bamboo that is all the better if cut to the ground, but if there are strong sound shoots of a year old, and greater height is wanted for the specimen, these may be shortened halfway. It is more often called *Bambusa Fortunei aurea*, but it seems wrongly, and is the most brilliantly variegated of all Bamboos, strong young leaves being for the most part rich golden-yellow. It will shoot up to the height of a yard in a season, and much larger leaves are produced by the new growths from the base, than on side shoots from the older stems.

Phyllostachys fastuosa is the noblest of all the truly hardy ones, but I feel sad twinges of conscience when I mention it, for it has not received the attention it deserves here, and exists under persecution waiting for a better day to dawn.

My Garden in Autumn and Winter

There is more likelihood of discovering a new planet than a site in this overcrowded, tree-root-robbed, dry old garden suitable for a Bamboo of luxurious tastes. That is why *fastuosa* sits like Patience on a monument almost starved to death by hungry trees. Some day we may be able to fill a deep hole with top spit and leaf-mould in a spot remote from robbers and translate the martyr with all due honour. Then we may hope for culms fifteen to twenty feet high, and rich deep green leaves from toe to top of each of them. The sheaths of this species are very remarkable; when young and active they are soft to the touch and rich purple in colour, but when they have done their work and are pushed off by the young branches they have sheltered, they are worth picking up, for their inner surface has a most marvellous glaze that is delightful to touch, a thing even a blind man could enjoy. Further, their light buff colouring is stained with a beautiful suffusion of crimson. I have a dried one in front of me as I write, picked up in 1907, that I use as bookmarker for Lord Redesdale's delightful book, *The Bamboo Garden*.

The old Scots Pine that is now smothered in Ivy is well shown in the picture opposite, and at its foot, on the left, can be seen three of the Palms that live among the Bamboos; the fourth and largest, shown in the other illustration, is so much behind them that though I can find two of its leaves, through knowing where to expect them, I doubt whether others can. They make a pretty group in this corner, and it is a very great pity that they are not more often planted in English gardens, seeing that they are so hardy, only asking for shelter from harassing winds,

A pillar of Ivy. (See p. 206.)

Evergreens

and are so beautiful even in the depth of Winter. They are not easy to procure in English nurseries without paying rather high prices for them, and I think it may be useful if I tell here how I get mine. Mr. Smith, of the Caledonia Nursery, Guernsey, has them of all sizes, and half a crown will purchase a nice young seedling in a pot. Another shilling on the price produces a plant that makes a good show at once, while if you care to go into pounds and risk the moving of a monster, you can get one tall enough to stand under, but I strongly advise planting them young. Their charms have led me away from the Ivies, and I want to put in a plea for some of them. I need not further praise the Tree Ivies I am so fond of, as they have already had their share, but I must return to the pillar of shining green up the old Pine. It is no doubt bad for the tree, but ever since I can remember the garden I can recall this tall Jack-in-the-Green, and the birds' nests it contained annually, and it is too late to worry about saving the Pine. It is the great roosting-place of all the sparrows and starlings of the place, and it is perfectly astonishing the number of them that fly out if a stone is thrown into the Ivy at dusk in the Winter. I have always hoped that by so doing I might induce them to migrate, but it seems to make no difference. Of late years my dog thinks it a fine thing to jump as high as he can into the Ivy and bark loudly at the clouds of birds that have never yet learnt that this attack of his cannot possibly harm them. Yet they all return again as soon as we move away, and quarrel and chatter over their roosting rights to certain twigs until everyone of

My Garden in Autumn and Winter

them is satisfied. The worst of old Ivy-covered trees is that some day the tree gets too rotten to hold the weight and over the whole thing goes. I have tried to save several fine old specimens here by having iron crutches made to support the Ivies' stout limbs, and I have tried to run Ivy up the irons so that it may thicken out and mingle with the mass above and bind it all together, and thus give it new legs of Ivy and iron. Nothing is more lovely in Winter than a fine old mass of Ivy with its slowly maturing berries, but if one has as many as exist in this garden there is a penalty to pay in the vast number of Ivy seedlings that appear everywhere and are so troublesome to get rid of among the stems of other plants.

Ivies are very good, if distinct forms are chosen, to cover bare patches of ground under trees. One of the best effects I have obtained is from a large mass of the form known as Bullock's Heart Ivy, from the size and shape of its immense leaves. On one side of this carpet is another patch of Ivy only about half as large as the other, and of a neat-growing, small-leaved form with beautifully variegated leaves, while on the other a good stretch of the variegated leaved Wood-Sorrel makes a good contrast with the dark green of the central mass of the huge Ivy. My dear good friend, the late Mr. Kingsmill, gave me this Ivy, but large as the leaves often are here, I have never seen one to equal two that set me on to beg for this form from him. He was sending me some plants, Violas, I think, and as he was digging them up he noticed two Ivy leaves that were twice as large as any he had ever noticed before. So he planned getting a rise out of me, and picked them

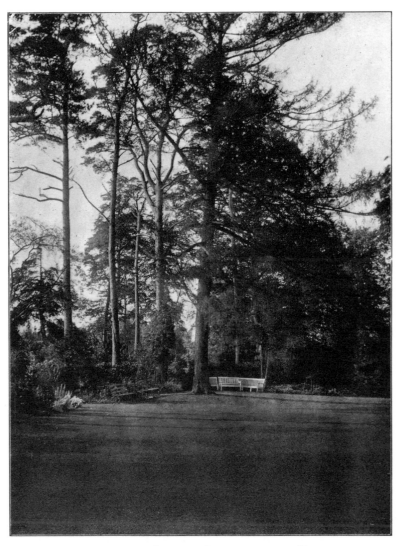

The old Bowling-green Lawn.   (See p. 208.)

Evergreens

both, and used them to wrap the Violas in, just as though they were the commonest productions of his garden. Of course I asked for a runner of this marvellous Ivy by return of post, and he sent the piece that has grown into this carpet, but with the explanation that those two leaves were the result of a special effort on the part of the Ivy. Anyway, it is a fine thing as it grows here, and reminds me of his kindly fun every time I pass it.

Veronicas provide much beauty for winter days, and I especially admire the thick round leaves of *V. Lindsayi*, and the beautiful way in which they overlap one another. It makes a low, rounded bush, and I like it planted among choice ferns, both for the contrast its solidity makes with their lacey open-work leaves, and also because it gives just the sort of shade, for some ferns that like it, as a stone would.

Then there is the best of all the so-called Whipcord Veronicas, in *V. Hectori*, whose leaves are so closely adpressed that the shoots are cylindrical and look just as though made of plaited green cord. It has a wonderful tone of yellowish-green quite unlike that of any other Veronica; it is a very distinct and beautiful plant, and I find it one of the hardiest of the family. Another one I often admire in the Winter, and sometimes cut sprays of its growth to place with *Iris unguicularis* or Snowdrops in vases. It is *V. pimelioides*, and, I think, an extra fine form of it. It has slender growths, and a rather light and straggling habit, that is much improved and made almost tidy and shrubby by this winter pruning. Its great beauty lies in the steely blueness of its tiny leaves and their deep reddish-purple edges. Very early in the year the young growths begin to deepen in colour and become almost crimson, and it is a lovely little thing to examine closely. Unless there has been a recent period of very sharp weather, *Briza maxima* provides one of the best patches of brilliant light green in the whole garden. It has already been praised for its large quaking-grass heads, but quite deserves a fresh pat on the back for sowing itself so freely and appearing in fresh greenness directly the autumn rains have soaked the ground enough to cause it to germinate. If it is thinned out a little and rounded into suitably sized patches where it is wanted for next season, it can be left alone, and relied upon to look cheerful and happy, whenever the weather is fit for a human being to look cheerful in a garden, until it ends up once again next July in a mass of red stalks and hop-shaped seed-heads that scatter and sow themselves with every touch. *Berberis dictyophylla* is a wonderful thing in the foliage line. Not quite an evergreen perhaps, but keeping its leaves for more than halfway through a mild Winter. Some of them turn brilliantly scarlet, while others remain as green as in Summer ; and all of them are as white beneath as if they had been whitewashed, and the white twigs make such a very distinct plant of it that any one meeting it for the first time is sure to wish to be introduced to it. The evergreen members of the Berberis family, sometimes called Mahonias, should be collected and planted in any garden, but the larger the garden the more species and varieties there should be. Even the common form of *B. Aquifolium* is worthy of a good open position, as then its leaves will turn to shades of bronze, purple, and

Evergreens

crimson worth rubbing one's spectacles to look at. Too often it is only used as padding where nothing else will grow. This reputation for good-nature causes the poor plant to be treated with as little respect as is often shown to human beings noted for long-suffering ways, but few plants repay the planter better if given a fair chance. *B. japonica* is a magnificent plant that grows well as a specimen in shaded but not overgrown places; but only too often one sees a rosette or two of its huge pinnate leaves peeping out among a vulgar crowd of Aucubas, Privets, and Portugal Laurels which have been allowed to overgrow the Berberis. Its straight stems, which seldom branch, with their crowns of fine leaves, have a most stately and tropical-looking effect in a good specimen, and the flower-spikes are formed so early that they are signs of Spring in the middle of Winter. Still handsomer, but very much rarer, is the true *B. nepalensis.* Its leaves, are much longer and have a greater number of leaflets, *japonica* being generally contented with nine leaflets, while a strong *nepalensis* will produce as many as twenty-five. The finest plants of it I have ever seen are at Enys, in Cornwall, raised from seed sent from Nepaul. A descendant of that true race accompanied me back from Cornwall after my last visit, and as it is not exactly a babe, it made rather a commotion at Paddington while we were trying to induce it to sit on a taxi. It is none the worse for its carriage exercise, and has produced a fine new crown of leaves in the sheltered corner I found for it; but then, of course, it has not fought for its life through one of our eastern counties' Winters yet.

There are some very charming dwarf forms of the Box

My Garden in Autumn and Winter

that are well worth planting to give a bit of shade to small ferns or even Daffodils that love not to be scorched. I collected the various forms rather diligently at one time, asking for a cutting of any variety I found in other folks' gardens and that was not represented here already. Many of them have no names attached in consequence, so I cannot tell you of a better way to acquire them than mine of begging. The good gardener should be the antithesis of the unjust steward. He cannot expect to do much good without digging for all he is worth, and unless he is as rich as Crœsus, he had better give up gardening if he is ashamed to beg.

Some of the narrow-leaved forms are very pleasing. I can tell you the name of the best of them, and it is *Buxus myosotidifolia*, which I remembered because it struck me as such an inapplicable name for a narrow-leaved Box. Silver-edged leaves and golden forms are among them, and they make wonderfully picturesque little bushes if left to grow as they wish. I planned out a bit of ground in a half-shaded position for ferns and Primulas, and managed to provide still more shade and coolness by digging something like a winding ditch through it, with a raised mound running along one side, and arranging so that all the sloping ground should fall towards the North. Little groups of these Boxes on the ridge of the mound, and a stone here and there, have helped to break the trench-like effect, and add to the shadiness. A charming companion for them is *Ilex crenata*, a miniature Holly with the general aspect of a Box, but easily distinguished by its small, round, dark-brown berries. Its green colouring is distinct—a soft

Evergreens

dull tone, that is pleasing among the glistening Box leaves.
I make a point of asking all the deeply learned scientists I
meet why the Box in all its forms is the only hardy evergreen I meet with in which the mature leaves are composed
of two separable layers. Some Eucalyptus are made on
the same plan, I believe—at least so the late Dr. Masters
told me ; but even he, with his vast knowledge of plants,
could suggest no useful purpose served by the separation
in the Box. If you wish to see it for yourself in a Box leaf,
choose " quite an old 'un, a last year's," as the nigger said
when he was reproved for stealing a tombstone to refloor
his oven. Cut it across the centre with a sharp pair of
scissors; hold one-half in your left hand, and press the
edges inwards with the fingers and thumb of your right,
and if it is as stale as the tombstone it should open, showing
a thick, leathery upper surface, and a thin, transparent, pale-
green under-layer, which gape widely when pressed apart.

Phillyreas are beautiful evergreen shrubs and trees
that seldom receive the respect from gardening folk their
merits deserve. I can recall some fine specimens at Shrub-
lands, near Ipswich, especially as I saw them once in May,
full of their tiny white blossoms, the delight of the pretty
Holly Blue Butterflies. As a rule one finds Phillyreas
jammed in among Laurels and other horrors of plants used
by early Victorian gardeners to fill up shrubberies, which
was their idea of landscape gardening. This means that
their fate is to be jostled and squeezed by undesirable
neighbours, and all their efforts to rise superior to their
surroundings are often annually snubbed by the shears.
P. latifolia grows into a small tree if allowed to, and looks

like a mixture of an Evergreen Oak and an Olive. It belongs to the order Oleaceae, so its Olive features are the
result of a family likeness, and I believe the form we have
most of here is known as the variety *ilicifolia*, which name
proclaims its other resemblance. A good specimen allowed
to develop naturally, but perhaps stripped up a bit to show
its legs, forms a graceful round-headed tree, the deep black-
green foliage lightened by its shining surface, which always
reflects sparkling high lights. There are two old specimens
at the back of the house here, and in the foreground of the
view from my study window. I can remember days when
they were shorn over or occasionally headed right back to
hard wood to form dense round blobs of greenery, almost
as graceful in outline as a haycock. Then for a season or
two their annual tonsure was overlooked, and it dawned on
me that it would be pleasant to strip their legs and show
the stems, that I might get the view across the meadows
away to the turn of the river and the blue distance beyond
through the tracery of the many stems, and the trees might
be allowed to grow as high as they wished above the
gothic windows formed by thin stems and branches.
Every year has added to their beauty, and I urge a plea for
all Phillyreas suffering from crowding and shearing, that
they may be allowed a chance of showing their owners and
persecutors how good they can be if let alone.

Bays, too, I have emancipated from the annual clipping
they used to receive, and they have formed noble specimens, and add to their interest by flowering ; but all three of
my trees are most likely but divisions or cuttings of one
plant, as they are all of the same sex, though I forget

Evergreens

which, and so I get no berries. One of the Bays I have treated like the Phillyrea and stripped it up, short-coated it. I was afraid it might catch cold its first Winter, but it has not suffered yet, and is very effective and unusual looking. Of course, it sends up hosts of suckers every Summer among its many stems, but they are so luxuriant and glossy they are good to see when quite short, and I like to cut them in Winter for sweetly scented greenery for the house, so they are not altogether an evil.

CHAPTER XIII

Ferns

THE choicer varieties of our British Ferns are to be found in far too few gardens, so please consider their good points for a minute and weigh them carefully in comparison with those of other plants.

1. *Hardiness;* inasmuch as they are native plants, no Winter will kill them.

2. *Beauty;* not only of fresh green colouring most of the year, but of form. The choicest varieties are the Mechlin laces and goffered frills of the plant world.

3. *Inexpensiveness;* one to three shillings apiece will purchase most of the good varieties.

4. *Suitability* for shady places, where little else as interesting could be grown.

5. *Interest as a study.* There is yet much to be learnt as to the cause of variations, the possibilities of crossing varieties when raised from spores, and there is also the fascinating work of hunting among wild ferns for good or new varieties. It is perfectly marvellous how many distinct forms even the common Hart's-tongue fern can present; and yet so far as one can see, none of these variations is of any real service to the plant, but appear to be evidence of the delight Nature has in variation.

Ferns

I used to believe one might as reasonably expect figs from thistles as good fern fronds in this dry garden. Then came a stage when, having dug out a deep valley in a new stretch of the rock garden, I tried to make a few ferns happy enough to keep up a struggle for existence in cool, shaded corners. A few settled down planted on the northern side of stones, and their roots pushed underneath them, where they were kept cool and moist. They never made much show though, and it was not easy to find many sites suitable for them. So there was no cause for pride in their achievements on either side! The first thing that inspired me with a longing to grow hardy ferns was a magnificent display of them at one of the winter meetings of the Royal Horticultural Society, shown by Mr. May of Edmonton, the greatest of all fern growers.

A kindly fate guided me further along the way to fern growing, for the next time my neighbour, Mr. W. B. Cranfield, came to see me and the garden, he asked why I grew so few ferns, and laughed to scorn my answer that it was because the climate would not let me; he convinced me that it was my fault rather than the climate's, as he grew plenty of them but a few miles off, and he left me no further excuse by most kindly offering to give me a good collection, and by pointing out a wasted bit of ground on the north side of a big Holm-oak, which he declared would grow them well if properly prepared. Full of faith in his knowledge, and fired further by a visit to his garden and an hour or two among the waving green plumes of his ferns, we set to work hewing down Laurels and Philadelphus bushes scrubby enough to be a disgrace even in a London square. Then the ground was trenched and a few cart-loads of the best approach to leaf-soil our woods contain were mixed in, and with a stone here and there I moulded the ground into slopes and hollows, and then my good friend sent me the promised cartload of treasures. I had begged him to send nothing but very hardy kinds, and was somewhat dubious as to his choice when I saw the finely cut filmy beauty of some of the Polystichums and the waved edges of the Hart's-tongues, that looked unfit to be trusted outside of a moist and shaded house. But what Mr. Cranfield does not know about ferns is not worth knowing, and I ought to have believed in him then as much as I do now ; for everyone of these beautiful forms have made good specimens, and they grow more beautiful every season. Planting and watching over these beauties has been fas-cinating work, and I have learnt to admire the wonderful varietal forms of our hardier British ferns. Further plant-ings have been made each season, and if only it would rain here once or twice during the Summer, I might even end by being as proud of my ferns as I am delighted with them. The poor plants suffer in our hot, rainless spells during July and August, but for all that they have always so far managed to throw up some extra fronds late in the season, at least the Polystichums do, and all through the Winter they are a source of great pleasure in almost all weathers, unless they are buried up in snow. An edging of hoar-frost adds to their beauty by accentuating the filigree of the finely cut ones, or the bold margins of those with waved edges, and they never look greener and more lustrous than on a wet day.

Ferns

Most of the choicer varieties of the Hart's-tongue are as easy to grow as the ordinary forms, and are readily propagated, so that every wild find that passes into the hands of a good cultivator will soon enrich our gardens with beautiful specimens. I wish all who read this could be induced to start with half a dozen really good forms in some suitable cool corner. I feel sure they would before long bless me for calling their attention to such fascinatingly lovely plants, and would keep an open eye for others in walks and drives in ferny country, and would find a new and pleasant interest added to life.

Write to Mr. May, Edmonton, or to Dr. Stansfield, Sale, Manchester, for their catalogues of hardy ferns; then purchase six of those I am about to describe, and treat them well, and I know you will never regret the purchase. If one grows a fern it might as well be the best, and certainly the *crispum* forms of Hart's-tongues or *plumosum* forms of Shield Ferns are as superior to the ordinary ones as a Crown Derby bowl is to a common flower-pot, cheese to chalk if you are hungry, and a silk purse to a sow's ear to anyone but the sow herself.

Variation in ferns can be divided into four distinct styles.

Variegation shall be first mentioned to get rid of it, for it is not at all common and not particularly desirable, as all the examples known thus far are very irregularly splashed with white or yellow, and the best are a few golden forms among the Hart's-tongues, none of which is sufficiently gilded to be brilliant, or even much more than sickly and jaundiced.

My Garden in Autumn and Winter

Next in lack of importance is *Reduction of frond surface.* This is again undesirable, when it only means a depauperation, and that some portions of the normal frond are missing, leaving gaps between the pinnae, or even shortening them so much that a stiff or clumsy frond results. There is a charming form of the Lady Fern (*Athyrium Filix-foemina*), however, in which the pinnae are reduced to neat little frilled rosettes placed alternately on either side of the midrib or rachis, which in a good specimen is over a foot in length. It was found by Mrs. Frizell in County Wicklow, and so is known as var. *Frizellae,* and is so remarkable in appearance and yet elegant, looking like a string of green beads, that I think it is worth growing wherever conditions can be found that are damp enough to suit a Lady Fern. But when the reduction produces a dwarf, sturdy, cobby little plant—a Shetland pony instead of a racehorse—one has a choice and useful variety to fit in among rocks, or in the front of the beds.

Better results are produced by *Cristation*—that is, the division of the extremities into varying numbers of points until they form a tassel. It may consist of only a forking of the main terminal, or be so much complicated that a frond becomes as dense as a ball of moss. I have not yet acquired the taste for tasselled forms of ferns with plume-shaped fronds, and think them more curious and interesting than actually beautiful, but I am charmed with the richness of effect cresting gives to the Hart's-tongue, and if only I owned a wood in a western county, I should like to carpet it with groups of every variety procurable.

Ferns

For the garden and its choicest corners, however, there are no forms that can compare with the form of variation known as *Plumation.* It is a comprehensive term, and covers a multitude of fern virtues and graces, but chiefly those that can be described either as a greater division into small sections among the ferns with finely cut fronds, or a greater amount of leaf surface due to an extra growth of the margins. This latter division is best seen in the Hartstongue and Polypodies, and results in effects that remind one of the frills and fringes and furbelows of millinery, while the former more closely resembles the patterns of various laces.

Let us go in imagination to the fern beds on some December morning while every leaf is still wet with recent rain or melted hoar-frost. The illustration facing p. 172 of the eastern end of the new wall that forms the boundary of the pergola garden, gives a view of the ends of three of the beds, and an idea of whereabouts they are situated. A solitary flower of *Colchicum speciosum album* in the right-hand bed tells us this photograph was taken in October, and the leaves are still hanging on the crooked old Spanish Chestnut that hangs across the right-hand corner. In the illustration facing p. 222, however, the ground is seen to be strewn with these leaves, and there we get an idea of the winter aspect of some of my favourite ferns. In the centre a good rosette of *Meconopsis paniculata*, the pale yellow-flowered species we used to call *M. nepalensis* in less enlightened days, makes a beautiful contrast with the ferns. Its silvery grey leaves were especially beautiful throughout the greater part of last

My Garden in Autumn and Winter

Winter, and when their stiff bristles held countless dew-drops, as happened on most days, few things in the garden were better worth gazing at. The drops can be seen with the help of a lens in this picture, and they give a good idea of the capacity of the plant for holding moisture without being wetted by it, for if you look carefully at the fallen Chestnut leaves, Primroses, and Hart's-tongues, you will see that they were quite dry at the time. There was a good group of a dozen or so Meconopsis rosettes even larger than this one here shown, in the opposite bed, that of the lone, lorn Colchicum flower; they were planted among Shield Ferns, and made a lovely picture all through the Winter, and flowered grandly in June. Since then they have scattered so much seed that I hope some self-sown plants may appear to replace their annoyingly monocarpic parents.

Now to look more closely at the ferns themselves. To the left of the Meconopsis rosette is a group of three plants of my best-beloved variety of Hart's-tongue. It is *Scolopendrium vulgare crispum Moly*, according to the way in which pteridologists name their treasures, a way rather appalling at the first hearing to the ordinary garden lover, but on the whole useful, as it distinguishes the main features of the form and also connects it with the finder. The late Mr. Moly was a most enthusiastic fern-hunter, the finder of over six hundred distinct forms, and he had a magnificent collection at his home in Dorsetshire. This collection has now passed into the hands of Mr. Cranfield, and that is how I come to be the proud possessor of these; for it is a form that is rare, and I believe not on the

Meconopsis paniculata among Ferns. (See p. 222.)

Ferns

market. Though not the largest and boldest of crisped Hart's-tongues it is yet one of the most beautiful, being of an especially brilliant green, and the goffered edge of its fronds is as perfect as those my old nurse used to produce for the frills of her caps. In my early days I used to watch the production of these frills with so much interest that I feel quite an authority on goffering; but for all that, I could not hope to see a better effect than this fern achieves without the use of the tongs. The variety that adds the word *latum* as another bead in its string of names is a bolder grower, and a good healthy specimen is a magnificent thing in the fern line, but its edge is less symmetrical and therefore coarser. It is the largest of all the forms I have growing in the open, for I have not yet dared to trust the precious youngster of *nobile* that Mr. Cranfield has given me, out in the burning summer air. Some day it will, I hope, rival its parent in size, but that will not be just yet. The patriarchal plant Mr. Cranfield brought up to the R.H.S. Floral Committee astonished the fern experts and obtained a first-class certificate; and deserved it too, for *S. v. crispum nobile Cranfield* is the finest of all Hart's-tongues ever seen. It was found on the limestone ridge known as Waston Crag, near Carnforth, and was most likely a sudden sport or mutation from an ordinary typical form, for nearly all these *crispum* forms expend so much energy on the production of extra leaf surface that they economise in the matter of spores and are perfectly sterile, and so far as I know there are only two forms that bear spores. One called *fertile*, and another appropriately named *diversifrons*, which bears two forms

223

My Garden in Autumn and Winter

of frond, the finely crisped ones being quite barren, and the fertile ones only slightly ornamented at the edges. Fortunately it has been discovered that Hart's-tongues can be propagated very easily by breaking off the bases of the stalks of old leaves. These leaves swell out a little just before they join on to the root-stock, and this enlarged portion retains life in it long after the frond has perished. If broken off and laid on damp sand in a closed jar placed in gentle heat, small white pimples will appear on the surfaces of these stumps, each of which will grow into a small plant identical in form with its parent. As many as thirty-six young plants have been obtained from an inch of base. So a fine form need not long remain an unique specimen if it gets into good hands. If you split the mid-rib of a Hart's-tongue frond you can extract a long black fibre from it that closely resembles a horse-hair. In some country districts this is accounted for by a legend that seems to savour of the good old days when monks had nothing better to do than to invent pretty tales about plants. It relates that our Saviour being tired rested His head on a tuft of this fern and left a hair of His head adhering to a frond, which immediately closed over it to preserve it, and ever since each frond has borne a counterfeit hair formed of its own fibres.

Two or more types of variation can be combined in one frond, and so we get such a plant as *S. v. crispum fimbriatum*, with tassels at the ends and fringes growing out of the frills, a very beautiful, soft-looking form, widely different from the untasselled crispums and from the ordinary plain-leaved type. We get forms in which the frond is divided

224

Scolopendrium vulgare ramosissimum. (See p. 224.)

again and again, until one can hardly believe a plant with so close a resemblance to some branching seaweed can have any relationship with the Hart's-tongue. *S.v.ramo-cristatum* is one of my delights in this class, and I have a long double row of this variety that are doing their best to make an edging of magnified moss to one of my fern beds. *S. v. ramosissimum* is one of the most extreme, and can be judged from its portrait facing p. 224, and also in the front on the left, below the Meconopsis, in the other fern illustration. It is the exact counterpart in a green fern material of the design of the Carrageen Moss, *Chondrus crispus*, the edible red Seaweed. Next to it I have planted, as shown in the picture, the narrowest of unbranched forms, *S. v. angustatum Moly*, in which the fronds are not more than half an inch wide, very thick and darkly coloured, a wonderful contrast to the beautiful *crispums*, and more interesting than beautiful. There are many other curios among the Hart's-tongues—some twist like corkscrews, others bear pouches at the end of their fronds, and are therefore named *peraferens*. A blunt-ending leaf with the midrib sticking out as a horn is the feature of the *cornutum* varieties, a surface covered with hard warty knobs of the *muricatums*, and a line of raised flaps on either side of the midrib the *papillosum* forms, and if these projections join to form even lines the form is called *supralineatum*. Of course my love for curious plants induces me to give a welcome to all these interesting and distinct forms, but for actual beauty I should advise others to plant the *crispum* and *ramo-cristatum* forms, and so provide for the dull days of Winter a luxuriant mass of glossy green fronds that are

My Garden in Autumn and Winter

beautiful both in colour and form. The highest pitch of
perfection reached by hardy evergreen ferns, however, is
to be found in the most plumose forms of the Polystichums
or Shield ferns, and the Polypodies. Among the former
there is such a wealth of glorious forms it is hard to say
which is the best. I have made two groupings of those
that 'please me especially, and will try to describe what
charms I find in them. It is no easy matter to find words
for these different patterns of fern filigree, and I can only
think of certain types of lace from which to draw terms to
express their delicate tracery. Perhaps it is a dangerous
thing to attempt, and the skilled feminine mind will detect
the superficiality of my knowledge ; but I will try to stick to
well-known makes that even a mere man might know
something about, and avoid technical terms, for I never
was able to master the exact use of the nouns and verbs of
feminine apparel. I can never remember whether one
gussets a gore, or gores a gusset, when a scarf becomes
more than a scarf and turns into a fichu, or how gimps
are distinguished from braids. But I think I know more
about lace. A little knowledge is dangerous, but it may be
turned to account, as it was by a small and mischievous
boy who, having heard his mother mention a placket hole,
created a feeling of dismay among several smartly dressed
folk at an afternoon party by whispering confidentially to
each in turn that he thought her placket hole was hanging
out, passing on quickly to leave them hunting for the
apocryphal offender.

First among my Polystichums I rank those varieties that
are like my idea of Mechlin lace—that is to say, so fine in

Hart's-tongue Ferns. (See p. 226.)

Ferns

division and pattern that, unless looked into, the general
effect is of soft delicate layers of network, as one finds
in a lace made up into a ruffle rather than when laid out
flat. This arises from the pinnae being so much widened
that they overlap one another, like the folds pleated (gus-
setted or gored?) into the band to form the ruffle. Now
here in the same border as the Bullock's Heart Ivy I have
praised already, is a group of some of the most Mechlin-
like, *P. angulare multilobum densum* would provide ruffles
and fichus fit for a queen, but nothing less than an
empress ought to wear such rich ones as are provided
by *Polystichum angulare divisilobum plumosum foliosum.* I
think this was the fern whose beauty attracted the criti-
cal eye of my good friend the late Mr. Kingsmill. When
he asked what it was, and heard the string of its names
recited, he said, "Well, if I can get a plant for a shilling
a word I will buy one."

P. a. plumosum magnificum is a new importation here,
but promises to be a fit companion for the others, perhaps it will do for either of the crowned heads while the
other ruffle is in the wash. *P. a. imbricatum* has so much
lace frilled up in its fronds that it stands on end as in an
Elizabethan ruff, and the effect is wonderfully mossy and
charming.

Then there is a lighter type of frond with more space
between the finely cut pinnules—this reminds one of
Honiton or Brussels lace, with a net background and
sprays of pattern on it. Two forms labelled *divisilobum
Padley* and *gracile Padley* are my best examples of this style.
For a contrast there is *P. a. quadripinnatum robustum*, which,

My Garden in Autumn and Winter

especially in the young fronds, reminds one of Venetian Point, as it has rounded lobes among the fine interstices that look something like the raised, solid, knotted decoration of that lace. Something in the same line, but more open in ground-work and finer—Point d'Alençon perhaps—is *P. a. laciniare Moly*, of which I have two fine big plants that spread out yards of lovely lace; and a little treasure that keeps breaking up into many crowns is *P. a. Bayliae*. I do not know whether this form ever grows into a large specimen; but I hope not, for the many crowns it makes are charming to divide in Autumn to extend the group, which makes a delightful edging to the fern bed, and its neat, narrow fronds and suitability for edging purposes remind me of Valenciennes lace. The form known as *crispato-foliosum* is particularly flat and smooth, and beautifully regularly and finely dissected; it looks too good to be used for ruffles, and would be better as a wide strip of insertion. *P. a. pulcherrimum* is quite distinct and hardly lace-like, more like a design for embroidery, but owes its charm to a wonderfully glossy green surface and brilliant colour, so perhaps we had better class it as beetle-wing embroidery. Ostrich plumes are well represented by some forms, especially one called *tripinnatum;* so by a judicious mixing and grouping of these a very rich and varied effect can be produced. Lilies seem to like the same soil and the shade to their roots of the big fronds, and look very lovely towering over the greenery in Summer; and I do not object to the winter aspect of their dead and yellow stems, marking the place one must watch in Spring for the

Osmunda regalis. (See p. 228.)

Ferns

reappearance of bronze-red shoots spearing through the fern fronds.

The Polypody provides wonderfully luxuriant beauty for the winter months, as it is the most thoroughly evergreen of our British ferns, and no cold seems to dull its brightness. One can understand this when noticing the thick and leathery texture of the fronds of the ordinary variety; but it seems to be quite inexplicable in the case of the form known as the Welsh Polypody (*Polypodium vulgare cambricum*), in which the frond is beautifully plumose, of a thinner texture, and looks hardly safe to trust outside a Wardian case on account of its delicate shades of light green. It is, however, hardy enough for an ordinary Winter, and retains its beauty of colouring until new fronds are pushed up to replace the old. It is, I think, the latest of all ferns to start into growth, and the beginning of June generally arrives before the tiny crosiers of rolled fronds break out from the creeping rootstock, and they do not reach their full growth and beauty before September rains give a finishing touch to their perfections. The original form was discovered many years ago near Cardiff, but similar ones, and some even more beautiful, have been found in other places. That known as *Barrowii* is perhaps the best of all, a more reliable evergreen in bad Seasons, and even brighter in colour and sheen and more deeply cut, making a finer plume than the older plant. All the same, it is possible to purchase it at the rate of two shillings a plant; so every garden that contains a fern and a shady corner ought to grow it.

My Garden in Autumn and Winter

The most finely cut of all the Polypodies is well named *trichomanoides*, for it is so filmy and finely divided that it has a great resemblance to the celebrated Killarney fern, *Trichomanes radicans*. But whereas the Irish rarity cannot be grown out of doors here, and is only happy in caves where water is ever dripping in its wild haunts, or Wardian cases, or shaded and damp enclosures in greenhouses when domesticated, its Polypody counterpart can be kept in good health if given plenty of leaf-mould in a well-drained but cool and moist spot. Every now and then a frond will bear a few pinnae as coarse in texture and as undivided as those of the common wild type, but most of the fronds should resemble tangles of the finest moss. Like the *crispum* forms of Hart's-tongues, these *cambricum* and finely cut forms of Polypody are quite barren, but of course their running and branching rhizomes provide an easy method of division and propagation. These forms of the Hart's-tongues, Shield Ferns, and Polypodies that I have mentioned are the best of the many known varieties for winter effect, but where there is room for a large planting of ferns, others, less evergreen, should be mingled with them for summer effect. That is not our business in this chapter, and I only mention them to emphasize the fact that these I have been praising are absolutely reliable for winter beauty.

In the rock garden smaller species can be used, and few things are prettier than a good grouping of *Asplenium Trichomanes*, our Maidenhair Spleenwort. It does best with me facing north-west, and planted so that it has a fair-sized stone covering its roots, and then it gives me

The Tawny-red of Osmunda and reflections in the Pond.   (See p. 230.)

Ferns

fronds four inches long. They are always beautiful, with their jet-black midrib and tiny pinnae, and in some parts of the rock garden spores have germinated and charming little colonies are springing up. *Asplenium Adiantum-nigrum*, so common and so beautiful in Devonshire lanes, dwindles away here in a year or two; but a rather finely cut form that came to me from Spain has lived for a dozen years, and has actually increased in size. I expect it came from a hot, dry wall, and had been obliged to struggle with southern sunshine, and so was prepared for the grilling atmosphere of our dog-days. *A. marinum* from sea-caves is too tender for outdoors, but I keep a few in pots, sunk in ashes, under the staging of a vinery, and they look very happy and glossy there, and have even managed to place out babies among cracks in the flooring. I bring home ferns from the Alps whenever I have room to pack in a few among my finds of flowering plants, especially the grand evergreen Holly Fern, which is not so hard to establish as most gardeners imagine, if only you can give it a northern exposure and cram its roots under a stone, or where that is not possible bury a brick on the southern side of its roots. Its long, narrow, deep-green fronds are very striking and distinct in appearance among other ferns, and some of mine look better and more glossy than they did in the bottom of those curious deep holes in the quartz rocks by the lake-side upon Mont Cenis, where they grow so plentifully, in company with the little pale-green beauty *Asplenium viride*. I always looked upon this as an impossible plant to keep in good temper here for more than one season; but I am now hoping that by making a sort of trough with two stones, and planting it in the crack at the bottom, it will continue to do as well as it has during the last three years. Even *A. fontanum* and *septentrionale* are living, now that I have taken the trouble to build up narrow crevices for some of my collected Saxifrages and Primulas, and have squeezed in these ferns at the lowest points. Of evergreen ferns that are not British everyone should plant the North American *Asplenium munitum*, and if it gets the woodland shade and moist leaf-soil it loves, great shining narrow fronds will reward the planter; they are stiffer and even handsomer than those of the Holly fern, and stand up more erectly, so that a good specimen is as beautiful as any fern. New Zealand provides some charming hardy ferns. I especially recommend *Lomaria alpina* and its variety *pumila* for a shady, peaty place, where they can be allowed to run about and make a carpet of their deep-green, pinnate, barren leaves, with a lighter layer above of the upstanding fertile ones, the pinnae of which are narrower and as thin as the midrib. A good companion for them is *L. crenulata* from Chili, which is rather larger in all its parts than the New Zealanders. I am using them as carpeting plants among my larger specimens of Hart's-tongues, and at present like the effect; but I am not quite certain they will not prove too strong-growing and inclined to strangle their larger neighbours when they fill the ground. I have been delighted, though, with the behaviour of a very fine form of *Soldanella montana* I brought from the wood above Misurina and planted among my choice ferns. Its round, deep-green leaves make a pleasant contrast at all seasons

Ferns

with the much-divided forms of fern fronds, and it likes
their shade, and the flowers the slugs spared me this
Spring were very beautiful with ferns for background. This
Soldanella with the large and markedly evergreen leaves
is always worth bringing home, as it is quite a plant of the
woods, and ought to thrive anywhere in English gardens
where *Anemone Hepatica* can be made happy. Some of my
patches of it can be clearly seen in the foreground of
the illustration facing p. 226, with a few tufts of *Cyclamen
ibericum* in front of them—all joining together to make a
brave show of various forms and shades of greenery even
on the dullest of winter days.

CHAPTER XIV

Berries

THE birds of this garden are such inveterate berry-thieves, that the amount of pleasure we derive from the consummated efforts of our berry-bearing plants is measured by the extent of avian charity and the share of a crop left for our enjoyment, after our feathered friends have taken all they want. They often strip off the Rowans before they have coloured to their full scarlet, and the fairy raspberries borne so sparingly by *Rubus arcticus* descend into the maw of some Saxifrage-destroying Blackbird, just as though they were the commonest of fruits.

As one cannot preach honesty to the birds, nor would wish to banish their songs and cheerful presence from the garden, it is best to philosophise mildly, and reconcile oneself to the loss of gaily coloured fruits by reflecting that as an actual fact we owe the beauty of colouring of bright berries as much to the birds themselves as to the plants that bear them. The very *raison d'être* of attractive colouring in a berry is to advertise it as a desirable meal for a bird, in order that, in one way or another, the seeds in the fleshy pulp may be carried into suitable places for their germination. But all the same, it requires more philosophy than I possess to prevent my feeling distinctly

Berries

annoyed when I have been watching some precious crop of fruit from day to day, and suddenly find it has totally disappeared. Perhaps it may be the first time the plant has set seeds, and I want them for sowing; or I may never have seen that fruit before, and wish to learn its ways and beauties, and there is but little satisfaction to be derived from the presumption that a family of thrushes must be suffering from repletion, if not a bad pain inside their speckled waistcoats, after such a heavy meal. *Vitis Coignetiae* fruited very freely here in the hot summer of 1911, and the bunches of green grapes hanging from the cross-pieces of the pergola gave promise of a delightful picture if they finally turned purple. I have never found out what colour they ripen to, however, for one day there remained nothing but bare stalks, and in every season since I have found a few seedlings in the beds close by as proof that at any rate the pips had matured.

There are but few showy berries that our birds will leave alone when once they have become coloured, and I notice a great difference between this and other gardens in that respect. The Rose hips that elsewhere are left alone until frost sharpens the birds' hunger are generally pecked to pieces even before the leaves have fallen. I brought a sucker of *R. Seraphinii* from Bitton, chiefly for the sake of its wonderfully brilliant crimson hips, having admired the glow of colour they made there one December. It has grown into a fine bush and bears hips plentifully, but some October morning sees a birds' break-fast party in that bush, and all that is left for me afterwards

235

My Garden in Autumn and Winter

is a mess of seeds on the ground and the torn bases of a few hips still joined to the twigs. Yet I do not like to spray the hips with quassia to make them distasteful, though I am trying to reconcile such a deed to my conscience by arguing that thereby the hips would be saved for days of greater need, and very likely the bitterness would have washed off before the worst frosts set in.

Up to the present the birds have not attempted to eat the bright orange berries of the plant we used to call *Cotoneaster angustifolia*, but which has now become *Pyracantha angustifolia*. Possibly they have a flavour palatable to none other than Chinese birds, and that has not yet become an acquired taste of the almost omnivorous sparrow. Anyway here, ever since my plant on the trellised wall was old enough to fruit, the berries have remained untouched, and have fallen off and lain on the ground in late Spring. If this immunity is universal, the newer orange-fruited species will be more useful than the older scarlet *P. Laelandii*, for unless that is grown on the wall of a house where birds are too shy to go to rob it, the berries soon get devoured. This is a pity, for *P. Laelandii* has berries that are gloriously brilliant, and if grown as a standard it is a very fine sight when well covered with them. *Cotoneaster rotundifolia* holds its fruit better than any other here, and as they are of a very rich crimson-scarlet, and large compared with the size of the leaves, it is a very good species to grow. In time it makes a large specimen, but has grown rather slowly here; that may be because my plant began life as a rooted side branch in the late Mrs. Robb's wonderful garden at Liphook, and

Berries

it is often difficult to get such a plant to start straight upwards and make a good stem. The berries contrast well with the deep-green leaves, and are very conspicuous from a distance, so it is rather curious that the birds leave them when one considers that they eagerly devour the much smaller fruits of *C. horizontalis* soon after they are ripe.

The newer *C. rugosa Henryi* has begun fruiting here after several years of resisting all my efforts to make it raise its head into the light. It must be a beautiful plant to start on the edge of a cliff, so that it might sprawl downwards as far as it likes. In an ordinary border, however, it insists on turning its growths downwards as soon as it has reached the top of the stake it is tied to, so that if let alone it will sprawl about on the ground among its neighbours' stems. I have forced one of my plants to stand erect for a height of six feet, and have shortened in its side-shoots, and now the sprays that arch from the top are worth looking at when laden with berries, even though they are not so bright in colour as those of the two other species mentioned above, being of rather a dull brownish-red. Although this chapter is headed Berries, I shall not limit its contents to the form of fruit it is strictly correct to call a berry—that is to say, a fleshy or juicy fruit with seeds immersed in the pulp, for such fruits are not very plentiful. Gooseberries and Currants are good examples of true berries, and many of those fruits we call berries have no right to the title. The Strawberry, for instance, has the seeds bare and naked placed on the outside of the fleshy receptacle. The famous letter to Mr.

My Garden in Autumn and Winter

Berry, who was a bit too previous in sending in his bill, might be set as a question in a botanical examination. Point out which are true berries in the following quotation : "I won't pay your bill Berry till it is due Berry. You have made a mull Berry, and are not like your father the elder Berry, but don't be a goose Berry, and look so black Berry, as if you were a rasp Berry, for I don't care a straw Berry."

One is accustomed to think of only small fruits as berries, but according to the botanical definition Oranges and Lemons, Tomatoes and Gourds are true berries. One speaks of a Cotoneaster fruit as a berry, but it would seem ridiculous to apply the term to an Apple, though it is constructed on an exactly similar plan. All the same, I must praise some of the Crab Apples for garden effect. Best of all is the old Siberian Crab, which in good seasons stands out from afar as a brilliant patch of red when it is laden with its crop of scarlet fruit, which the boys about here aptly call Cherry-Apples. They will eat them, too, and declare them "'licious"; but if I try one it entails a super-human effort to get my eyes open again to see in which direction to spit out the horribly astringent mouthful. After a touch of frost they are mellower, but they seldom get left long enough for that, as they make uncommonly good jelly that has a pleasant acidity about it and is excellent for sandwiches for afternoon tea. It is a curious but unexplained fact that, with one exception, all the brightest-coloured apples are borne by varieties that have the palest flowers, and *vice versa*. Thus the Siberian Crab has practically white flowers, to be followed by fruits that

Berries

deepen from scarlet to a rich crimson, while its near relation, *Pyrus Malus floribunda*, and its double form var. *Scheideckeri*, that are so brilliantly red in bud and rosy-pink when in full flower, bear miniature apples that never do more in the colouring line than turn a dull greenish-yellow. It is the same with the real apples grown for eating, and which a small boy from Berkshire used to delight me by calling "yarples"; so far as I have noticed, the greenest of cooking varieties have the reddest flowers. Sir Harry Veitch once showed a large collection of flowers and some of their fruits before the Scientific Committee of the Royal Horticultural Society to illustrate this, and the only instance to the contrary that any of us present could recall was *Pyrus Niedswetskyana*, the awful name of which I have heard anglicised as Needs Whisky and Ned's Whiskers. In this species the whole tree shows traces of red colouring, the young bark is purple, the leaves are tinged with red, the flowers of a deep uniform crimson, and the fruits are, even when quite young and small, a bronze-purple on the outside, and if cut open when ripe the flesh is seen to be stained all through with red. I sowed some pips from fruit ripened here one season, and am rather surprised to find that two of them have produced plants with light green leaves and no trace of red on the stems, and I am looking forward with interest to seeing flowers, as according to the ordinary usage of apples they should be extra brilliant in redness, if the fruits, like the leaves, are to be green. Anyway, it is very curious that the apple family should be so peculiarly constituted as to use up all its red colouring in either flower or fruit, not having enough to go round for both

239

oourses. The Crab Apple John Downie is well worth a
place in a garden, on the edge of a lawn or in a shrub-
berry. It has a good compact habit of growth, and makes
a handsome small tree fairly quickly. Its flowers are large
and pale and very ornamental in their season, but in August
and September one feels that John Downie is more than a
"yarple." Then the oval-shaped fruits grow in a way of
their own, their colouring ranging from bright yellow
through orange shades to absolute scarlet, and it is the
mixture of such fiery hues on one fruit that gives them so
much charm. I have used them for Crab jelly, but thought
it lacked the piquancy of that made from Siberian Crabs,
so we now enjoy their beauty on the trees till the birds
enjoy their flavour. *Cydonia Maulei* is anxious to annex
the range of the rock garden it has been allowed to found
colonies in, and tries to do so both by running underground
and seeding itself about. One of the seedlings is an improvement on its parents, being larger in all its parts, but
of the same fiery orange hue as to flowers. The colour of
its quinces, too, is as fine a yellow as those of the little wild
form, and the stems when wreathed with them, just after
the leaves have fallen, are very pleasant to behold, and their
scent is delicious. A very good point in favour of these
Maulei forms is that, instead of the appalling odour of
mingled onions and overripe apples given out by the
ordinary culinary quinces, they have a delicious fragrance,
with a touch of Violet or Orris-root scent about it. Two or
three freshly fallen ones placed on one's writing-table will
scent the room very pleasantly, for it is one of those
mysterious fragrances that is intermittent, and only appears

Berries

in little bursts and whiffs, and it never becomes over-
powering or sickly. I have tried them in apple-pies, but
came to the conclusion there was not enough flavour
produced to pay for the trouble of picking and peeling, but
they make a good jelly that is pleasant with roast mutton
as a change from that made from the orthodox Red-currant.
Yellow fruits are not very plentiful in the late autumn
and winter garden, so these *C. Maulei* bushes are worth
thinking about when planting for effects that are good late
in the season. The orange hips of *Rosa Soulieana* on their
tall tree with *Pyracantha angustifolia* and *Cydonia Maulei*
might be used to make a very effective grouping beside a
good specimen or two of the Sea Buckthorn, *Hippophae
rhamnoides*, which is the best of all orange-fruited plants
when it fruits well. It is unfortunately a dioecious plant,
and so one must have both sexes represented to get a good
set of berries, and of course that means the staminate tree
will be bare in Winter. There is a golden-fruited form of
the Yew, and its waxy, semi-transparent golden urns,
holding the deep green seed, are wonderfully beautiful to
look at closely, but not so effective from a distance as the
red ones of the Common Yew. This form of the Yew is
but little known ; it is well worth planting where an evergreen is needed, as it can be kept small by pruning if
desired, and the fruits are surprisingly charming, in their
brilliant yellow, among the black-green leaves ; unfortunately the birds look upon them as an extra delicacy, and
finish them off as soon as they are ripe.

The yellow-fruited Holly is a much better known tree,
and useful to make a change where many Hollies are

241   Q

grown, but a far more beautiful form with orange berries is very rarely seen. It is supposed to be a seedling form of the yellow-berried Holly, and is known as *Ilex Aquifolium fructu aurantiaco.* There is a fine old tree of it in a shrubbery on the outskirts of my brother's garden that looks as though it may have been self-sown. It would be worth my while to graft some of it, as it is a beautiful bit of colour when bearing a good crop, and it would be unlikely to come true from seed even if I had patience to wait for it, for the Holly being a dioecious tree the pollen that sets each berry must come from some other tree, and one would have to spend a lifetime to find a male tree with the mixed blood of a red and yellow race in it ; and even then half one's seedlings would be males. Many years ago Canon Ellacombe gave me a Bramble, *Rubus xanthocarpus,* which was then a novelty and reported to have fine yellow fruits. I have often wished he had not been so generous with it, for I shall never get rid of it now. It is worse than Bindweed and Mare's-tails for running underground and resurrecting itself from any broken scrap ; and is a nasty scratchy thing to touch, while its inconspicuous flowers and the boasted yellow fruits are so seldom produced it is not worth growing. Beware of the wretched thing, and never introduce it to your garden unless you wish to spite your heirs and assigns. Some of the new Chinese Brambles have yellow fruits, but too small to be very attractive, and the wicked wandering ways of the coarse plants that bear them appear so aggressive that it seems best to march them off to the bonfire heap, before they fill the garden and push up through the floors and scratch one's legs under the

Berries

dinner table. We have quite enough rough bramble stems in our own woods to trip us up and scratch us when taking short cuts, without wanting any more varieties, even though they come from China. I grow a very curious plant under glass for the sake of its yellow fruits. It is *Debregeasia velutina*, a close relation of the Mulberries. When grown in a stove it fruits in mid-winter, and the whole length of the year's shoots is covered with round, orange-yellow fruits that at first sight look like the flowers of some Acacia and are very curious in texture, as though they look soft and velvety, yet they glisten beneath the down from the juice in their cells. If cut back annually and good strong growths are encouraged, it makes a charming pot plant to bring into the house, and will last in full beauty for several weeks.

White berries are not common either among hardy plants. The Mistletoe and Snowberry are perhaps the best known. I have saved the Christmas bunch of the former for many years after it has played its part among the decorations in the house, and I hang it up in the garden and hope the birds will help themselves to the berries and sow them for me on various trees. The only plants I know of so far, however, are those that sprang from my sowings. It is of course rather too early in the season for certain success, as the Mistletoe berries are not really ripe before February, but unless they have withered badly by the middle of January it is reasonable to expect a good number to germinate. I sow them by squeezing a berry until it bursts and the horribly viscid contents come out along with the flattened grey-green seed. This should be stuck

243

My Garden in Autumn and Winter

to the underside of a smooth and healthy young twig by means of the natural glue it produces for itself. Apple and Poplar make the best hosts for it, chiefly because their bark is soft and they grow rapidly, but I have been very successful in starting it on Hawthorns. Here it is best to choose a twig on the shaded and cool side of a tree, as our dry atmosphere is unsuitable to the growth of the young plants before they have got well established, and most of them dry up if in too sunny a position. The little seed adheres wonderfully firmly when once the sticky pulp has dried; and if all is well with it, it will become greener when the April rains soak it, and then will push out the radicle, which is shaped like a finger with a wide flat disc for its tip. This disc bends over and presses hard against the bark, and that is all the seed appears to do during the first season. The year's growth of the twig goes on round the disc but not below it where it presses against the bark, so that by the end of the Autumn the disc is either enclosed by the bark, or resting in a shallow pit in it. The centre of the disc has by then protruded a little point, called a "sinker," into the bark of the branch until it reaches the wood. It pushes in no further, but simply waits until the addition of layers of woody tissue gradually buries it deeper and deeper. By the following Spring the sinker is able to absorb nutriment from its host, and all is ready for the plumule to be pulled out of the old seed coat. The little green finger now straightens itself out, the tiny cotyledons open and the first two leaves grow out above them to start their work in the world and help the host plant with the housekeeping by extracting carbon for themselves out of

Berries

the air. For the Mistletoe is not fairly treated when it is called a parasite, in that it does not exist entirely at the expense of the host, but being an evergreen plant does a good deal all the year round towards its keep, by the absorption of carbonic acid gas and retention of carbon. At first it is a very slow growing plant, and two seasons are taken up in producing the one pair of leaves, but in the third, two branches and two pairs of leaves are produced from between the original pair, and then increase proceeds at the rate of a geometrical progression. Besides this a flourishing Mistletoe sends out suckers in the cambium layer of the host, just under the bark, and should anything destroy the original shoot, these suckers will break through the bark and produce young shoots, much in the same way as certain plants will if their central shoot is cut away. One of the first of my successfully sown berries proved so attractive in its infant stage to my Sunday-school boy visitors that it was pointed out every Sunday afternoon by the older ones to newcomers, and often got poked by a finger in the process, and it was a sad day when we discovered an extra vigorous poke had inadvertently knocked the young shoot and its six leaves off altogether. But a couple of months later sorrow was turned into joy by the appearance of three tiny Mistletoe shoots at short distances on the branch close to the broken stump of the first shoot. Two summers ago this plant set some berries for the first time; but those dishonest birds ate them early in the Autumn just as they began to look transparent, and before they were really white. Large numbers are swelling up this season, and I think must be sprayed with quassia

245

My Garden in Autumn and Winter

soon lest they too help to fatten a greedy thrush. A much older and larger plant on a Crab-apple has never borne a berry, so I expect it is the male plant. It is too far away to fertilise those on the thorns, I feel sure, so that good work must have been done by one or more of some smaller tufts higher in the thorn trees. In starting Mistletoe on a tree it is wise to squeeze on as many berries as possible, as not everyone will start to grow if taken from dried Christmas bunches ; many will get knocked off before they are safely fixed, others may dry up in Summer, and if you get only one to grow, that will not be sufficient to provide berries even though it be a female plant. If you can get freshly gathered berries in February or March, the chances of getting them to grow are much greater. Some people advise cutting or scraping the twig before placing the berries on it, but I have found the best results arise from choosing a healthy shoot with naturally smooth and clean bark.

The common old Snowberry, *Symphoricarpus racemosus,* was as much of a plague in this garden as the Laurels and Aucubas when I began gardening, and I have not yet cleared all the shrubberies of its rampageous runners. As it is generally seen, mixed among evergreen shrubs and suckering up among them only to produce spindly and starved shoots that bear more leaves than flowers and berries, it is a most depressingly dull plant. But if it is fairly treated in an open bed, and allowed to form a large shrub, it is very beautiful when freely covered with its bunches of white berries so much like bladders of lard of the right size for the kitchen of a doll's house. A new form has been introduced lately, and at first called *S. mollis,*

Berries

but now considered to be only a superior variety of our old garden enemy and should be called *S. racemosus*, var. *laevigatus*. It has a rather more compact habit, and is so free and generous with its berries that the shoots are weighed down with them, and if it will continue to behave as prettily when it feels more at home, will refrain from running into all its neighbours, and from making a preponderance of barren shoots, it should find a place in every garden. I have one on trial here, and at present it is delightful, only five feet high and fuller of bladders of lard than any pork butcher's window.

Among lowly plants suitable for the rock garden or to hang over a rough wall, there are two with pretty white berries. *Margyricarpus setosus* is the neater in habit, producing slender shoots with minute leaves that have a look of some small conifer about them, and in late Summer little dead-white berries cover the length of each shoot. They are strange pasty-looking affairs with a kid-glove sort of texture, and are spongy and dry to touch, and its generic name signifying pearl-fruit is rather too flattering, for they have none of the brilliance of a pearl, and in fact are much more like tiny chips of the *Pâte de Guimauve* lozenges that are so good for a cough and taste so pleasantly of orange-blossom.

The other plant forms in time quite a fair-sized bush with gouty, much branched stems and small, dark-green, leathery leaves. The flowers are produced on the undersides of the thick branches, and are inconspicuous green affairs quite hidden by the leaves in their natural position, and not worth the trouble of looking for. Their structure,

My Garden in Autumn and Winter

however, proclaims that they belong to the Violet family, and gives them a certain amount of interest. They are the forerunners of small round berries which are bright green until about the middle of September, when they are full grown and assume a curiously dull, inky shade of grey. Later in the year they begin to turn white in patches, always commencing to do so on the surface towards the ground; they present a very curious effect when they have become piebald, and like a black and white rabbit in colouring. From above they are hardly visible while in this stage, but if a bough is raised and turned over, the white under-surface is very conspicuous. When fully ripe the upper surface also turns white in most of them, but I have noticed that even then a good many retain the black marking on the top, and at no time are they conspicuous as viewed from above, being so much hidden by the stout branches and the leaves. So what can be the meaning of it all? It puzzles me very much, for I can hardly believe that, being a New Zealand plant, this first colouring of the underside is arranged on purpose to attract Kiwis or some other wingless bird that would see them from the ground when looking up into the bush, for I fancy Kiwis are nocturnal feeders, and a white berry would not show up much when viewed with the sky as a background even at midday. Still it can scarcely be an accident, and nothing worth to the plants, that so many New Zealand leaves are brilliantly white on the under surface, and these berries follow that antipodean scheme of coloration also.

Blue seems to be a colour rarely met with among seeds

Berries

of hardy plants, and I know of none that freely produce really blue seeds or berries, and whose character is free from some trait of horticultural perversity. *Tropaeolum speciosum* is possibly the least difficult of them to grow, and yet it is not everybody's plant, for it needs fussing with, a shady root run in cool leaf mould, or some such hardly achieved garden luxury, before it is really happy, and will produce a good crop of its blue seeds, so remarkably conspicuous on the deep red of the matured calyx. *Gaultheria trichophylla* did well here for many years, planted in accordance with Mr. Buxton's instructions, at the bottom of a small trough-shaped depression, whose two sides were flat stones. As he prophesied would be the case, as soon as the plant had filled the space of cool soil behind each stone with its underground runners, healthy shoots appeared on the level ground which were not long in becoming strong enough to flower, and then to bear the wonderful blue berries which are the chief point of beauty in this lowly plant.

My old clump wearied of its position, and I have not yet succeeded in replacing it. *Billardiera longiflora* from Tasmania should be tried by everyone with a space of warm southern wall to give to it, as its large, deep violet fruits are of such a marvellous colour. *Dianella coerulea* has produced fine heads of blue berries among its deep green Iris-like leaves, when grown in pots in a cool house, but the large clump that takes up a good space in the Peach house border has not yet paid tribute in beads of lapis lazuli. Surely it will do so soon, having assumed such a patriarchal appearance, with its outlying tufts of youngsters

My Garden in Autumn and Winter

invading the space rightfully owned by neighbouring plants. Two Coprosmas, that at Glasnevin give a yearly offering of semi-transparent berries shot with blue and lilac shades like some cold fireless opal, are very chary of their fruit here. *C. acerosa* is a trailing species, with fine wiry stems and minute, coppery leaves. It is supposed to be dioecious, but the Glasnevin form always fruits well without having a barren plant within hail. So, as my plant is a cutting from the fruiting Irish one, I fear climate has much to do with its niggardliness, and that is a harder obstacle to overcome than the provision of a husband for a widowed pistillate Coprosma. *C. propinqua*, also came here from Glasnevin, and has grown into a handsome, stiff-stemmed bush, but never a berry has it given me yet. Still I hope some extra fine season, or the mere matter of age, will some day set right these wrongs.

Ophiopogon japonicus, often called *Convallaria japonica*, gives us beautiful bunches of deep blue berries when grown indoors in a pot, but nothing but deep green, grassy leaves out of doors, and *Vitis humulifolia* has never given me a single grape yet, though at The Holt, Harrow Weald, on Mr. Kingsmill's verandah, and at Bettws y Coed, and also in Dr. Lowe's garden at Wimbledon I have seen the plants laden with bunches of berries of the colour of the turquoise.

I must remain contented with other berries then, and few can rival the beauty of the newly cracked pods of *Iris foetidissima*, especially those of a yellow-flowered variety, that produces larger and more brilliantly orange-vermilion berries than the common wild form of the plant.

Berries

Few other plants produce red seeds inside green pods, at least I can recall but few. *Littonia modesta,* a climbing Liliaceous plant I grow in a house, and always hope to try outside, has seeds that greatly resemble those of the Gladwin, *Iris foetidissima.* The seeds of *Anomatheca cruenta* when ripe are a rich crimson, and very beautifully polished. In spite of their good looks I always hurriedly bury them directly I see them, as they will then grow and spread the colony of this delightful little plant.

Some Paeonies have brilliantly red bodies in the newly split pods; these are not the fertile seeds, but those that have failed to ripen and are taking on themselves the work of advertising to some kinds of birds that the pods are open. It is not easy to see the exact design of this advertisement, for the good seeds are very hard and black when ripe, and have no pulp or skin on them that birds could digest. The plant can hardly wish to deliver its seeds over to some bird with a beak strong enough to crack and devour them. Is it possible then, that, attracted by the brilliant colour, some young and inexperienced bird may visit the pods, and in sampling the red, empty skins, jerk the black seeds away for a foot or two round the mother plant? But this strikes one as too small a gain to be worth the elaboration of so much colour.

The best of all plants that bear deep scarlet berries that will last throughout the Winter are some forms of *Skimmia japonica* and the Butcher's Broom. Of the former species the variety known as *S. japonica,* var. *Foremannii,* is most lavish with fruit here, and is certainly brighter in the tone of its red than any of the others. Its deliciously scented white flowers are as good as those of the pollen-bearing forms generally seen, and often appear on the plants in Spring while the berries are still fresh and glowing, making a very pretty picture.

Ruscus aculeatus, the Butcher's Broom, is a wonderfully fine thing in midwinter if it berries freely. The deep myrtle green of its leafless shoots is then at its best in two or three year old stems—and looks as glossy and happy on a bitter day with an icy wind blowing as it does at midsummer, perhaps even more so, from the contrast afforded by the brown or dull foliage of other plants.

It is but seldom, however, that one sees a garden in which the Butcher's Broom fruits freely. This is mainly due to the fact that for the most part the plant is dioecious, and the stock in any one garden seldom contains both of the sexes. Everyone who wishes for its bright scarlet berries should examine the flowers of their plants. One needs a magnifying glass for this, at least I do nowadays, and during March or April there should be no lack of open flowers ready for examination. The male flowers show a beautifully arranged star of anthers at the summit of the curious, purplish central body formed of the filaments welded together in one hollow sac.

In the female flower this sac has an open end blocked up by a greenish flat disc, which is the stigma.

After several seasons of close examination I came to the conclusion that, though this garden contains more Butcher's Broom than any other I know of, we had nothing but the female form, and that was why we so rarely saw a berry.

Berries

I begged male plants from all the gardens I found containing them. The little gentlemen looked very insignificant at first, sitting as a clump of only two or three shoots near the masses of many yards width of their wives, and as though they might be terribly henpecked with such a harem to look after; but they are growing into fine sturdy clumps, and I am beginning to enjoy the beauty of glowing berries on the older clumps.

I knew a single plant of Ruscus in Mr. Gumbleton's garden near Queenstown that always bore a fine crop of berries in spite of its being an isolated specimen. All I could learn about it was that he got it from a garden in Wales. After some years I learnt, by pestering my Welsh friends, that it was Mrs. Mainwaring who gave Mr. Gumbleton this precious possession, and through the kindness of Mr. E. C. Buxton in communicating to her my longing for this plant she generously sent me a clump of the same form. It is indeed a treasure, for I find that each of its flowers is perfectly hermaphrodite, and therefore with any sort of luck produces in due course a glistening scarlet berry. For most months of the year it is bright with berries, and when the last of the red ones drops or is carried off by an admiring visitor to be sown in his garden, the bright green youngsters are already growing along and sufficiently conspicuous on the dark cladodes; to be pretty as well as interesting. Lately I have acquired from two different sources a monoecious form of the Ruscus, that is to say both forms of flowers are produced on the one plant, and though the berries are of course not so plentiful on this as on the herma-

253

phrodite form, yet they are sufficiently abundant to make it a very showy plant. I sow all the berries I see fallen of all my varieties, and though they take a long time to germinate and are very slow in growth for their first year or two, I hope before long there will be none but the actually staminate plants that will not make a brave show of berries. Already some of the clumps of pistillate plants are setting fruits freely, evidently influenced by the male flowers of the monoecious plants a few yards away. The gorgeous orange-red Chinese lanterns of the Winter Cherry, *Physalis Alkekengi*, are too well known to need my praise. Both in the autumn garden when freshly ripened and in the winter months, when the outer covering has become skeletonised and shows the red berry inside through its delicate network of veins, it is a beautiful object. Also it is useful to cut and dry for vases. I have given up growing the old form, however, and prefer the hybrid raised between *P. Alkekengi* and *Franchetii*, which is named *P. Bunyardii*. It has the advantage of combining the tall slender stem of the former with a fruit almost as large as that of the latter. I have given up a little square bed close to the farmyard gates to this plant, as it is such a troublesome bedfellow for any other plant, always endeavouring to monopolise the whole bed; and if it cannot push out its companion, finishing it off by smothering it as ruthlessly as Richard III smothered his nephews.

The finest red fruit the garden gave me this Autumn was that produced by a very large form of the Himalayan May Apple, *Podophyllum Emodi*.

The white flowers on tall stems, with the leaves hanging

Opuntia camanchica on the Rockery. (See p. 255.)

Berries

below them like the silk of a closed umbrella, were wonderful enough in May, but throughout the autumn months each stem bore a dangling fruit as large as a hen's egg that changed from bright green to orange, and ended as a brilliant vermilion with a waxy bloom on it that gave it a bluish hue in certain lights. It was with much regret that I plucked those fruits and extracted their seeds for sowing, on the day that I discovered some horrid bird had pecked a great hole in one of them.

The Opuntias in the rock garden generally set a brave show of fruits in favourable seasons, but most of them take two years to ripen and turn to the deep red or purplish crimson that is their final colouring. In most winters there are some that have got along sufficiently with this coloration to look attractive among the prickly shoots out of which they grow.

CHAPTER XV

In the Grip of Winter

IF one could but arrange that Winter should arrive with snow and ice, say a week before Christmas, and remain with us for three or even more weeks, and then go away, taking the cold winds and snow to the North Pole, allowing the temperature to increase in warmth gradually from day to day until Spring was due, very little harm would befall the treasures of our gardens. Nowadays Winter has such tricky ways that one never knows how to be even with him.

If one covers up the *Crinums* and *Salvia patens* with ashes too soon, and an especially warm spell sets in, there is a chance they will start to grow under their coverings. Hand lights and coverings make a garden very unsightly, and except during the most severe weather are often more of a danger than help to certain easily excited plants. I try to use as little winter covering as possible here, and to enjoy the natural aspect of the plants in their winter state as much as the short dark days will permit.

There is a wonderful beauty in the old dead stems, the kecksies, of many plants in a soft winter evening's glow. A ruddy light on brown Grasses or Eryngium stems, or against bare Lime twigs, is a source of great pleasure when

256

In the Grip of Winter

it is just too dark to see to weed or dig among the small plants. It is delightful to watch the glow fade off the tall Scots Pines, and to listen to the blackbirds chasing one another about among the evergreen shrubs, and noisily claiming their right to certain desirable roosting places. Then when they have settled down, the robins have a few words to say in their harsh clicking winter voices. It may be only a kindly good-night to their friends, but it always has rather an angry sound, as though it referred to the encroachments of neighbours on their roosting rights. Then comes the stillness of a winter evening. A dim grey vision of one of the Winter-moths flits by, and it is time to move towards the house and the tea-table as the tawny owls wake up and call for physic or start hooting. Then again on a frosty morning, every stem, weed, blade of grass or cobweb has its edging of pearls or diamond dust, and I am always glad if I have not yet tidied away the dead stems that look so lovely in their coats of hoar-frost. Freshly-fallen snow is best of all, if it has not been too heavy, and has come at the right season, and not just as the spring flowers are trying to make a show. The beauty of Cedars and Pines, bent under its weight into strange and new angles and curves, is nearly as pleasing as looking at some great remodelling of the garden plan just as it begins to show the effect of the new planting. The bare trees coated in light snow stand out in a way one never could have predicted from looking at their bare brown limbs, and all sorts of unexpected beauties are revealed. The worst of snow, however, is that one feels its beauty has to be paid for in the slush and mess that follow the thaw, and the

My Garden in Autumn and Winter

bent, if not broken, evergreens that it leaves behind if its weight has bowed them down for several days.

Some of the conifers, such as Irish Yews, Junipers and Cypresses, take years to recover in shape from a heavy fall of snow. It is possible to shake some of the weight off many of them, but it is difficult work to perform without breaking some of the most important branchlets. So, beautiful as snow is at its first coming, I never long for it, and am always glad when I see the last patch, lying on the north side of some hedge, dwindling and becoming transparent under the influence of a westerly wind.

I like to see snow on the top of some mountain in June, when I go there to find it, but in my garden I can very well live without it; for even on the dullest of winter days there is always some stem or bud that is worth looking at, or some job that wants doing. On the very worst days of all, those of determined rain, or frost that hardens the ground, I scrub the Yew stems and soon get warm and feel the benefit of the exercise, their spreading heads serving as an umbrella. Another job for a really bad winter day, and one that most gardens can provide, is the removal of adventitious buds, or outgrowths covered with buds, from the stems of old trees, especially Limes and Horse Chestnuts. I much dislike to see the bole of a large tree disfigured with sprouts of young growths, as though they had green whiskers that needed shaving.

I find a chisel and mallet the best tools to use to remove these moles, wens and warts, and if they are cut away as cleanly as possible, in many cases the evil habit of forming them is given up by that portion of the bark.

In the Grip of Winter

On fine days there is always enough work in the rock garden for the hours of daylight, where the most omnipresent weeds are always waiting to be pulled up before they reach flowering and seeding age. One of the worst here is that evil little Cress, *Cardamine hirsuta,* that is not common in uncultivated ground, but seems always to appear in the choicest bits of rock gardens. Sometimes I feel the possibilities of reducing its hold on my moraines is so hopeless, that I had better try a sort of horticultural Christian Science about it, and pretend to myself it is not really there. I do not believe it would do much harm to *Gentiana verna,* and the smaller Primulas it nestles up among so cosily, and it is not very unsightly except when yellow in leaf and a mass of irritable explosive seed pods. So perhaps one could get used to it, and all that would be necessary to save oneself from the jeers of garden visitors would be to solemnly assure them no such plant exists to the mind that is raised above it by Christian Science.

Poa annua and Chickweed are always in full growth in this garden all the year round, and both are tiresome to detect and extract among certain small plants; especially the Poa when it gets a hold among *Edraianthus graminifolius* or some Dianthus with dark green leaves. So when there is not much to be looked at among flowering plants, one can always employ an hour or two uprooting weeds, clearing the dead wood out of shrubs or trees, or doing some job that does not appear sufficiently attractive when plants are growing and flowering, and there is something fresh to be watched and enjoyed every day.

My Garden in Autumn and Winter

If you can be content with quiet-toned colouring, and the beauties of surface and construction, there is much even in the darkest days of the year that is worth looking at. At no other time do the stems of certain plants look better. The Whitewashed Brambles, for instance, are generally then at their best, and have lost none of the coat of paint Nature provides for them. I still think *Rubus biflorus* the best of them all, as it cannot be beaten for whiteness, is no runner, and thereby unlike so many of the new garden worries Chinese collectors have added to our lists of tiresome weeds. *R. tibetanus* is one of these, and a young plant with grey-coated stems, ferny leaves and gracefully arching side shoots, is so beautiful that people will crave the tips of these shoots when they have reached the ground and begun to root. But when one discovers in Spring that the whole border for several yards round the pretty specimen is a mass of grey and purple suckers of this Bramble, and that it will become a regular jungle unless cleared of them, one goes back to one's first love, the staid old stay-at-home *R. biflorus*. *Rosa Willmottiae*, on the contrary, is a wonderfully well-behaved plant, only asking that old wood should be severely cut out annually to make room for two or three sturdy shoots of the year, which will then thicken out enough to stand without staking, and will cover themselves with a coat of waxy powder of a very beautiful soft shade of grey, making the bush almost as beautiful when bare in Winter as it is when smothered in its tiny pink blossoms in the end of May. Most of the Dogwoods assume purple or red shades on their smooth bark in Winter, and the several silver or golden variegated

In the Grip of Winter

forms I have grouped together look quite ruddy and cheerful when completely bare. The best red-barked plant I have is a golden-leaved Alder—*Alnus incana aurea*—which, when it is growing strongly, rivals the red-barked Willow in brilliancy.

The twigs of a dwarf form of Guelder Rose are also very attractive when bare and lit up by sunlight. The most wonderful bark coloration I have ever seen is to be found in some of the Maples, one of which has thereby earned the name of the Snake-bark. It is *Acer pennsylvanicum*, and in its variety *erythrocladum*, the young shoots are of the most brilliant crimson imaginable, and look as though they had just received a new coat of varnish on the top of their paint. It is very rare in Britain, and one of the specialities of the wonderful nursery of Mr. Späth of Berlin, but unfortunately is unobtainable from thence during these unhappy days of warfare.

Some plants can achieve a certain amount of growth even during the deepest gloom of Winter, and it is pleasant to observe their changes day by day, and to be thereby led to feel there is activity and promise of Spring.

One of the newer introductions from China, *Stachyurus chinensis*, provided itself with interesting looking bunches of buds even before its leaves coloured to a fine bronze last Autumn. After the leaves had fallen, these pendant buds looked rather like young Hazel catkins of a deep glossy brown. After every spell of mild days it was easy to notice just a slight lengthening of these pendants, and after a time the swelling out of flower buds on their central stalks. The cold snaps arrested their growth, but did them no harm, and they at length developed into pretty hanging tails of pale yellow bells like threaded Cowslips, and were very charming for a few days in March, until a sudden and extra severe frost caught them and blackened and ruined them. It seemed extra sad that they should have perished just at the pitch of perfection, after braving all the wintry days so well.

Euphorbia biglandulosa is another plant I enjoy watching during the Winter. It makes semi-prostrate stems, larger and less procumbent than those of *E. Myrsinites*, but of an equally beautiful steely-blue colour. These stems take two seasons to mature, and then form terminal buds that unfold during November and December bract by bract, till in January they are a mass of bright golden yellow, making a wonderfully good contrast with the glaucous leaves. It seems so strange that a flower stem that takes two years to come to perfection should choose January of all months for its flowering here in our sunless clime rather than give up its habits of punctuality acquired in Greece, its native land of sunny winter months.

Euphorbia Wulfenii also gives us constant pleasure in Winter by the daily changing tints of red and purple, green and gold that appear on its terminal flowering heads.

So if only the owner of a garden will plant enough plants of the most different types and habits procurable, there ought to be never a day in which he cannot find some pleasure in watching growth or decay, structure of bud, leaf, blossom, fruit or stem, no minute of the daylight hours of the working days in which there is no interesting

In the Grip of Winter

and health-giving work to be done ; and no bed of the garden that will not provide some offering for a friend, whether it be cut flowers, ripe seeds or divisions of roots. That is my idea of what a garden should provide for its owner and his friends, and my desire in writing these notes on my garden during the four seasons is that others besides myself, who like a plant for its associations and interest as well as for its own individual beauty, may be encouraged to grow collections of plants that are often overlooked in the present-day desire for masses of colour. Of course I confess humbly that, owing to hindrances and limitations due to soil, climate, purse and space, the art of gardening for colour effect is too hard a one for me to attempt here. I do not wish to belittle the great successes others have achieved nor the pleasure I dorive from seeing their beautiful gardens. I only wish to show how much pleasure I have derived from this by no means remarkable garden, and to encourage others somewhat similarly cir-cumstanced to collect and grow plants of all kinds, to watch and note their peculiarities, mark their charms, and hand on the best of them to others who love a plant for its own sake.

I conclude with the wish that they may find as much joy in bright and happy days, and as much relaxation and consolation in periods of pain and anxiety as I have derived from this my garden, in Spring, Summer, Autumn, and Winter.

INDEX

My Garden in Autumn and Winter

Index

My Garden in Autumn and Winter

Index

269

My Garden in Autumn and Winter

Index

My Garden in Autumn and Winter

Printed by BALLANTYNE, HANSON & Co.
Edinburgh & London

NOMENCLATURAL UPDATE
by Peter Barnes

A gardening book does not have to be very old for some of its names to be considered out-of-date; indeed, nomenclature and taxonomy may both be considered rather fluid art-forms rather than precise sciences. It seems inevitable that this should be the case, since they are dealing with living organisms, by their nature also constantly varying. Consequently, the reader must not be surprised to find many name-changes from this book's original index. A few words to explain the reasons for these changes may be worthwhile.

It is a commonplace among gardeners to ask, Why must they keep changing our familiar names? We must remember that names familiar to one generation may be very strange to an earlier one. All the many rules governing the naming of plants are directed towards stability of names but, inevitably, their application sometimes results in new names being required (or, more often, older names being revived) for familiar plants. There are two main justifications—taxonomy and nomenclature.

Taxonomy is the study (I hesitate to call it a science) of the relationships between different plants. It is taxonomy that encourages us to bring together, in the family Rosaceae, apparently differing genera such as *Rosa*, *Potentilla*, and *Fragaria*, not to mention *Malus*, *Prunus*, and *Spiraea*. From time to time, more detailed study, perhaps new techniques, may suggest that previously held

My Garden in Autumn and Winter

ideas cannot be sustained, and a plant may then have to be given a new specific epithet, or be transferred to a different genus.

The rules ("Codes") of nomenclature determine what names may be applied to a particular plant, and especially, which name of many that may have been used for it over the years should be considered the correct one. A basic principle of nomenclature is that of priority, whereby (in general) the earliest name properly published for that plant is to be considered the correct one.

Rules notwithstanding, room often remains for argument as to the correct name for a particular plant, hence the differences between some modern publications. From time to time, proposals have been made to adopt a standard list of names, seldom with any lasting effect. Therefore, the reader must not be surprised if a name here given as "correct" is disregarded elsewhere.

The reader must bear in mind that when Bowles wrote this book the concept of the cultivar (i.e., "cultivated variety") had not been adopted. Consequently, the typography of the original index differs from what is now the norm. I have listed, in their proper style (capital initial letters and single quotation marks), those latinized epithets which are now treated as cultivar names, to distinguish them from botanical epithets belonging to subspecies, varieties, or forms. Non-latinized names, such as tulip 'Bleu Aimable', are not listed again. Bowles generally capitalised botanical epithets derived from proper nouns, a style I have not adopted. I have also corrected a few misspellings.

In general, names in this supplementary index have been brought into alignment with *The Plant Finder*, which is now increasingly used as a standard nomenclator by the nursery trade, but I have reserved the right to differ in a very few instances.

Nomenclatural Update

Furthermore, a surprisingly large proportion of the names used by Bowles represent plants not listed in that work. Some, evidently, are not currently in the nursery trade; a few others are names which, as far as I can determine, have either never been validly published or are of uncertain status. Some may be errors of the compiler of the index, of the printer, or even of the author's memory, but the text does not always help to determine their true identity. In a few instances, incorrect page references have been rectified. At the least, these supplementary notes should make it easier to track down further information about almost all of the plants that feature in this eloquent and enduringly readable trilogy.

NAME USED IN *My Garden in Autumn and Winter*	PAGE	CURRENT NAME
Acer pennsylvanicum	261	*Acer pensylvanicum*
Acidanthera bicolor	109	*Gladiolus callianthus*
Aegle sepiaria	168	*Poncirus trifoliata*
Ailanthus glandulosa	43, 44	*Ailanthus altissima*
Alnus incana aurea	261	*Alnus incana* 'Aurea'
Alyssum maritimum	9	*Lobularia maritima*
Amaryllis belladonna var. *rosea perfecta*	146	*Amaryllis belladonna* 'Rosea'
Amaryllis belladonna var. *speciosa purpurea*	146	*Amaryllis belladonna* 'Purpurea'
Amaryllis belladonna var. *spectabilis bicolor*	146	*Amaryllis belladonna* 'Spectabilis'
Amaryllis Parkeri	146	×*Amarygia parkeri*
Amelanchier canadensis	164	*Amelanchier lamarckii* (which is often confused with *A. canadensis*)

My Garden in Autumn and Winter

Nomenclatural Update

My Garden in Autumn and Winter

Nomenclatural Update

My Garden in Autumn and Winter

Nomenclatural Update

My Garden in Autumn and Winter